ART AND YORKSHIRE

FROM TURNER TO HOCKNEY

JANE SELLARS

GREAT NORTHERN

Great Northern Books
PO Box 213, Ilkley, LS29 9WS
www.greatnorthernbooks.co.uk

ISBN: 978-0-9576399-9-7

Design and layout: David Burrill

CIP Data
A catalogue for this book is available
from the British Library

Contents

Preface by Alan Bennett 5

1. Introduction 9

2. The Yorkshire Landscape 27

3. City and Industry 71

4. The Sea 93

5. Yorkshire's People 107

Acknowledgements 141

Bibliography 142

Index 143

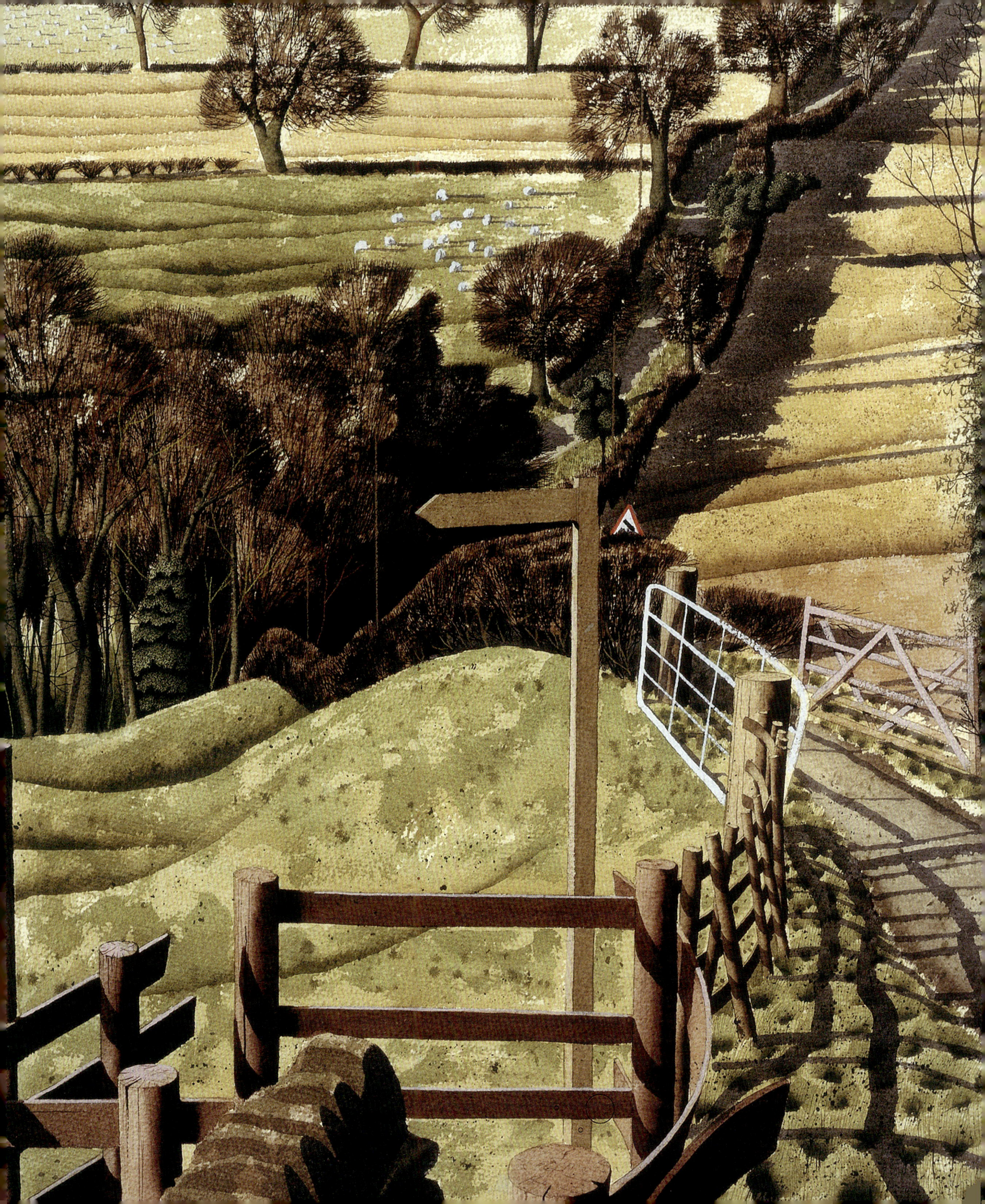

Preface
by **Alan Bennett**

When I was a child growing up in Leeds art was quite thin on the ground. It was wartime and though we were quite often in the art gallery on school trips it was seldom to look at the pictures most of which had been put away for the duration or altogether evacuated. In London the National Gallery's collection had been glamorously spirited away to a cave in the depths of Wales. In Leeds, with glamour as usual not on the agenda, our pictures had just been put on a tram and taken up through Halton past the golf course to Temple Newsam.

So if we came down from Armley to the art gallery in the Headrow it was not to be uplifted by art (difficult anyway for me aged 6) but to be given a dose of propaganda, exhorted to Dig For Victory! or to Save the Ark Royal! in a series of exhibitions which included at one point a mock-up of a coal mine. If art did get a look in it was only via the paintings we had to do when we got back to school with the promise, never made good, that the best of them might end up in the art gallery themselves.

More satisfying was to be taken by my grandma as we regularly were on the same journey as the city's paintings up to Temple Newsam House where some of the braver paintings could still be seen. Not that I was much interested. Far more fascinating was the broad brimmed felt hat that was on display all through my childhood and which purported to be that of Oliver Cromwell, with a bullet hole in the crown to prove it.

I can see, though, that simply for want of anywhere more exciting to go one did as a child begin to acquire the habit of art, without … and this was important … necessarily thinking art was anything special. And this persisted, so that when as I got older I used to do my homework in the City Reference Library I often took a break in the art gallery next door, where quite early on art in Yorkshire began to rub off.

The most notable artist in this book is, of course, Turner though it's not the Turner of the huge stormy canvases of his later years. These are kinder paintings and of views we can still recognise. What makes the Yorkshire Turners immediately accessible is that they are so topographical. Here is Kirkstall Abbey, pretty much as we know it today (though not quite as black). Here is Bolton and the transept at Fountains with the setting at this stage of Turner's development not subordinated to some

Simon Palmer, b. 1957. Detail from *Above Leighton Bridge* (JHW Fine Art)

vast meteorological drama or a battle between darkness and light which reduces the ostensible subject to a corner of the canvas and even there seen through a fitful haze. They aren't picture postcards either but they are views, prospects and works that Turner's patrons at Farnley and Harewood could readily appreciate. They are … dare one say it … down to earth.

Down to earth, too, in a different way is Henry Moore, much lauded now in his home county … his home Riding one should say … though it was not always so. When in 1951 the Festival of Britain included one of Moore's reclining figures outside Leeds Art Gallery it was regularly defaced and was the subject of acrimonious correspondence in the local papers. Nowadays it's hard to see what people got so upset about but that's simply because the public has caught up with him, with some, glibly, even claiming to have left him behind.

Moore's thoughts are said to have been turned to sculpture when, as a boy, he was taken to services at Methley church where there is indeed plenty of stonework to occupy a boy's attention during a boring sermon. One would like to think it was something so ordinary and so local but I'm never sure that one can pin down the source of an artist's inspiration as precisely as this even when the attribution comes from the actual artist. It's certainly not true of literature where characters, however vivid, are rarely based on one particular person, and seldom yanked out of life into art as readily as readers think. Art is a mystery even to its practitioners, a sculptor's inspiration in the hand as much as the eye.

I remember when we were on holiday in Bridlington in the late 40's going with my mother to Burton Agnes Hall which we were enchanted by ('It's like somewhere Down South' said my mother). Less enchanting then were Marcus Wickham-Boynton's Post Impressionists which I can remember visitors, myself included, being shocked by. The comments were as they say nowadays 'robust' with 'I wouldn't give that thing house room' a typical remark. I think, even at 14 I had enough sense to keep my mouth shut, knowing instinctively that with art it was often a case of catching up.

Besides, reputations come and go. The virtues of Atkinson Grimshaw nowadays go without saying whereas even as late as the 1950s he was taken to be old hat. I've always liked his pictures if not for purely aesthetic reasons. All too often he brings back what we have lost and his painting of Park Row in Leeds Art Gallery is a sad reminder of what Leeds used to look like before the developers got to work, his painting of Boar Lane similarly. Then too his studies of suburban Roundhay and Shadwell recall my lonely teenage walks through Woodhouse and Headingley, their leaf-covered lanes redolent of my youth. In the early 60's Grimshaw used to be recommended in the colour supplements as a good investment, an artist whose stock was going to rise. And so he was, if that is what you were after. But at his best he captures Leeds and Harrogate as I can remember them, nostalgia as fitting a response to paintings as an appreciation that is more purely aesthetic.

Where pictures are concerned I have always found my appreciation is linked far too closely to possession. I know if I like a painting when my instinct is to walk out of the gallery with it under my raincoat. It stamps me as aesthetically immature, I can see that, and not being a Russian billionaire it's not a craving I can indulge. But if I did own even the modest pictures I've fancied it would be both a distinguished and pleasing collection numbering, among others, the Camden Town paintings I first saw in Leeds Art Gallery, the Cotmans I saw at Temple Newsam and the aforesaid Grimshaws of Park Row and Boar Lane. There would also be the odd Pompeo Batoni, which figure in so many country house collections, quite silly though some of them are and a bit big for the raincoat. I'd also like one of the early drawings of Lucian Freud and the Patrick Heron portrait of Herbert Read that figured in the celebratory exhibition about Read a few years ago.

I can see this desire for possession is ignoble, particularly if possession involves as it so often does a large degree of showing off, though if the showing off includes admitting the public to the collection as it does in so many country houses it can perhaps be forgiven. What recommends ownership of even the most modest painting is that it allows the virtues and the beauty of the picture to creep into one's affections. It's another reason to visit and re-visit galleries as a reminder of one's old friends. Many of these pictures we know so we don't have to cudgel our sensibilities into some sort of response; this is not a fresh encounter, it's a reunion. Here is Fountains as Turner saw it and we remember him seeing it from last time. Here is Grimshaw's autumnal lanes and on the Tube platform Moore's sleepers cuddle up as the Blitz rages above.

I had too many cold, wet holidays at Bridlington as a child readily to succumb to that locality's undoubted charm and the latest phase of David Hockney's development. I prefer (only once having been there) his California or his paintings done in Paris. They are the ones that would go under the raincoat. No room for his circumambient trees anyway.

The weather in Katharine Holmes' pictures is what rings a bell as she lives not far from us in Craven and we share the often grim climate of the Western Pennines which she seems to brave on a daily basis. Simon Palmer's Yorkshire is a more idyllic landscape though I can't say he idealises it any more than Katharine Holmes does hers. The corner of North Yorkshire round Jervaulx, Masham and Coverham is indeed blessed and with his evocative titles Palmer invests it with an additional layer of mystery. I can congratulate myself on having acquired two of his pictures when I'd never heard of him. This was thirty years ago in a print shop in Camden Town. My two pictures are entitled Between Lane and Field (which isn't very exciting) and After a Late Breakfast with on the edge of the picture a spectral figure who looks as if she has strayed from a novel by Barbara Pym. One could almost dramatise Palmer's world; they would be small dramas … women waiting on the edge of woods, solitary figures at bus stops … but always in this rapturous landscape, poems in paint with life almost stopping but going on.

Rather than bare white rooms I like domesticity in the presentation of art, which few galleries go in for. I like paintings in rooms and even behind a vase of flowers. It's a notion of pictures as furniture which art historians would deplore but suits me because, liking pictures to rub off I'm happy to catch them out of the corner of my eye. Leading on from that, I don't think it goes against the spirit of a book of this kind if I put in a plea for art to be more taken for granted.

Not long ago I wrote a play *People* in which Dorothy Stacpoole is the aristocratic owner of a rundown Yorkshire country house which the National Trust and other interested parties are anxious to acquire. Dorothy wants things left as they are, reconciled to a degree of decay and neglect as preferable to having the place, its pictures and its furniture spruced up and made a showcase. There are masterpieces here, she admits that but she shrugs them off as they are what she has grown up with. It's Art, yes but she doesn't want her nose rubbed in it. She'd rather go on as she always has, taking it for granted.

It's a point of view with which many people found it difficult to sympathise but I think (an author not always the best person to know what he or she has written) I was putting in a plea for the ordinariness of art as opposed to the super-stardom of pictures in particular that has been wished upon them by the great auction houses. Any one of the Turners in this book, the one of Fountains for instance, would sell for many hundreds of thousands of pounds but to the casual viewer it's a familiar prospect of a well-loved place. It's good but it's also ordinary. Is it a masterpiece? I don't know and I don't much care because that gets in the way. Here where we know these paintings and often know the places they depict we can and should ignore the rest. Paintings can be friends.

You may not agree but still, I hope you'll enjoy the pictures.

1. Introduction

Art and Yorkshire are two of the main ingredients of my life; I am an art curator and writer and I was born in Yorkshire. I live here still, and although I will admit to a protracted love affair with Liverpool, where I lived and worked throughout the 1980s, and a long-running flirtation with Italy, it is Yorkshire that runs in my blood. This is the personal history that gave me the ambition to write a book about art and Yorkshire. Another art historian may well have chosen different artists. The following story of my life as a curator will, I hope, provide the background to why I chose what I did.

I grew up in Tadcaster on the banks of the River Wharfe, a town famed for its breweries, where the smell of hops lingered in the air and public houses lined the High Street from end to end. My family was rather at odds with the town as we had no connection with the breweries and both my parents were academics. We lived in Tadcaster because my mother's father had had a house built there in the 1930s and it was going spare in 1953, soon after my parents married. It was a mock Tudor detached house in a big garden that looked spacious from the outside, but inside it was quite small and my two sisters and I never had enough space for all our activities, such as doing homework, practising the piano or playing loud pop music. My mother taught the infants in a village school a few miles away and my father was a lecturer in History in York. We three girls went to Tadcaster Grammar School, which, despite the name, was a comprehensive school, built in the early 1960s on the outskirts of the town. I found it terrifying at first, going to this huge school with 2,000 pupils from across a wide area, from posh Leeds suburbs to bleak coal-mining villages. But once I had established that I loved English and art, was hopeless at maths and science and even worse at any kind of physical education, I found my niche as a reserved girl who read a lot of books, otherwise known there as a stuck-up swot.

Our house was full of stuff, not useful things like furniture or radiators, but books, Staffordshire figures and pictures. By pictures I do not mean valuable oil paintings, but reproductions of Old Masters and the great moderns, and Victorian prints that my father had picked up in junk shops. I can remember falling asleep every night in my cupboard sized bedroom watched over by a particularly sour looking green-faced Virgin Mary by El Greco. In my sisters' bedroom there was a reproduction of the Matisse still life in the Glasgow Art Gallery, which puzzled us all for its lack of knowledge of perspective. Over the fireplace in the dining room we had an Arts Council print of Lowry's The Public Shelter, also baffling for its pin-men figures, which had we drawn them at school would have brought forth scorn from the art teacher. In the front room there was Van Gogh's The Yellow House, whose Mediterranean colours described a glorious sunlight generally unknown in Tadcaster. I must have spent a lot of my time gazing at these Post Impressionist prints because, imprinted on my memory, they are set off against a background of my parents' 1960s interior design choices of pale green walls or William Morris wallpaper. I was eleven years old when I finally got to see the real thing in the National Gallery in London. I would like to say that I was dazzled and excited, but I wasn't; I just felt at home. Obviously the National Gallery Van Goghs and Monets looked vastly different to the reproductions that I had grown up with – much bigger for a start – but it was enough to make me realise that what I wanted to do one day was work in an art gallery.

My parents were both teachers, so they felt duty bound to take their three girls on mandatory educational excursions. My father was a keen walker and rock climber and an architectural historian, so he dealt with the landscape and ruined abbeys. My mother preferred walks that included a visit to a junk shop in search of blue and white plates and Staffordshire figures, which nobody else wanted in the 1960s and 1970s. We girls liked to go to the sea, but that was only allowed once a year when we paid homage to an ancient family tradition by spending a week's holiday at our grandparents' caravan at Robin Hood's Bay. Living where we did, midway between Leeds and York, we had access to the rich and diverse choice of towns, cities and landscapes that make Yorkshire so appealing to artists. When we got our first car, a blue Volkswagen Beetle in the early 1960s, Yorkshire was our oyster. As a child, tramping across the North Yorkshire moors or wandering dreamily around Fountains Abbey, I did not of course make any connection with the paintings that I would come to know later on when I studied history of art, but the memories of those days and the physical connection with nature stayed with me in many ways that have informed my view of the paintings described in this book.

Wharfedale was our true stomping ground. Pool in Wharfedale had a particularly strong place in our affections, because it was there that my paternal grandfather Charles Sellars had been the stationmaster, until Dr Beeching came along and put paid to all that in 1965. The blue VW Beetle would climb up Pool Bank over the bridge at the site of the old railway station, which was rapidly demolished and replaced by a housing estate,

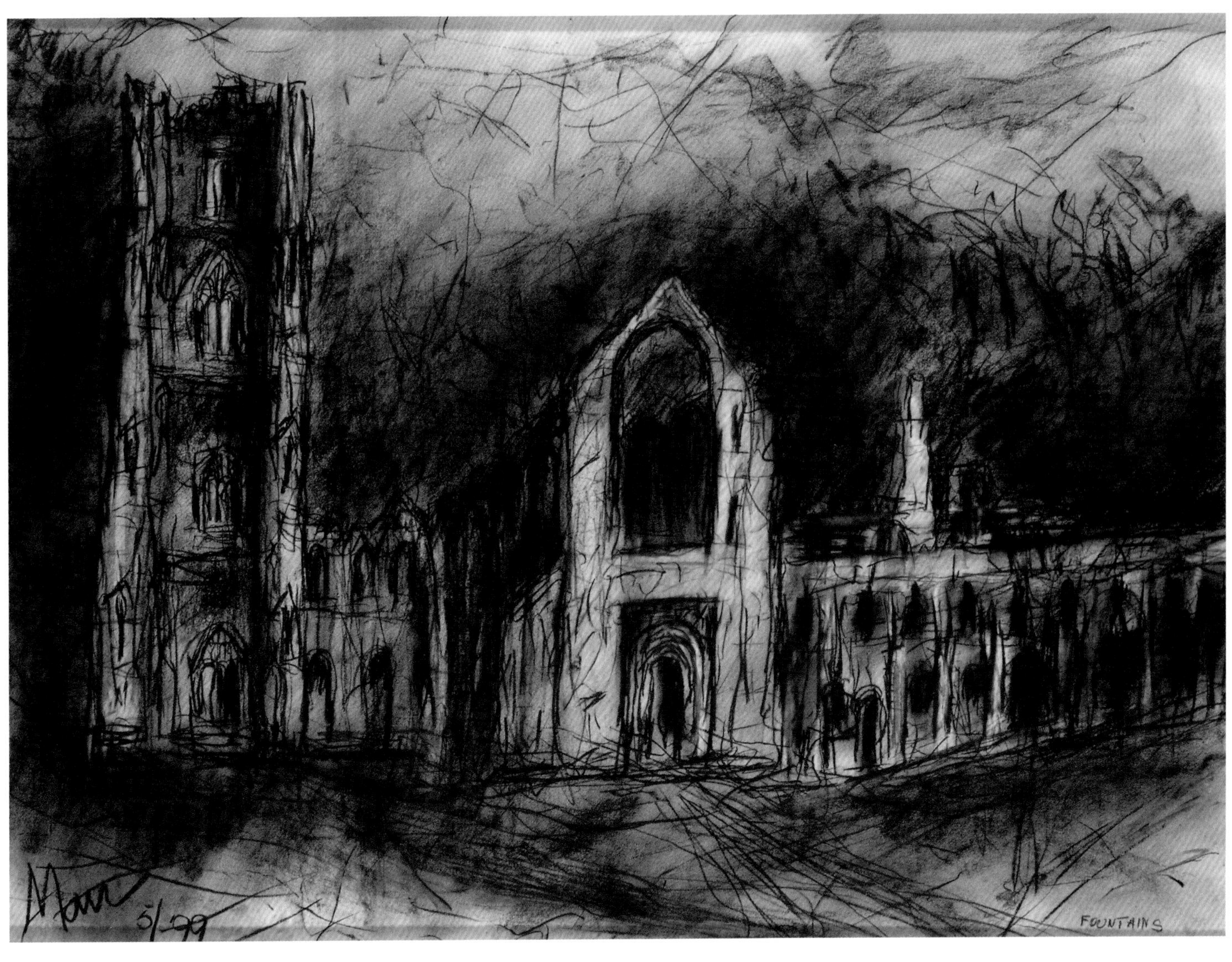

Leslie Marr, b. 1922. *View of Fountains Abbey* (1999). Charcoal on paper, 56 x 74.5cm (Mercer Art Gallery, Harrogate Borough Council)

down into Otley then into the Washburn Valley for a hike around the reservoirs. Swinsty was a favourite, and Thruscross, where a village was submerged when the valley was flooded on completion of the dam in 1966. Falling for the local folklore, we always hoped that the level of water would be low enough for the old church bell tower to be seen, its ghostly bell ringing out a sinister lament. Not so far away from here is Almscliffe Crag, an extraordinary promontory of millstone grit rock set in the sweep of lower Wharfedale and one of my most coveted destinations, as, surprisingly for one so non-athletic, I was the only Sellars girl who had any aptitude for rock-climbing. I had my father's attention for once, and

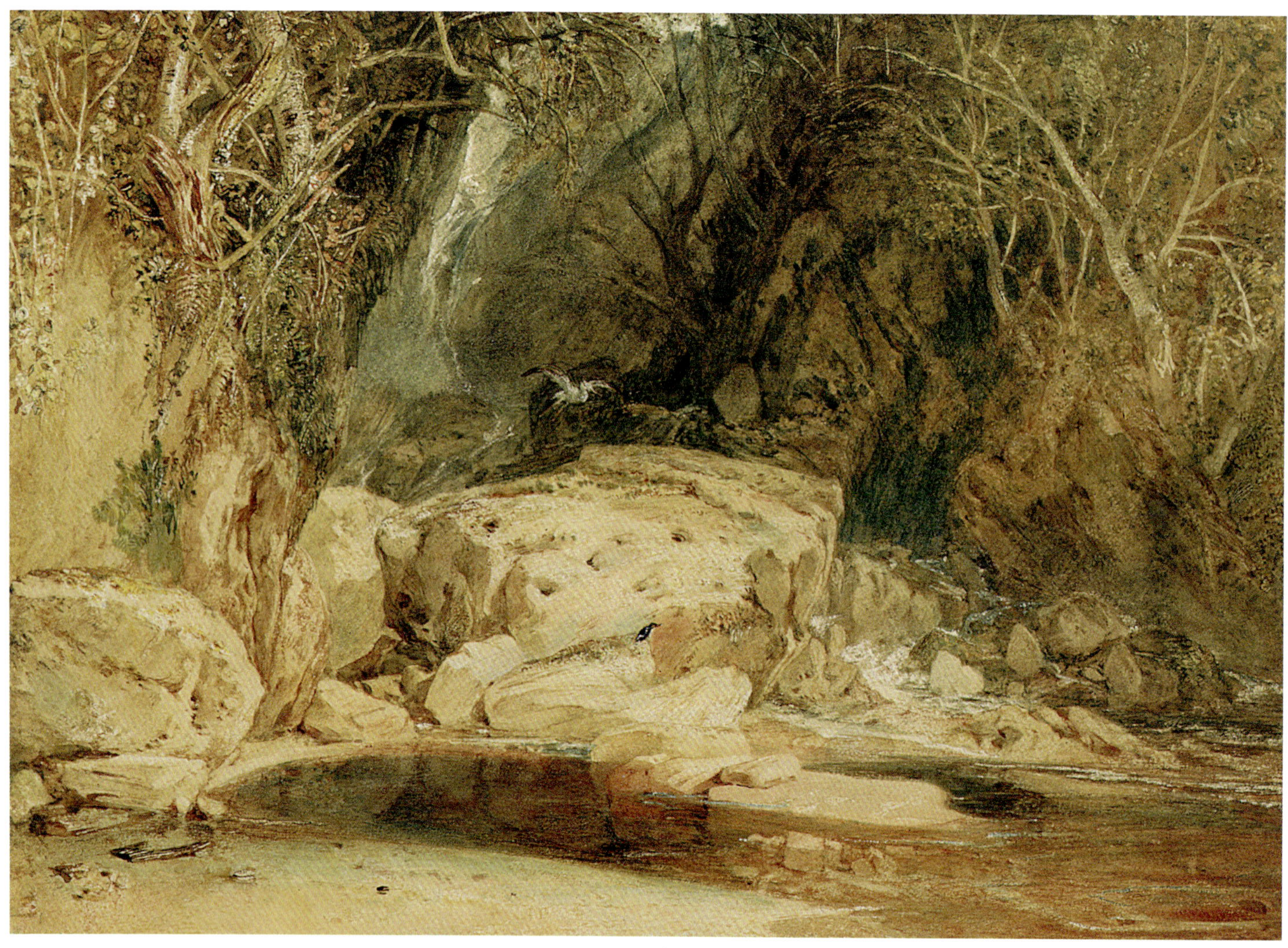

the other two straggled on behind as I clambered to the top for a truly breathtaking view. What I did not know then was that the dramatic presence of the crag in the soft valley setting had caught the eye of England's greatest landscape painter, Joseph Mallord William Turner in the early nineteenth century. Unwittingly, I was walking in the footsteps of Turner, as he had tramped around the valley, sketchbook in hand. Over a period of twenty-five years, Turner had been a regular visitor to nearby Farnley Hall, home of the Horton Fawkes family, where he made watercolours of the house and its Wharfedale surroundings. Thomas Girtin, Turner's dazzling contemporary, had also walked this way. When the Victorian writer and art critic John Ruskin visited Farnley in 1884 he wrote, 'Farnley is a unique place, there is nothing like it in the world – a

J M W Turner, 1755 - 1851. *A Lonely Dell, Wharfedale* (1815). Watercolour on paper, 27.8 x 39.5cm (Leeds Museums and Galleries)

place where a great genius has been loved and appreciated, who did all his best work for that place, where it is treasured up like a monument in a shrine.' What I did not know then was that I was destined to become almost as familiar with the stately homes of Yorkshire as Turner had been.

Fast forward some thirty years: I was the principal curator of Harewood House and I was driving my car somewhere in Yorkshire looking for an obscure country house. Lost, in other words. Beside me sat Caroline, assistant curator, trying to read the map upside down. On the back seat behind us was a Turner watercolour, which that morning had been carefully packed in tissue, bubble wrap and polythene and delicately manoeuvred into my Peugeot 206 and tucked in with blankets. I was driving slowly and carefully but a hopeless sense of direction meant that I had to do a five-point turn on a wintry country road when we realized that we had gone past the gates of our destination. With massive sighs of relief we drove up the gravel drive at the speed of a hearse.

When you arrive at a grand house in the country you always encounter the same problems; the front door looks as though it is never used and any other door is hard to find; immediately you get out of the car a troupe of at least three different sized dogs appears from nowhere, barking madly and joyfully jumping up at you with filthy paws; you find a door and yank at a rusty bell-pull, then you wait, as in this case. After about ten minutes, as we peered through the glass, His Lordship appeared at the end of a corridor wearing a long overcoat, waved at us vaguely and disappeared, to re-emerge five minutes later from a hidden door onto the terrace round the corner.

'Good morning, we've brought the Turner back.'

'Oh dear, I had quite forgotten you were coming. Come in, come in, let me give you a hand with the picture.'

It was not a very big painting, but we curators are rather fussy about how art objects are handled, especially by their owners. We cringed as he whisked the package out of my hand and carried it by one corner into the blissfully Aga-warmed kitchen where he casually propped the picture against the fridge.

'Have you been here before? No? Well do let me show you round.'

Another thing about country houses is that as soon as you leave the kitchen the temperature plummets to just a few degrees above freezing. Always hang onto your coat. The house was icy but beautiful, with an elegant curving staircase in a huge hall with doors opening off in all directions. His Lordship opened door after door, we walked into darkness and then, as he flung open the shutters, pictures on the walls were revealed and picturesque views of a rolling landscape could be seen through large plate glass windows. Eventually we went into an upstairs room with an empty space above the fireplace, apart from one lonely nail.

'Now, that's reminded me, we must re-hang the Turner. I'll go and get

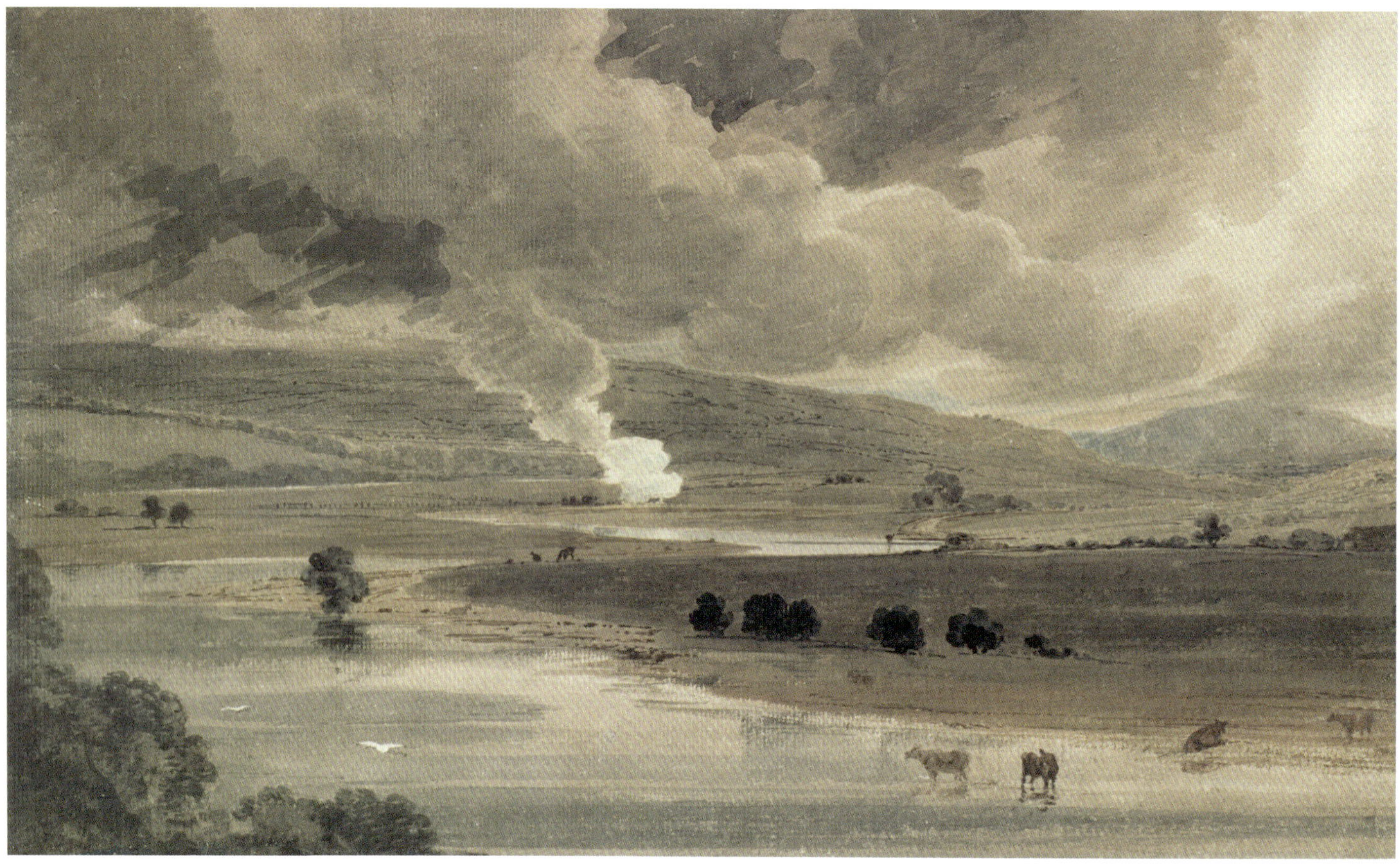

Thomas Girtin, 1775 - 1802. *On the Wharfe* (c. 1800). Watercolour on paper, 31.6 x 52.7cm (Private Collection)

the stepladder if you two wouldn't mind bringing the picture up here. Where did I leave it?'

Luckily we managed to find our way back to the kitchen just as the dogs rushed in. A golden Labrador whisked the picture with a huge muddy tail and knocked it over, but Caroline managed to catch it just in time. Back upstairs, a large stepladder was flailing about with His Lordship underneath it. I rushed to help whilst Caroline, wide-eyed, clung to the picture, reluctant to unwrap it.

'Just two shakes of a lamb's tail and we'll have it back on the wall,' he called from the wobbling stepladder.

The nail was quite high up on the wall, but luckily he was quite tall, even though his balance was a bit shaky. Caroline clung to the stepladder as he climbed up it and I stood on a Sheraton chair to hand the painting to him. He stretched forward, picture in his hands, and for one gut-wrenching moment I thought that he would not reach and closed my eyes to say a prayer. When I opened them again the Turner was hanging on the nail, swinging ever so slightly, but back on the wall. There were a few more minutes of slapstick as I directed His Lordship in getting the picture straight, then at last it was done. We said our goodbyes, got into the car and drove the long way home to Harewood in total silence.

Curators tend to have different perceptions of art history depending on when and where they studied. When I was an eleven-year-old girl from Tadcaster looking wistfully at the French Impressionists in the National Gallery I knew about history, and art, but I had never heard of such a thing as history of art. Unfortunately, neither had the teachers at Tadcaster Grammar School. By the time I was fourteen my parents were busy deciding which university I was going to go to. By then I had decided that I wanted to be a hippie and go to art college instead, but that aspiration was rapidly squashed. My father bought a book called *Opportunities After O Level* and discovered that I needed to study art history to work in an art gallery; that there were not many universities in the 1970s that taught it, and that I needed French and Latin for starters. The good news was that Manchester University offered a degree in art history, and Manchester was not only a big, exciting city, it was conveniently quite a long way from home as well. I got a copy of Gombrich's *The Story of Art* and taught myself art history and scraped my way through Latin and French. Dressed in maxi-skirt and platform-soled boots, I landed at Manchester University, into a profoundly traditional academic course. We learned our art history starting with the Ancient civilisations, stumbled through the Middle Ages, then found the source of everything in the Renaissance. We slowed down a bit to gloat over the excesses of the Baroque and Rococo, shifted uneasily through the eighteenth century, then leapt joyously over the Pre Raphaelites, then not so fashionable, to find my beloved Impressionists and the start of Modernism at the end of the nineteenth century. We did not get much further because our tutor did not think anything terribly important had happened in art since Abstract Impressionism in the 1950s, and the Modern Art course ended with Jackson Pollock getting killed in a car crash in 1956.

Art galleries, to my surprise, did not seem to feature in Manchester's teaching methods. Why could we not go and sit in front of the paintings in Manchester Art Gallery or the drawings in the Whitworth to talk about them? Rather than peer at blurred, black and white slides – not even colour – in a darkened room. A few of us used to slope off to the galleries whenever we could, and so we got to know and love the Pre Raphaelites after all. We discovered that there was such a thing as British art, something that our tutors generally disdained in favour of the French, and I even spotted my first women artists, who of course had never been thought worthy of a mention. Those forays down Mosley Street to see the city's art collections confirmed me in my ambition to be an art curator, now that I knew what a curator was.

I launched my career with a tough couple of years teaching in a comprehensive school in Hull, which introduced me, and my sixth formers, to the Ferens Art Gallery. I would talk to the group about a handful of the major works - by Frans Hals, Lord Leighton, the then newly acquired The Tyro by the Vorticist Wyndham Lewis – then once they were settled down with their sketchbooks I would sneak away to indulge my secret passion for Edwardian sentimentality and spend a few minutes in front of Fred Elwell's **The First Born**. Elwell was one of those British, nay Yorkshire artists, whom you never hear about when you study art history, but they become your daily bread once you work in a public art gallery. After Lincoln College of Art, Elwell had a continental training in both Antwerp and Paris, hence the Impressionistic effects of the light filtering into the cottage bedroom and the intimacy of the domestic interior. This touching painting of a young man arriving to see his wife and child, tenderly laying down a bunch of primroses on the counterpane, was painted in 1913 and purchased by Hull the same year. There is a greater poignancy about the work; just a year later the First World War was to erupt, taking many like this young man away from their wives and children forever.

The Walker Art Gallery in Liverpool gave me my first gallery job, as an education officer of almost missionary zeal. It was the 1980s, and a difficult time to be living and working in Liverpool; the time of the riots, a militant city council and urban poverty on an astonishing scale. The Walker, with its Old Masters, traditional academic values and reputation for showing challenging contemporary art, was generally regarded as an unapproachable ivory tower. My boss and I shared an office that was two halves of a former cloakroom at the back of the lecture hall, one on top of the other. There was one tall window with a gap between the floors that was handy for passing papers through and shouting to each other. We also had a close-up view of the entrance to the Magistrates' Court next door, so every day we could watch an endless parade of human misery. My first assignment was to give talks to classes of Liverpool teenagers about an exhibition of David Hockney's prints, which included portraits of his friends, the Grimms' fairy tales and, unfortunately for me, one or two rather explicit homoerotic subjects. I devised various routes around the exhibition to avoid having to explain the latter, but fifteen-year-olds gravitated towards them like moths to a flame, so I gave in to their demands. My talks gathered quite a crowd. In time, Hockney's painting **Peter Getting Out of Nick's Pool**, which won the John Moore's painting prize in 1967, became one of my best-loved pictures in the Walker's

Opposite: Fred Elwell, 1870 - 1958. *The First Born* (1913). Oil on canvas, 102.3 x 127.3cm (Ferens Art Gallery, Hull Museums and Galleries)

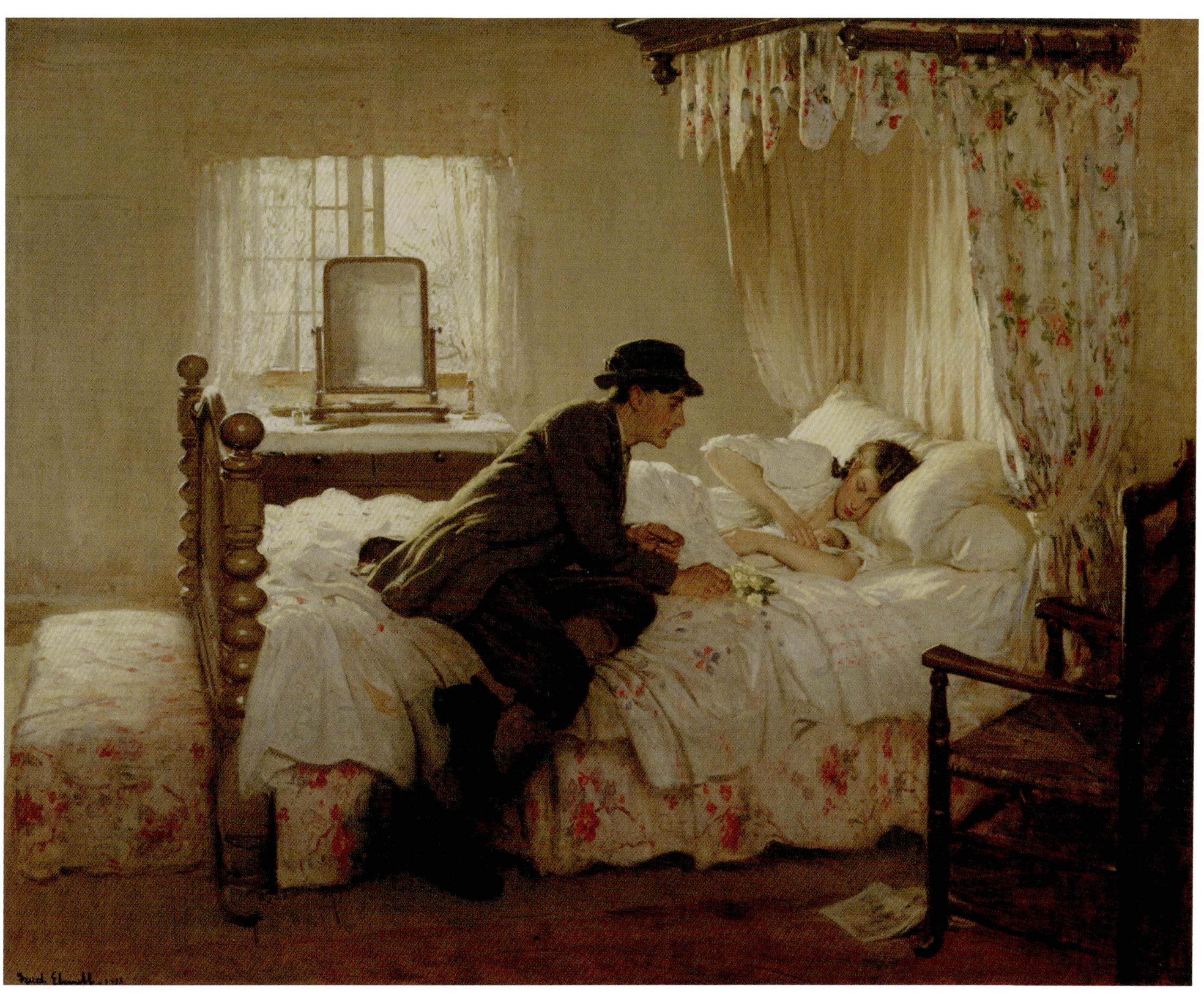

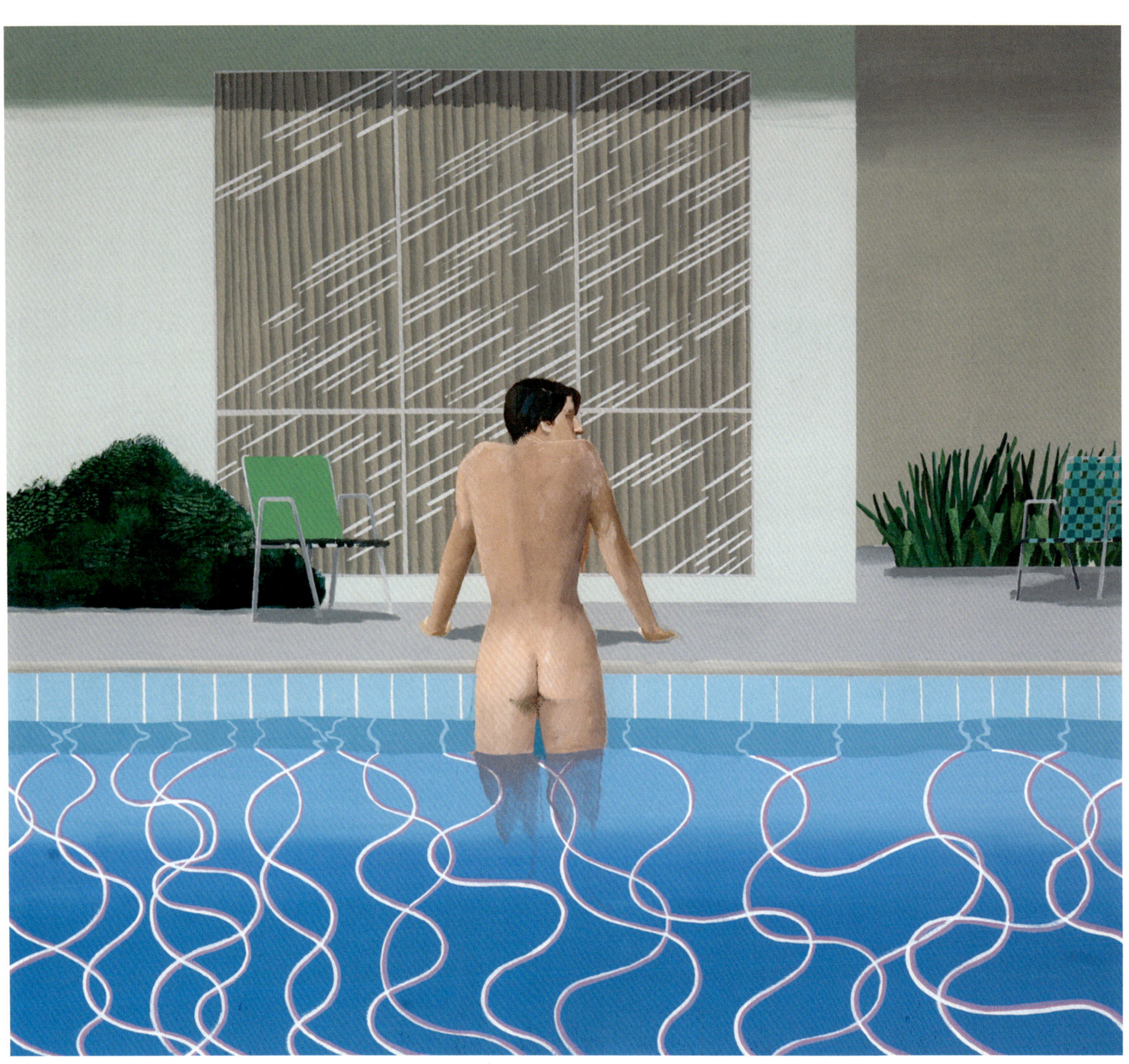

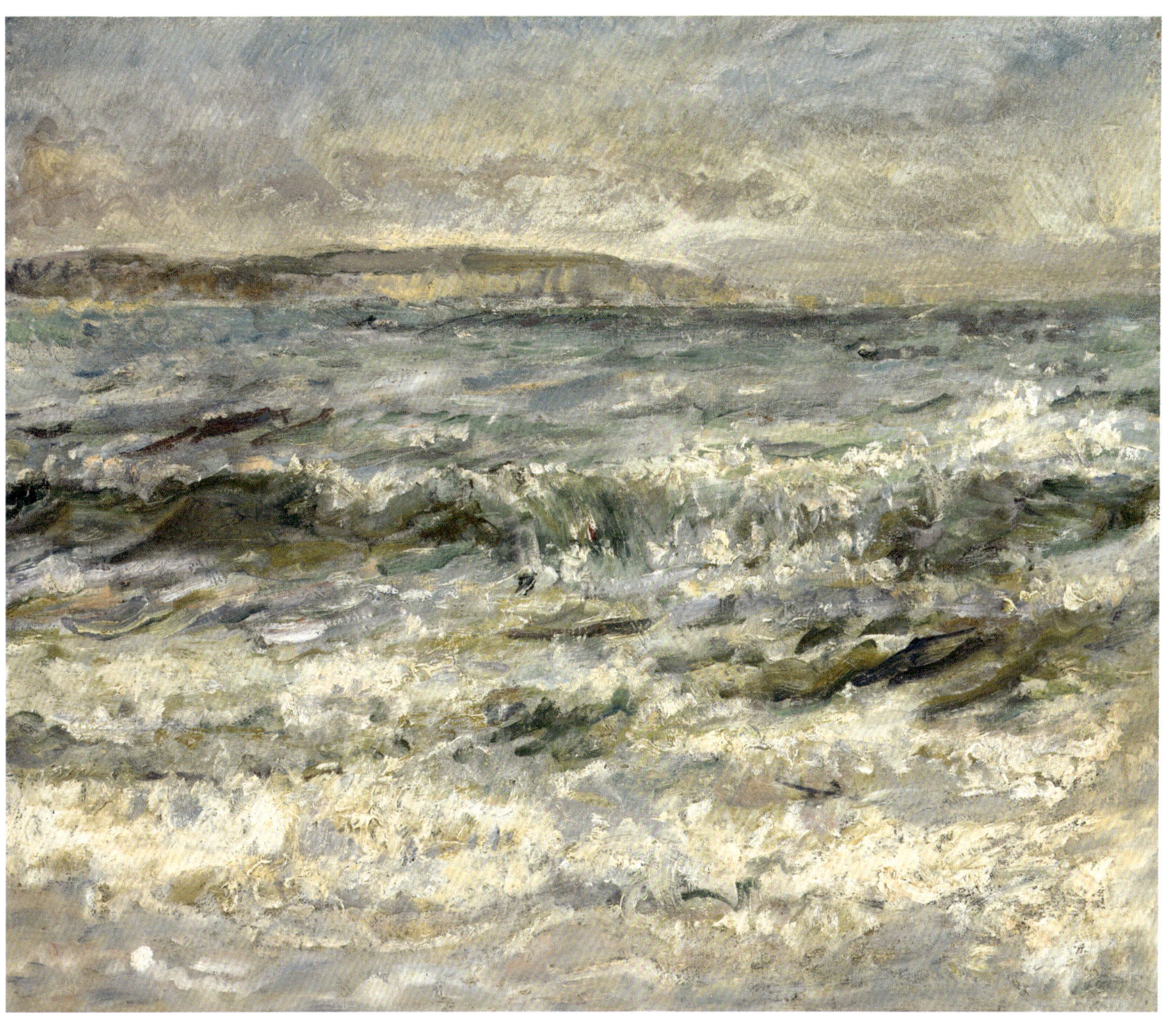

Ethel Walker, 1861 - 1951. *Seascape* (c. 1950). Oil on canvas, 51 x 61cm (Walker Art Gallery, Liverpool)

Opposite: David Hockney, b. 1937. *Peter Getting Out of Nick's Pool* (1966). Acrylic on canvas, 152 x 152cm © David Hockney (Walker Art Gallery, National Museums Liverpool) Photo Credit: Richard Schmidt

collection. Not least because I felt that I had a compatriot's understanding of Hockney's longing for the never-ending sunshine and blue skies of California as a release from the grey climate of Bradford, where one would not willingly get into an outdoor swimming pool whatever the time of year.

At the Walker I found my own calling: the research and promotion of women artists, those strange creatures whom art historians seemed not to have noticed for a couple of hundred years. I came across the Walker's wealth of women's art not by looking at what was on the gallery walls, but in my explorations of the picture stores in the basement of the building. Down there were huge rolling racks hung on each side with mostly huge paintings, and not something I could easily move myself so I used to squeeze between the racks with torch and notebook and see what I could find. I found Sophie Anderson, Jessie MacGregor, Henrietta Rae, Laura Knight, Ethel Gabain, Sheila Fell, hundreds of them, enough to fill a book and an exhibition, which is exactly what I did. When I was feeling

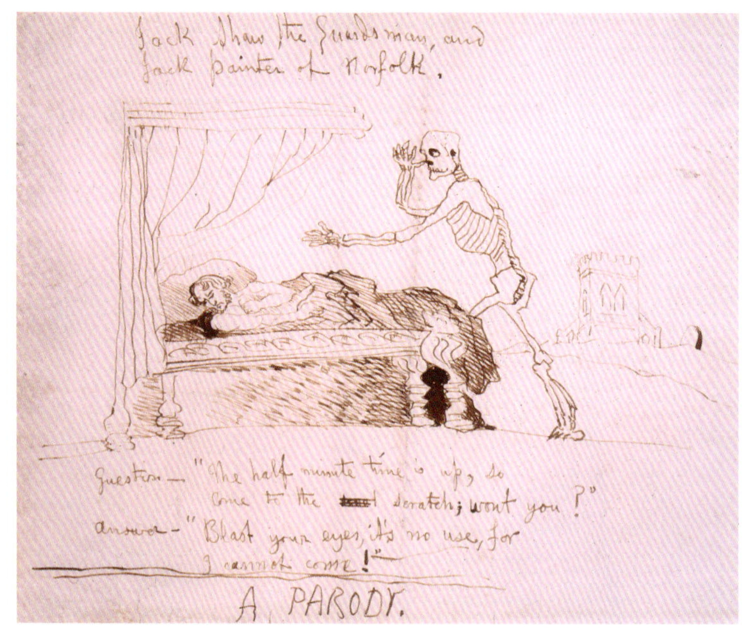

homesick for Yorkshire there was one female artist's painting that I could rely on to take me back there in spirit, Ethel Walker's **Seascape** of Robin Hood's Bay, where she had a house so perilously close to the edge of the cliff that it has long since fallen into the sea. During summers there Ethel Walker painted numerous views of the sea and sky in all their different moods; the angry green-grey look of the North sea and the views of the cliffs stretching in the direction of Whitby immediately put me in mind of holidays at the Bay, when a spot of wind and rain never kept us away from the beach in our one precious week there. Robin Hood's Bay was our childhood heaven, where we were left entirely to our own devices, which mostly involved turning over rocks on the beach to reveal scuttling crabs and wafting sea anemones. Sometimes we were forced into the Volkswagen Beetle and driven to other picturesque places, such as Staithes further up the coast. In the 1960s the old women there were still wearing Victorian gingham bonnets and there was an antique shop to occupy my mother, but I never liked the place; it had a sad feeling. The first time I went there a body had been washed up and we watched as the police carried a red coffin away from the foot of the cliff. Another time there was a house on fire, and when on the third visit there were enormous waves crashing into the shore I decided never to go there again.

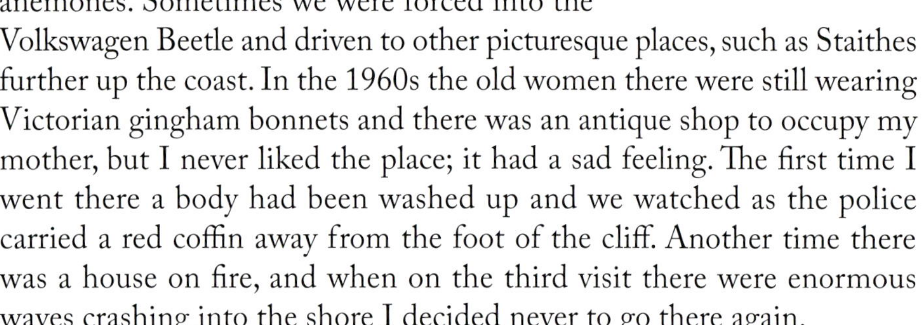

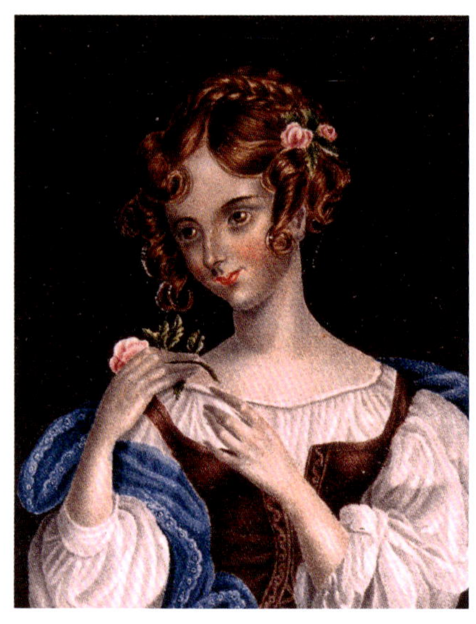

In 1990 I entered the world of the Brontës when I went to Haworth to be the director of the Brontë Parsonage Museum. When I decided on the move to Haworth I believed that I would be developing my career as a feminist historian. I was looking forward to reshaping the museum into a place that celebrated women artists in general and the Brontës in particular. Never has a woman been more wrong. After about a week into the new job I realised that I had unwittingly walked into a whole new place that I knew nothing about – that is, Brontë country. My first mistake was in thinking that the Parsonage was a museum: it was not, it was a shrine – a shrine full of quasi-holy relics, such as Charlotte's tiny shoes and her wedding bonnet; the brass collar that had been worn by Emily's dog, Keeper, and at least fifty locks of hair that purported to have been snipped from the heads of various Brontës. There was also of course a large collection of important Brontë letters, books, drawings and manuscripts, but my overwhelming impression was that the personal possessions and paraphernalia were more highly regarded for their physical connection with the Brontës than was the material that related

Branwell Brontë, 1817 - 1848. *A Parody* (c. 22 July 1848). Ink on paper, 18.9 x 23.7cm (Brontë Parsonage Museum, the Brontë Society)

Charlotte Brontë, 1816 - 1855. *Portrait of a French Brunette* (14 May 1833). Watercolour and body colour on paper, 16.2 x 12.9cm (Brontë Parsonage Museum, the Brontë Society)

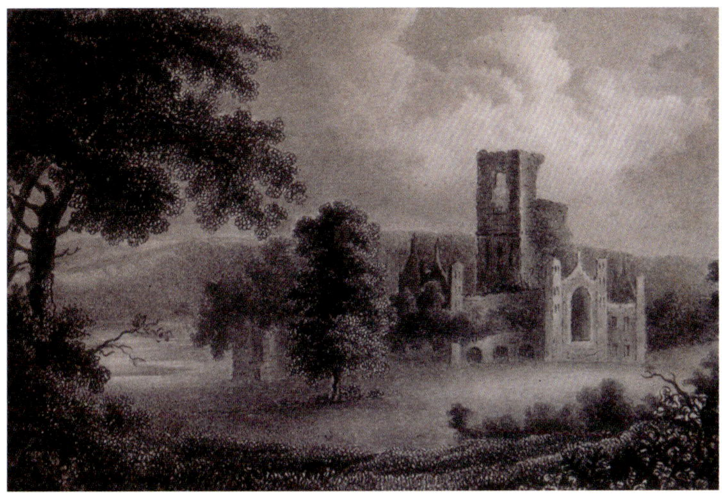

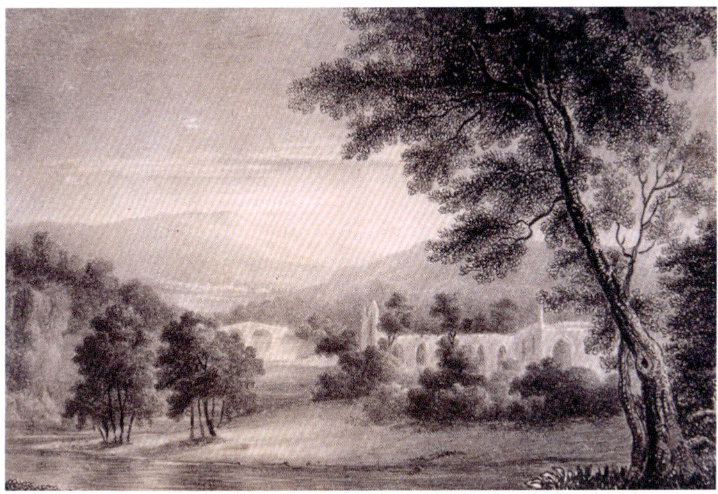

Charlotte Brontë, 1816 - 1855. *Kirkstall Abbey* (c. May 1834). Pencil on card, 9.9 x 14.1cm (Brontë Parsonage Museum, the Brontë Society)

Charlotte Brontë, 1816 - 1855. *Bolton Abbey* (c. May 1834). Pencil on card, 9.9 x 14.1cm (Brontë Parsonage Museum, the Brontë Society)

to their achievements as some of the greatest writers of the nineteenth century. There was a sense that there was nothing more to be learned about the Brontës. There was, of course.

I knew that Branwell Brontë had made an unsuccessful attempt at a career as a portrait painter in Bradford in the 1830s but I was relieved to discover that the Brontë sisters, Charlotte, Emily and Anne, had also been artists as well as writers, with a large collection of paintings and drawings at the Parsonage and other works scattered around the world. The art of the Brontës became my next project. Branwell's portraits of local worthies were less than average in quality, but his drawings could be wildly inventive, especially the ones that he made just before his death, that tracked his drug fuelled demise. Charlotte, it emerged, had a serious ambition to be an artist and even showed her meticulous pencil drawings of Bolton Abbey and Kirkstall Abbey in the summer exhibition of the Royal Northern Society for the Encouragement of the Fine Arts in Leeds in 1834. Charlotte would have been well aware that Turner frequently sketched the ruins of Bolton Abbey and that Wordsworth wrote his poem *The White Doe of Rylstone* after a visit there with his sister Dorothy. Indeed, Charlotte visited this famous picturesque site, but her drawings are not from nature; this drawing is a copy of Edward Finden's crisp engraving of the scene, based on Turner's well-known drawing of 1809 in the British Museum, which Charlotte found in the magazine *The Literary Souvenir*, 1826. The Brontë sisters learnt to draw from copying, which was the method of the day, intent on gathering drawing skills that they could use as teachers and governesses, but at the same time art was immensely important to them as writers. Although none of them ever saw much original art – except for Charlotte who, in her years of fame after the publication of *Jane Eyre*, had more opportunities to visit the National Gallery and the British Museum in London – visual art was inextricably entwined with their literary outpourings. As children they made tiny books of illustrated stories, and Charlotte copied portraits of lovely ladies in *Heath's Book of Beauty*, transforming them into the heroines of Angria, their shared imaginary world. Emily, the animal lover, painted her pet bullmastiff Keeper 'from life' in painstaking watercolour, and Anne made drawings of trees that evoked her love of trees as much as the lines of her poem *Lines composed in a wood on a windy day*, written in 1846. Art was a constant theme in the Brontës' novels: Anne Brontë wrote one of the few books in Victorian literature with a woman artist as heroine, *The Tenant of Wildfell Hall*, and in *Jane Eyre* in a number of key scenes, such as when Mr Rochester insists that Jane shows him the drawings in her portfolio, art is used to expose elements of Jane's character and to allude to her growing feelings for her employer.

The Brontës have inspired generations of creative artists – painters, illustrators, musicians, composers, film-makers, photographers and dancers - through their novels and their own life stories. In recent years an innovative contemporary arts programme has brought some of the best writers and artists in the land to work and exhibit at Haworth, including Paula Rego, who in 2002 began a series of theatrical and subversive lithographs made in response to Charlotte Brontë's *Jane Eyre*. Rego's prints were partly inspired by Jean Rhys's 1966 'prequel' novel *Wide Sargasso Sea* about the first Mrs Rochester, the West Indian Creole Bertha who becomes the madwoman in the attic. Rego has repeatedly drawn on well-loved stories as inspiration for her work; she takes a narrative and turns it into a picture, using sitters, costumes and all kinds of props until the composition symbolises her original idea. In **Come to Me**, in which we see Jane's face twisted in anguish as Rochester seems to call to her, the sense is that the artist is beckoning to Jane to join her. The image is constructed in a visual style that mimics the manner of Victorian illustration. This graphic style is in keeping with the period of the novel, but subverted by Rego, thus bringing Jane into the artist's own world of dark imagery, with an eye for the macabre and a disdain for the novel's happy ending.

Leeds is the first city that I got to know as a child; it was where we were taken to buy new winter coats at Marshall and Snelgrove, tweed with a velvet collar and a ghastly matching round felt hat. Later, it was where we went to buy miniskirts at Chelsea Girl; to drink frothy coffee in a café on the Headrow or a furtive half of lager in the Victoria pub behind the Town Hall; to clubs to hear bands such as Jethro Tull and Quintessence, and, of course, to go to the art gallery. As a post-graduate student I

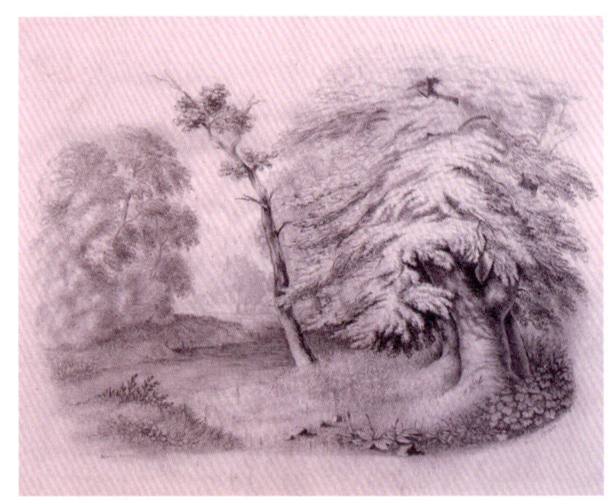

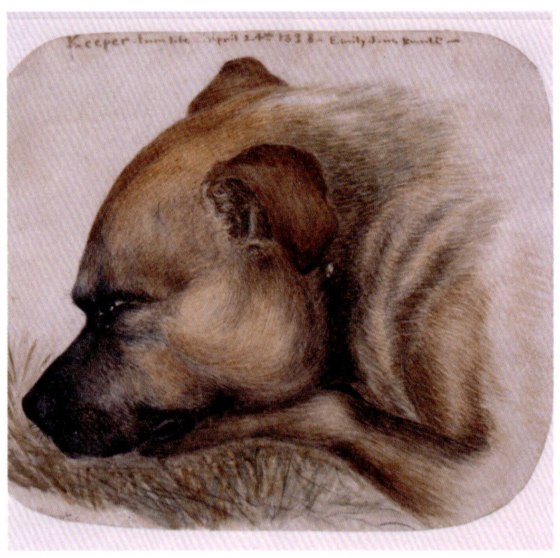

Anne Brontë, 1820 - 1849. *Landscape with Trees* (16 December 1843). Pencil on card, 25.2 x 32.7cm. (Brontë Parsonage Museum, the Brontë Society)

Emily Brontë, 1818 - 1848. *Keeper from Life* (24 April 1838). Watercolour on paper, 13.2 x 15.7cm (Brontë Parsonage Museum, the Brontë Society)

Opposite: Paula Rego, b. 1936. *Come to Me*, from Jane Eyre print series (2001 – 2002). Lithograph, 89 x 59cm (Marlborough Fine Art)

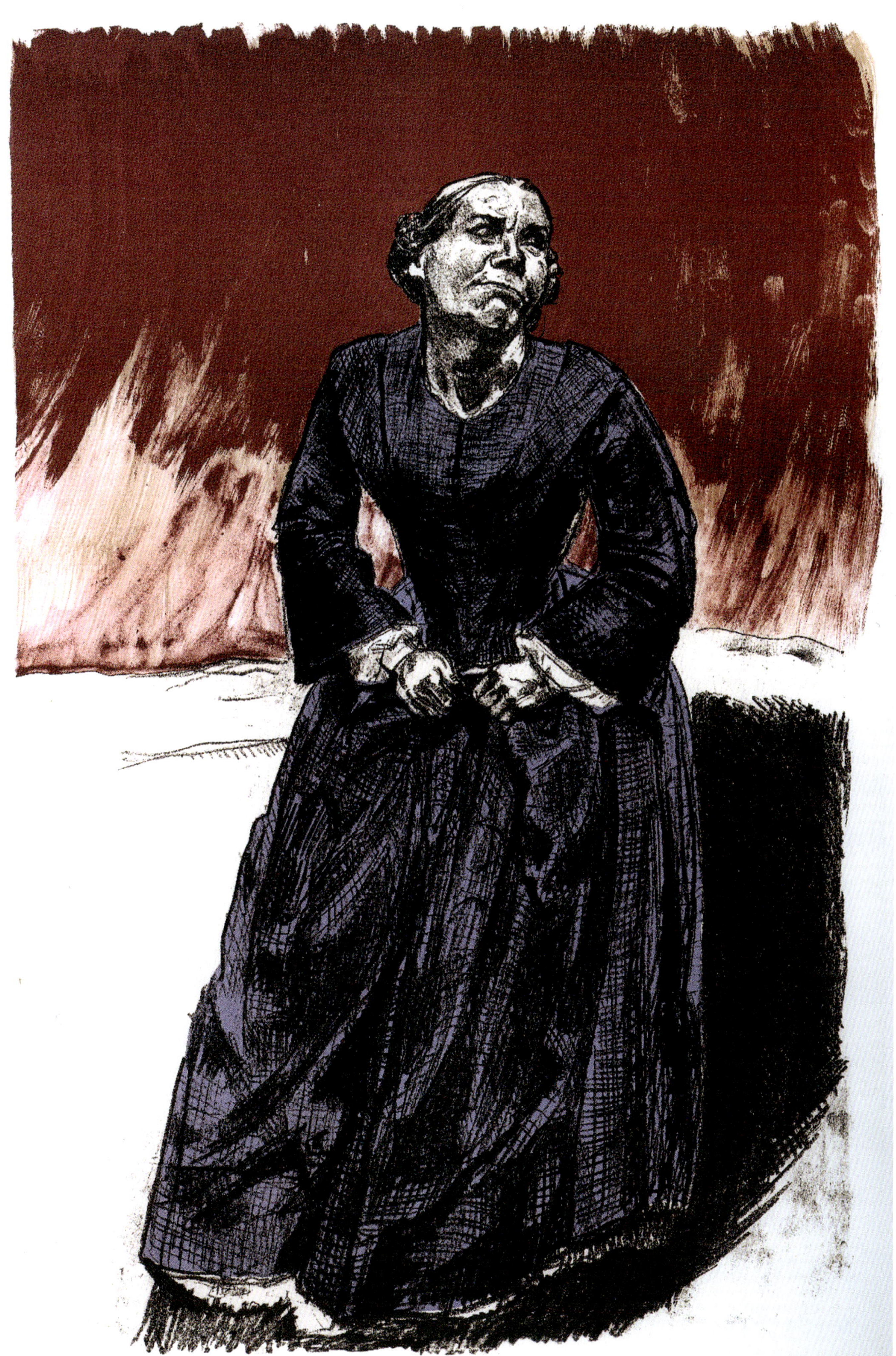

worked as a volunteer at Leeds Art Gallery, Temple Newsam House and Lotherton Hall, a rich and varied work experience. At Lotherton I modelled dresses in the costume collection so that they could be photographed, including eighteenth century silk gowns, which were so tiny that I had to breathe in hard to get the bodice fastened and bend at the knees so that the skirt covered my legs. Nowadays a costume curator would faint with shock at the very thought of real people slipping into pieces from the collection. At Temple Newsam I worked on an exhibition of fans and was thrilled to see my name in an exhibition catalogue for the first time in my life. Working in Leeds Art Gallery was when I first got to know Atkinson Grimshaw, the painter of moonlight.

Atkinson Grimshaw is an artist whose success in his lifetime as a provincial painter of moonlit urban scenes and landscapes died with him in 1893. Indeed, he barely made it into the history books until the reputations of Victorian painters began to be restored in the early 1960s. Grimshaw was born in Leeds, hence the city's large collection of his paintings. In the 1970s, when I worked in Leeds Art Gallery, I lived in Headingley in Leeds in a flat in a big house behind a high stone wall, surrounded by trees. As far as I was concerned, I lived in a Grimshaw painting, and the girl walking along a moonlit road could be me. The melancholy of Grimshaw's paintings appealed to me, fitting in with my love of Gothic novels and romantic poetry. This subjective view of an artist's work was eventually knocked out of me by years of research and curatorship. Later I learnt that Grimshaw's shadowy lanes are generic views accumulated from his knowledge and observations of the city's streets; that his life was troubled by grief and financial worries. But whenever I look at his paintings, particularly **Silver Moonlight**, which I know so well because it is in the collection of the Mercer Art Gallery in Harrogate where I am currently the curator, my instinct is to be drawn into a sense of a Yorkshire city that persists to this day. Grimshaw is one of the many artists I have chosen for this book, all of who, for me, have that same very special sense of Yorkshire. I hope that you, the reader, will feel the same.

Atkinson Grimshaw, 1836 - 1893.
Silver Moonlight (1880). Oil on canvas, 83.2 x 121.9cm (Mercer Art Gallery, Harrogate Borough Council)

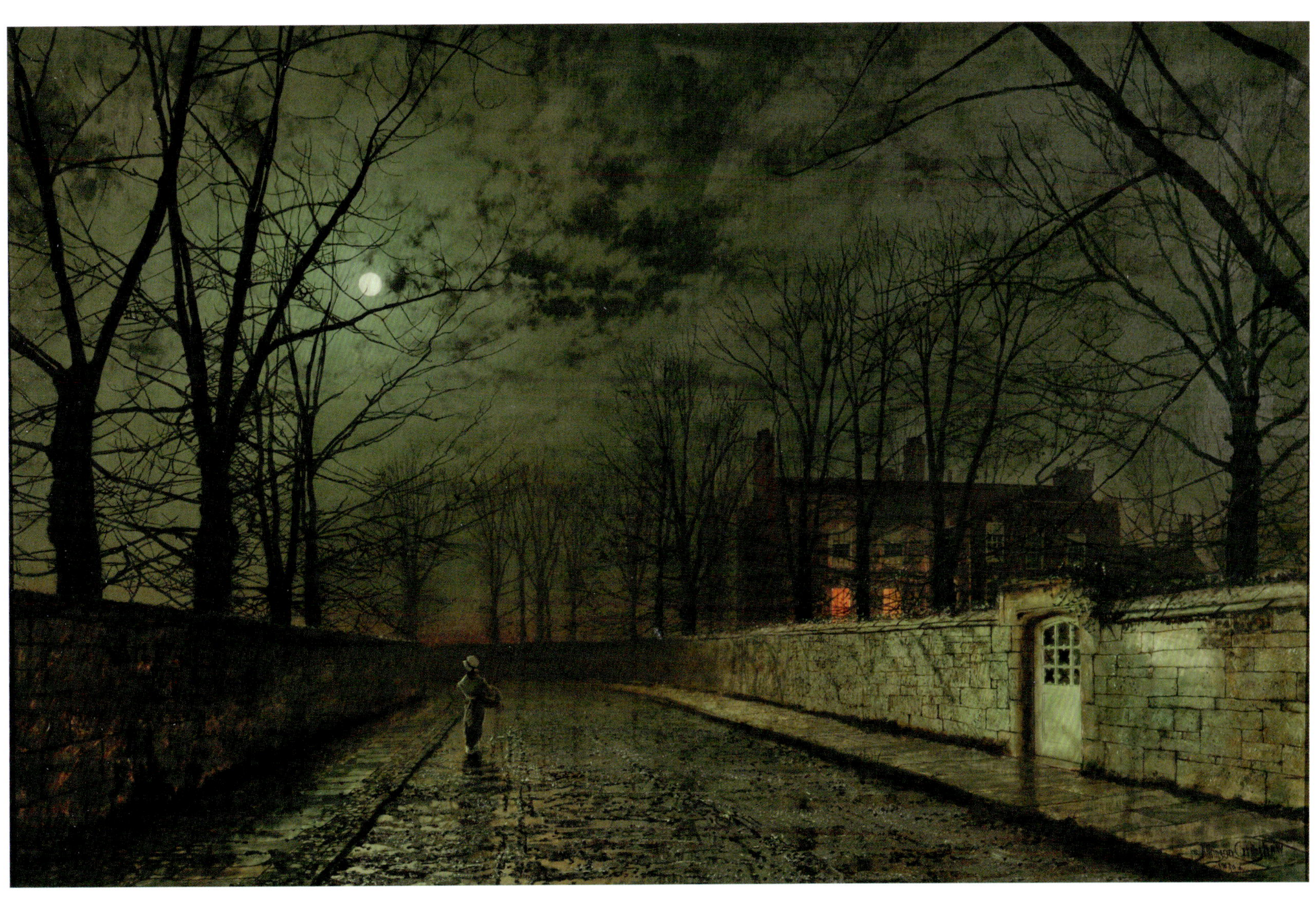

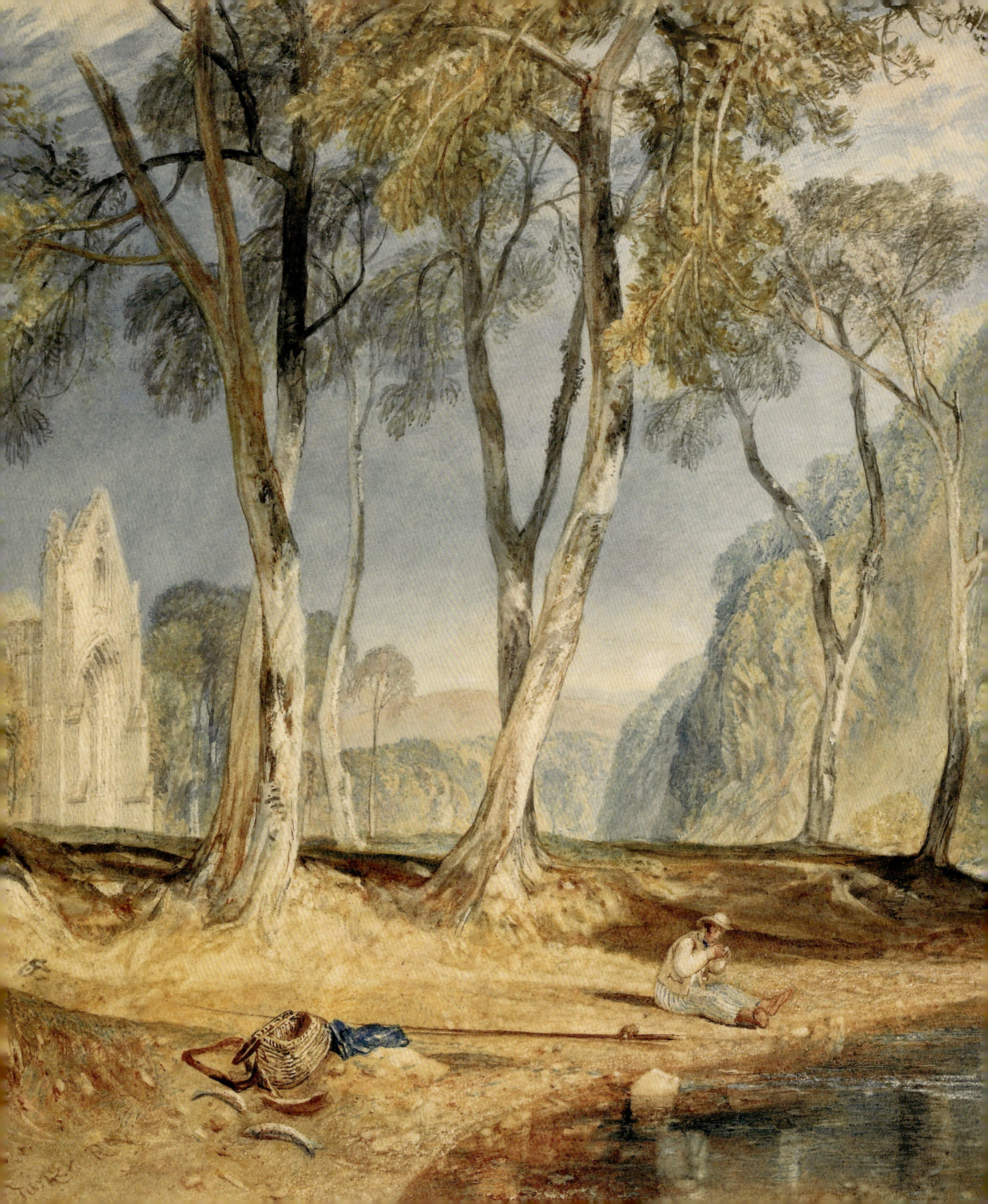

2. The Yorkshire Landscape

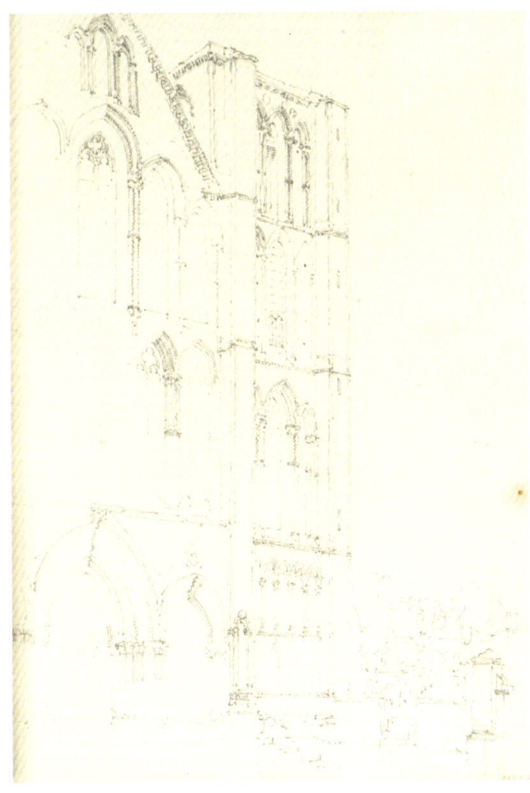

J M W Turner, 1755 - 1851. *Ripon Cathedral: West Front from North of England Sketchbook* (1797). Graphite on paper, 27.2 x 21cm (Turner Bequest, 1856 – Tate)

Opposite: J M W Turner, 1755 - 1851. Detail of *Bolton Abbey* (c.1825). Watercolour with extra gum Arabic and scratching out on paper, 28.1 x 40cm (Lady Lever Art Gallery, National Museums Liverpool)

'… those shores of Wharfe which, I believe, he could never revisit without tears; nay, which for all the latter part of his life, he could never even speak of, but his voice faltered'
John Ruskin, *Modern Painters* Vol IV, Part V.

The Yorkshire landscape has inspired legions of British artists to create some of their very best work. John Ruskin, writing about Joseph Mallord William Turner's drawing of **Bolton Abbey** of 1825, which he then owned, described how the mere mention of the beauty of Yorkshire's landscape moved the great British painter to tears decades after he had first seen it. Indeed, Turner's tour of the North in 1797 is known to have inspired his artistic creation until the end of his days. In the late eighteenth century the Yorkshire landscape was the subject for the art patronage of Yorkshire's aristocratic families, followed in the nineteenth century by the wealthy industrialists of the Victorian age. Later, in the twentieth century, Henry Moore and Barbara Hepworth carved and cast their monumental sculpture with memories of the rough-hewn landscape of West Yorkshire. Then in the twenty-first century we find David Hockney painting vividly coloured trees beside a road near Bridlington in the east Yorkshire Wolds.

Yorkshire is a vast county with a diversity of landscapes that seems to define the character of the people who live in them. Mrs Gaskell, for instance, in her *Life of Charlotte Brontë*, 1857, describes 'the peculiar force of character which the Yorkshiremen display. This makes them interesting as a race; while at the same time, as individuals, the remarkable degree of self-sufficiency they possess gives them an air of independence rather apt to repel a stranger.' The Yorkshire Dales have a rounded summer green softness that is belied by jagged limestone outcrops that in winter are transformed into harsh snow-scapes. West Yorkshire has its characteristic masses of dark stone houses, old mill buildings both ruined and regenerated, and areas of moorland in every shade of bleakness, but it is not just a gritty stereotype. A journey across

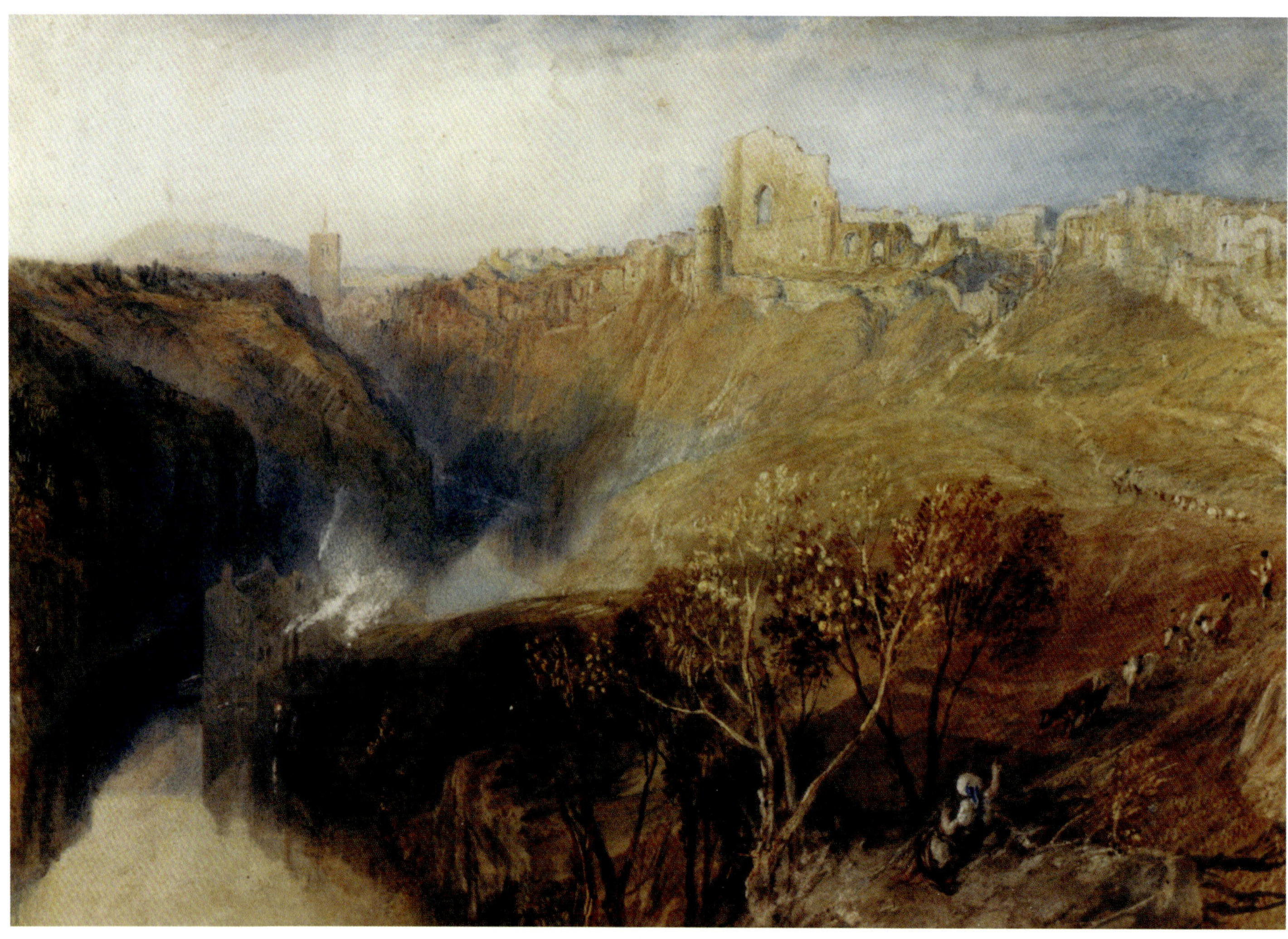

Yorkshire reveals every stage of its industrial history, from the ironstone mines of the northeast moors and coast to the shiny service industries of contemporary Leeds. There are areas of Yorkshire that have attracted artists from far afield with their sheer beauty, and others that have sent creative natives packing, in search of brighter colour and a more benign light.

In 1797 Turner spent eight weeks on a sketching tour of the north of England; a journey that was to prove to be one of the most important expeditions of his life because its influence on his art was to remain with him forever. He took with him two large drawing books - now in the Tate, accepted by the nation as part of the Turner Bequest 1856 – which he filled with over one hundred and sixty sketches of the landscape in pencil and watercolour. The artist travelled from London up through the centre of the country, passing through Leeds and Wakefield, then to the north of Yorkshire where he made drawings of Knaresborough Castle, Ripon

J M W Turner, 1755 - 1851. *Knaresborough Castle* (c. 1797-98). Watercolour and graphite on card, 7.5 x 12cm (Private Collection)

Opposite: J M W Turner, 1755 - 1851. Detail of *Harewood House from the North East* (1797). Graphite and watercolour on paper, 49.5 x 64.5cm (Harewood House Trust)

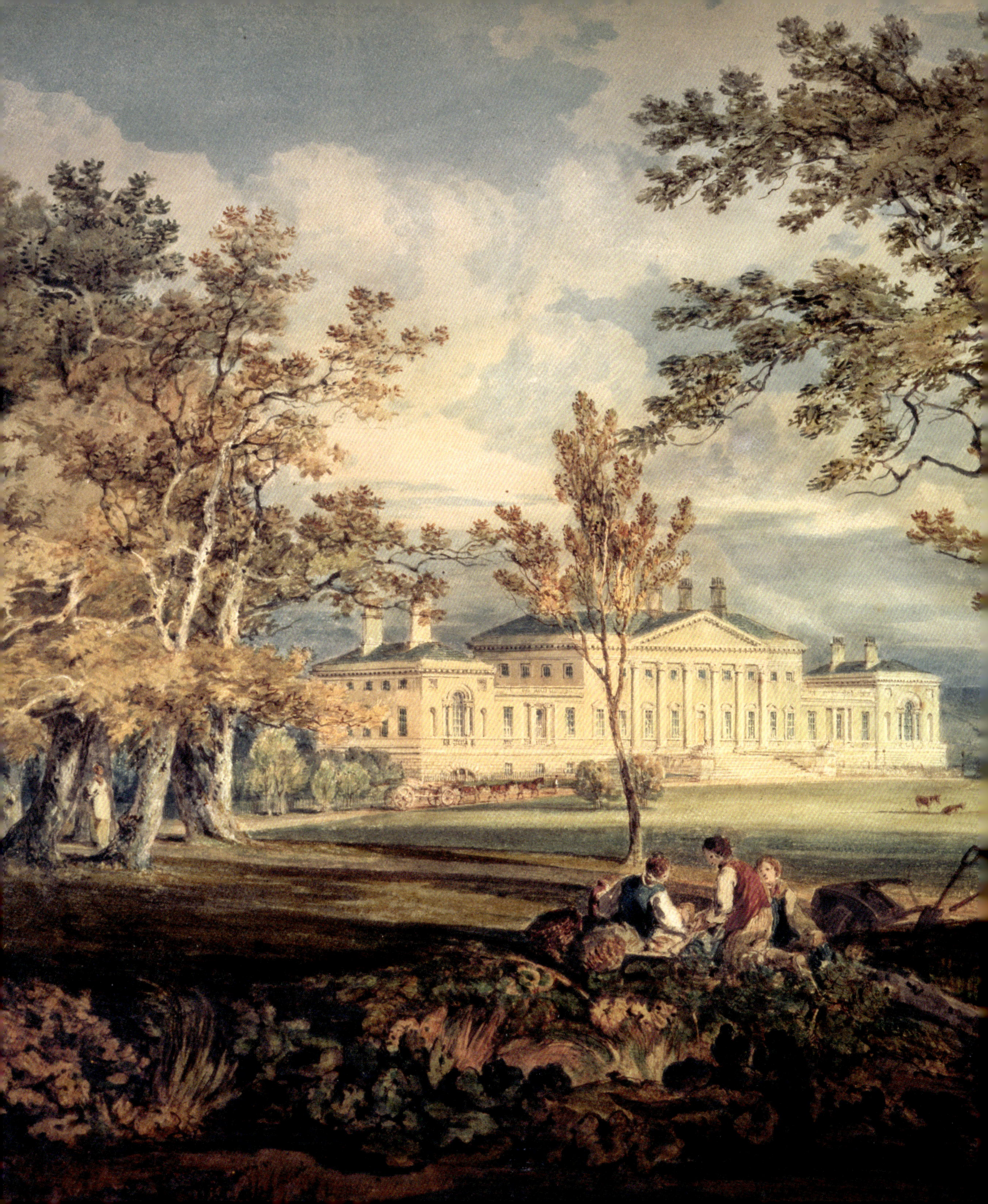

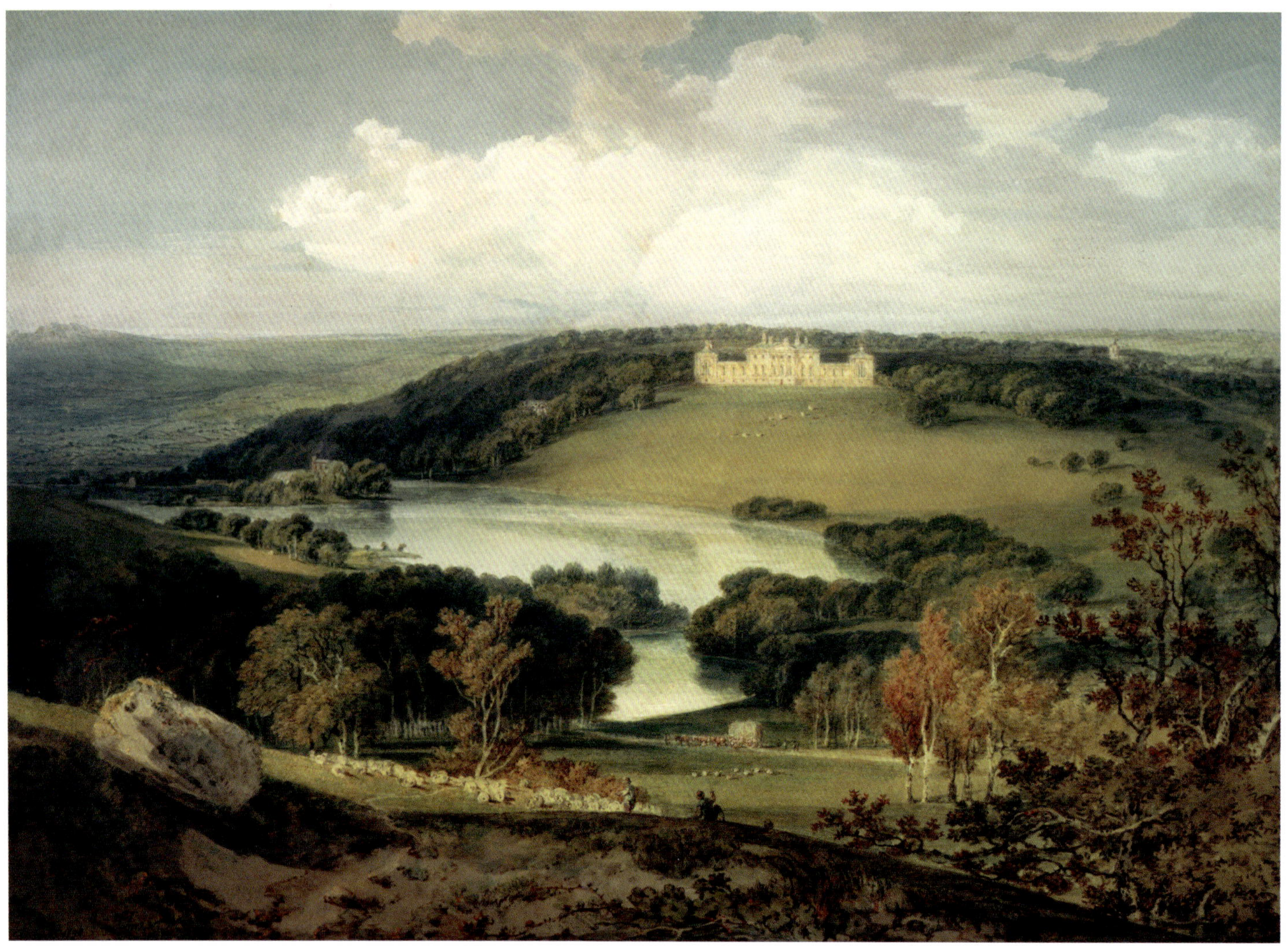

J M W Turner, 1755 - 1851. *Harewood House from the South* (1798). Graphite and watercolour on paper, 47 x 66.1cm (Harewood House Trust)

Cathedral and Fountains Abbey, all of which he returned to later as the source for large finished watercolours. Turner travelled on into Northumberland, along the east coast as far as Berwick upon Tweed, then west into the Lake District. He then struck off back in the direction of York, visiting Bolton Abbey en route, arriving finally at Harewood House near Leeds, home of the 1st Earl of Harewood, where he had been summoned by one of his earliest patrons, Edward Viscount Lascelles, to create a group of watercolour paintings of views of the house with its Capability Brown designed surroundings, and the looming ragged shape of Harewood Castle. Turner was then only twenty-two years old, highly successful in the business of making topographical and architectural studies of the great buildings of England, and it was this outstanding skill that had brought him to Lascelles' attention, but by the time he reached Harewood his art was about to change forever. Enthralled by the desolate, romantic ruins of the abbeys and castles seen on his tour of the north,

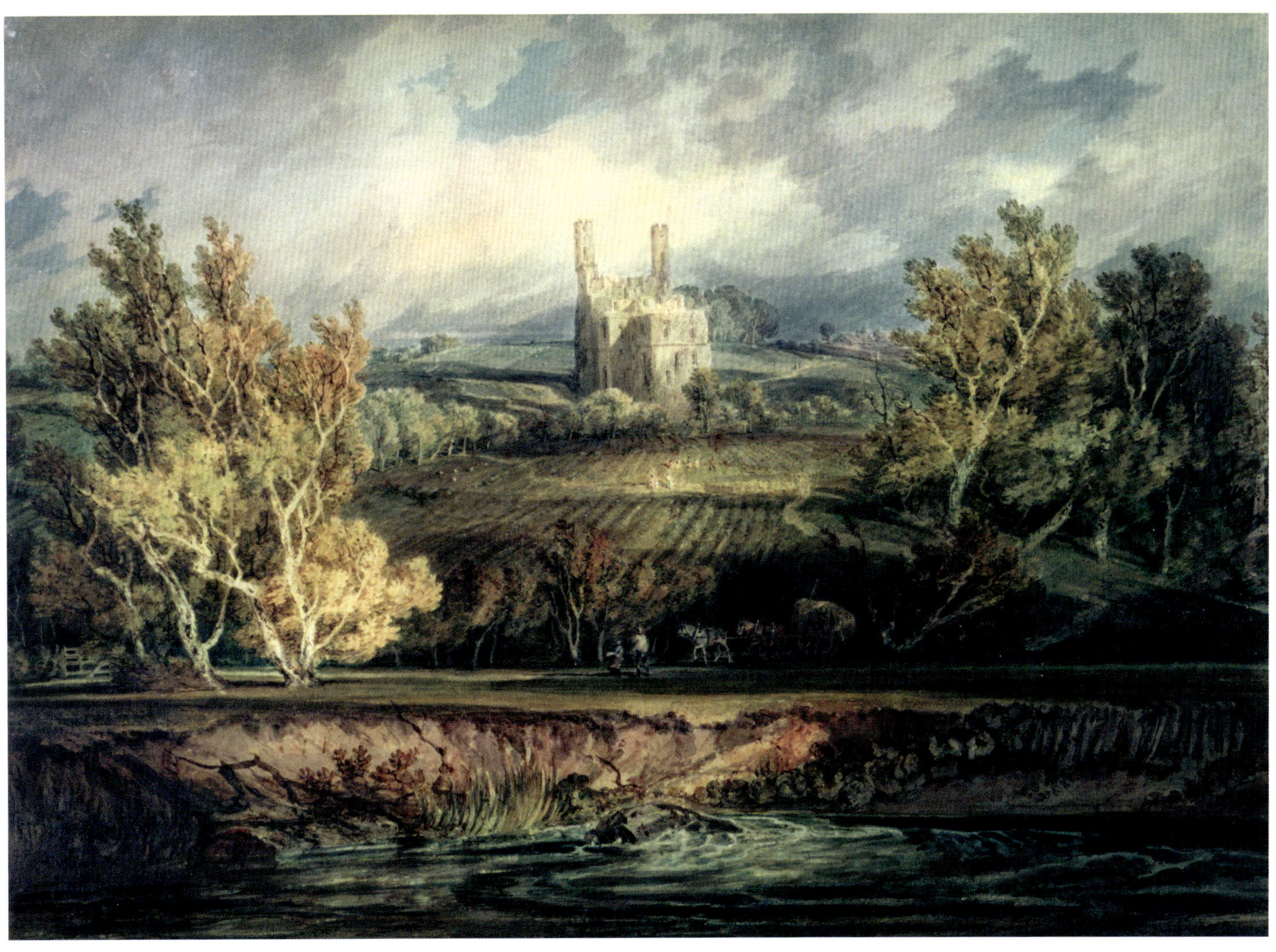

J M W Turner, 1755 - 1851. *Harewood Castle from the North* (1798). Graphite and watercolour on paper, 45.7 x 65.2cm (Harewood House Trust)

enraptured by the ever-changing light of the great northern skies falling on the greyness of the North Sea and the towering drama of lakes and mountains, Turner had discovered his own great potential as a landscape painter.

At Harewood Turner was more attracted to the landscape than the magnificent house, and roamed the park making expansive views of its surroundings. On his return to London, in November 1797 Turner despatched the first two of his Harewood watercolours to Lascelles, one depicting the house seen from the northeast and the other from the southwest. These works displayed a new density of colour, with the effects of light and weather described in an atmospheric manner that was to become the hallmark of Turner's genius as a painter. In all of the Harewood works, Turner moves away from the conventional manner of depicting the country house as the dominating feature of the view and concentrates his attention on the landscape, on the trees, the foliage, the

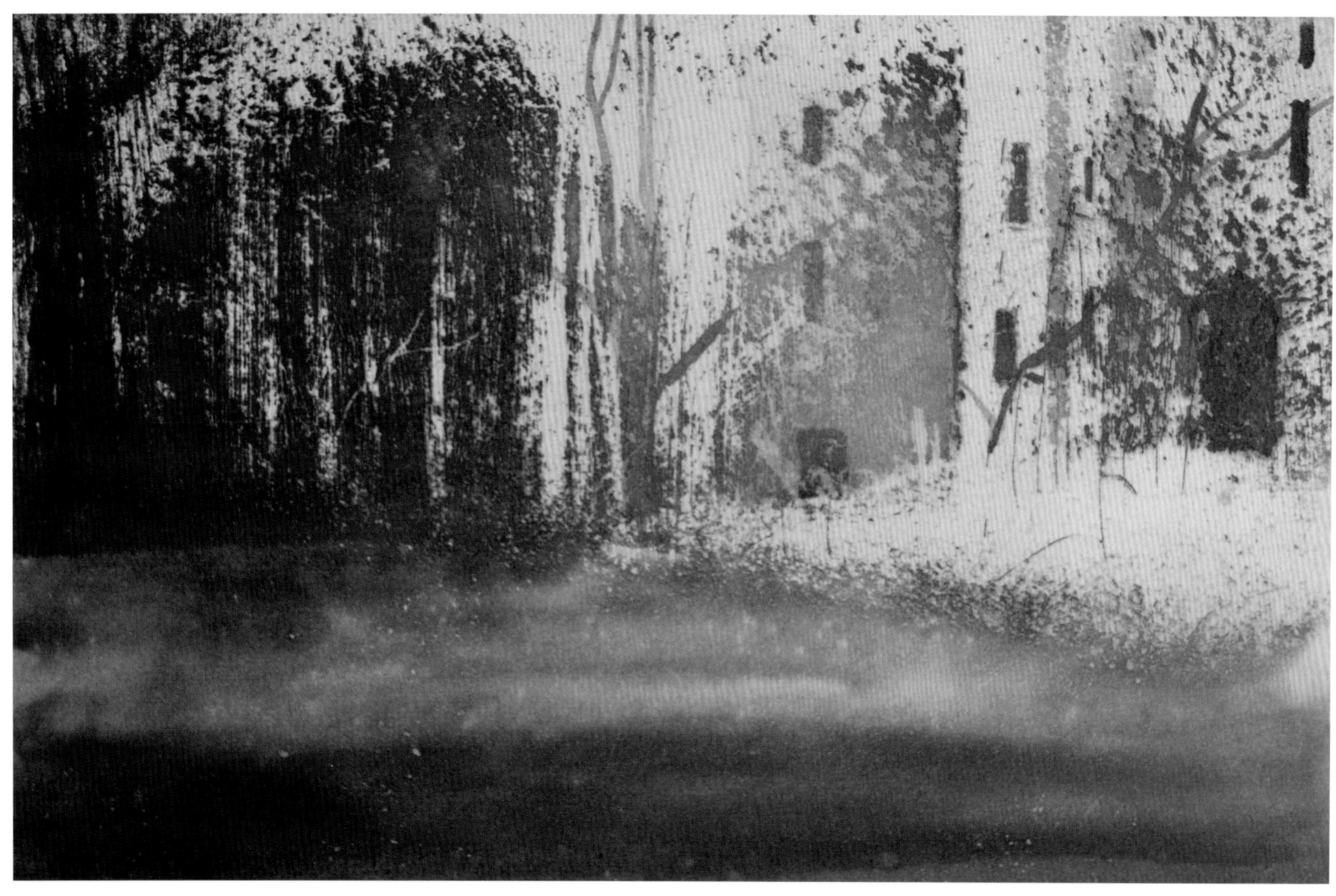

boulders and, innovatively, he places groups of workers going about their daily business prominently in the foreground. Turner was a man of humble origins, the son of a Covent Garden barber, and in **Harewood from the North East** it is clear from his choice of human content that his interest lies with his own class. For him Harewood is not just an elegant park to be enjoyed by people of wealth and culture; it is a place where the working classes toil to maintain the viability of the landscape, such as the group here in the foreground, resting from the day's labours of felling a tree as the sun begins to fade and the trees cast their cool shadows over them. In **Harewood House from the South**, delivered to Lascelles six months later, the house sits like a distant coronet, sublimated by the sweeping view of Wharfedale where the natural form of Almscliffe Crag sits in splendour. In the foreground the eye is captured by the wealth of detail with which Turner describes the texture of the earth and trees, a landscape once again inhabited by the workers.

Harewood Castle may well have appealed more to Turner than the house itself, with its dramatic rugged shape and commanding position

Norman Ackroyd, b. 1938. *Harewood Castle* (1997). Aquatint, 28 x 37cm. (Courtesy of the Artist)

Opposite: Norman Ackroyd, b. 1938. *Harewood in Autumn* (1997). Aquatint, 28 x 37cm. (Courtesy of the Artist)

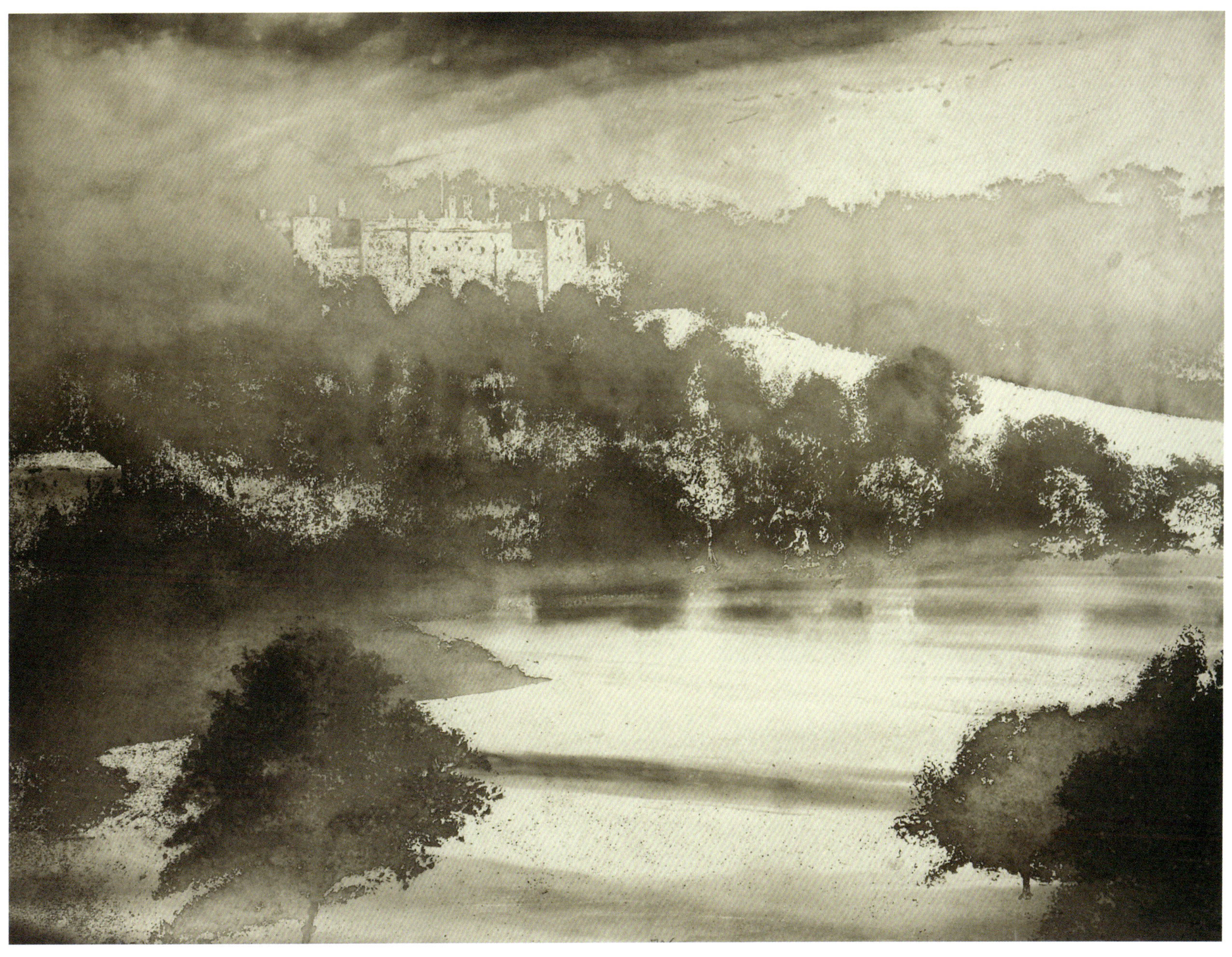

overlooking the River Wharfe. In **Harewood Castle from the North**, 1798, he conveys a sense of movement throughout the view, the water seeming to swirl in a gathering wind as the sky above darkens with threatened rain, causing the haywain to hurry to cover the load on his wagon. As the figures in the fields respond to the forces of nature around them, it is Turner's intention that the viewer is also compelled to engage with the sense of human vitality in its relationship with nature.

In the twentieth century Harewood became a royal residence when HRH Princess Mary, The Princess Royal, married Henry Lascelles, the 6th Earl of Harewood. Princess Mary died in 1965, but even in her lifetime Harewood had started to reinvent itself as a modern tourist attraction. George Lascelles, the 7th Earl of Harewood, Princess Mary's son, was highly cultured, and despite the massive death duties that fell upon him in 1947 when his father died, Lord Harewood managed to keep the most important art collections of the house intact, including Chippendale furniture, Old Master paintings and the Turner watercolours. Later George and his second wife Patricia, Countess of Harewood added significant international modern art, paving the way for Harewood's present day reincarnation as a centre for both historic and contemporary art. From the 1980s artists continued in the tradition established by Turner and Girtin and were invited to Harewood to make work inspired by the house and landscape. Leeds born Norman Ackroyd, celebrated landscape artist and printmaker, was first invited to Harewood in 1997 to mark the bicentenary of Turner's visit. Like Turner, Ackroyd has roamed Britain, visiting its remotest corners to find his subjects. Ackroyd followed in Turner's footsteps around the park, house and castle and produced a set of etchings that seemed to use the acid on the metal plate as fluidly as Turner used watercolour. Ackroyd's prints possess that same sense of engagement with nature in all its moods with swirling dark ink clouds rearing overhead with deep cuts into the plate to depict the light breaking through. The printmaker, interestingly, never includes the human figure in his work.

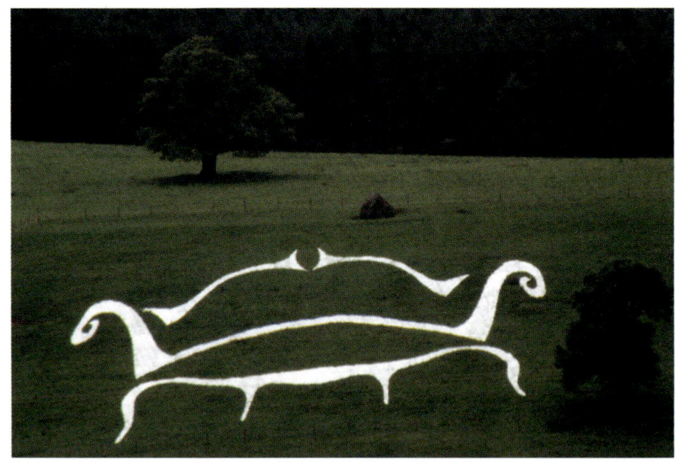

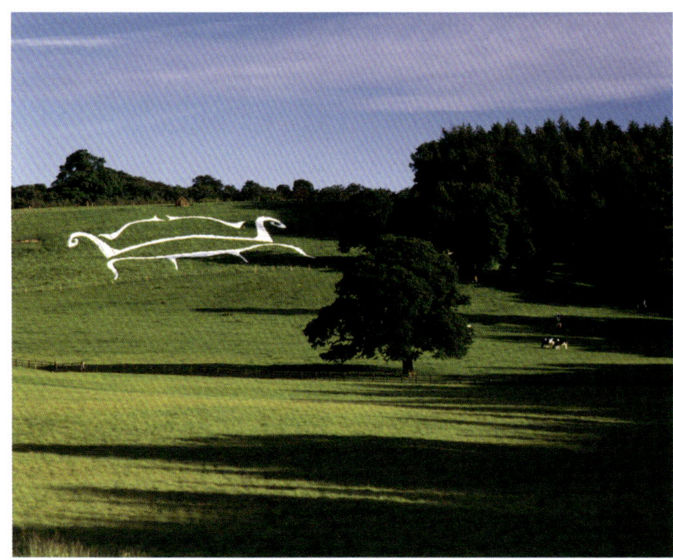

In 2000 the spotlight at Harewood turned on Thomas Chippendale, the master furniture maker born just down the road in Otley, who was commissioned by Edwin Lascelles to furnish the newly built house from top to bottom. The vast majority of this furniture survives to this day, some major pieces having been rescued from barns on the estate where the Victorian generation had consigned them to oblivion. Since the 1960s much restoration work has been carried out and magnificent mirrors and suites of furniture have been rehabilitated in their original locations. The 2000 Chippendale exhibition celebrated the new millennium with the restoration of the lavish Chippendale State Bed along with a visual arts programme that invited a number of artists working in all media to create their response to Harewood's multi-faceted history.

Artist Kate Whiteford has always had an interest in the relationship between landscape and history, which made her a natural choice to create

Kate Whiteford, b. 1952. *Sitelines, Harewood: After Chippendale. Land drawing close view* (2000). (Courtesy of the Artist)

Kate Whiteford, b. 1952. *Sitelines, Harewood: After Chippendale. Land drawing distant view* (2000). (Courtesy of the Artist)

Opposite: Kate Whiteford, b. 1952. *Sitelines, Harewood: After Chippendale. Chippendale Sofa* (2000). Watercolour on paper, 55 x 70cm (Courtesy of the Artist)

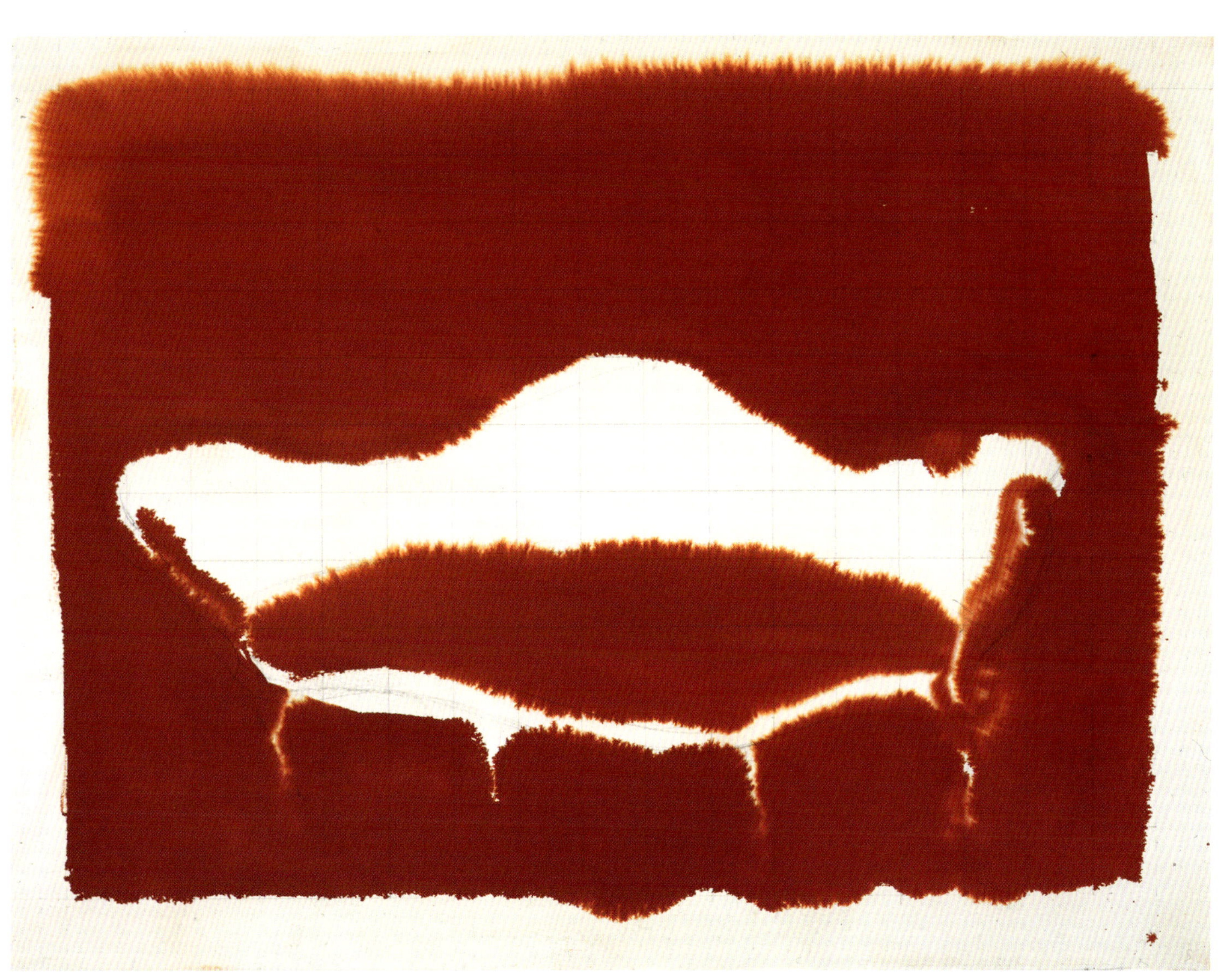

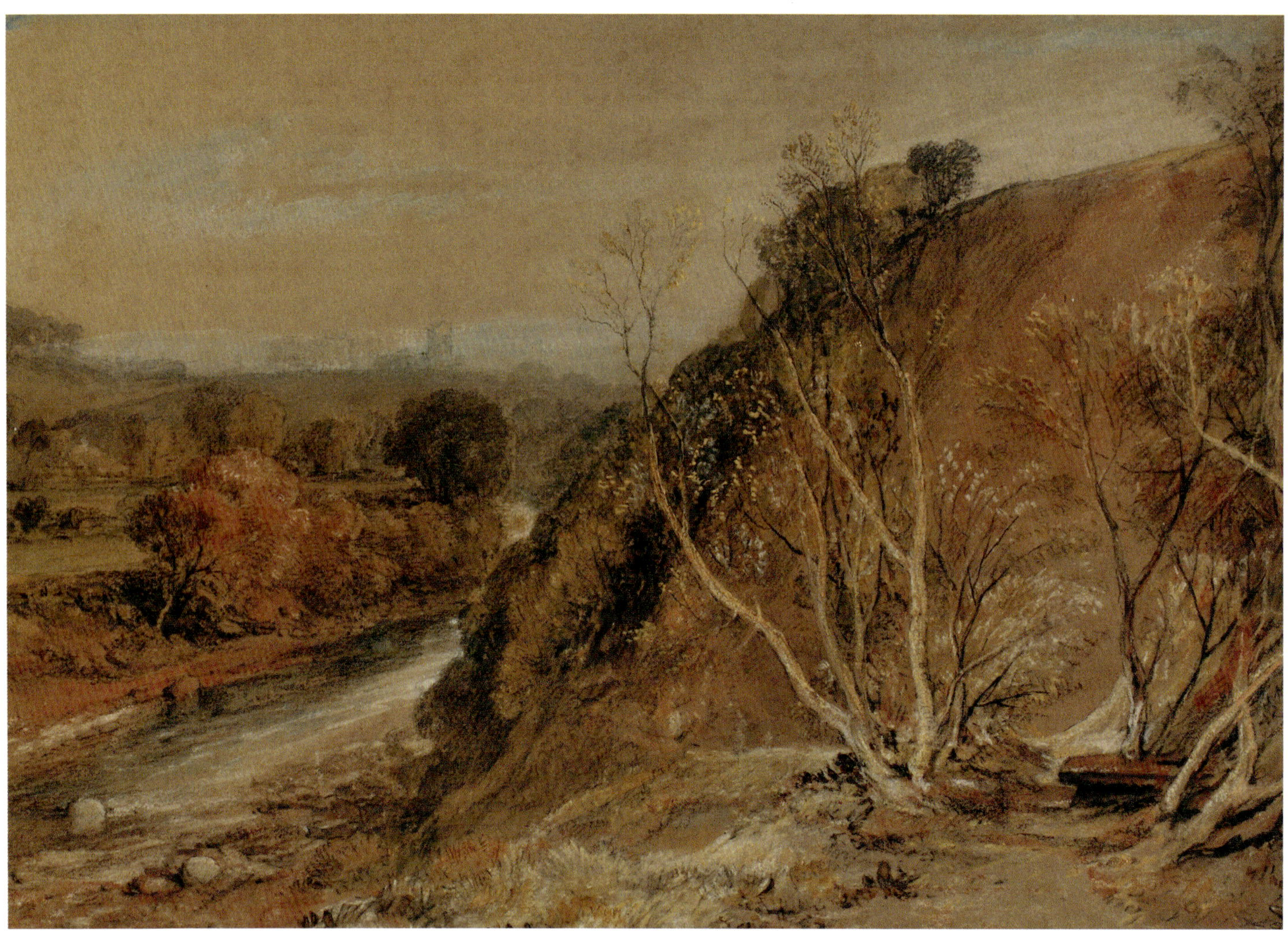

a work of art for Harewood that developed a vital interplay between the historic house, its collections and Capability Brown's contrived illusion of the perfect landscape. Several months of research, with regular visits to record the collection, especially Chippendale's furniture, led to an ambitious plan to create a land-drawing. This drawing, sited on the hillside immediately opposite the house, combined ideas centred on the serpentine line employed by both Chippendale and Capability Brown. The drawing evolved from a series of translucent monochromatic watercolours inspired by the recurring curving shapes found throughout the collections. From these the quintessential design emerged: *a sofa triumphans*, graceful in its artificial curves, made to prance across the equally contrived lines of Brown's faux-classical landscape. Whiteford's monumental land-drawing sculpted from hi-tech architectural fabric for a classical landscape in view of one of the great stately homes of England was a witty reflection on the artifice of the landscape itself, posing

J M W Turner, 1755 - 1851. *Valley of the Washburn and Leathley Church* (c. 1818). Chalk and body colour on paper, 27.2 x 38.5cm (Private Collection)

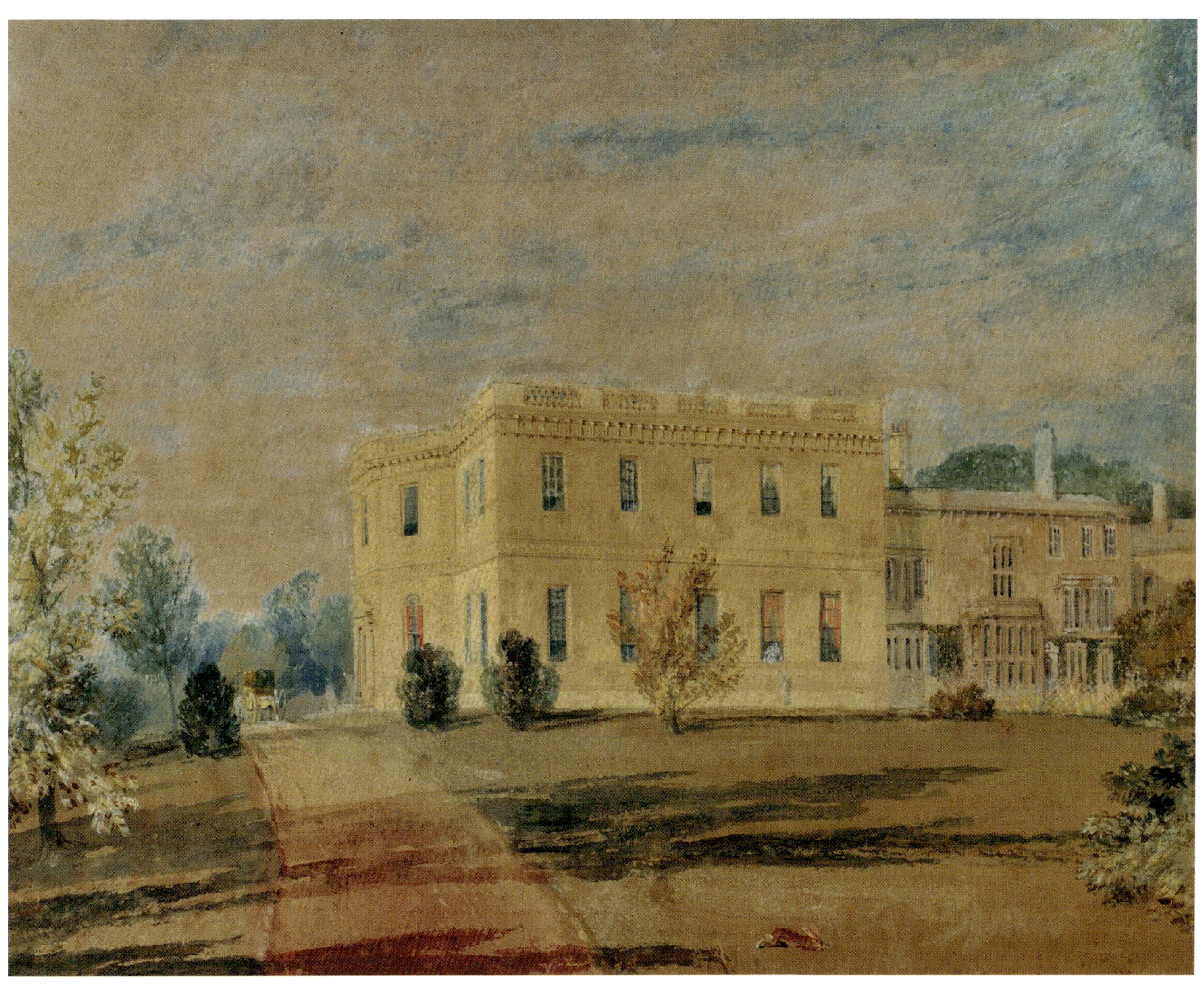

J M W Turner, 1755 - 1851.
Farnley Hall from the East
(c. 1818). Body colour and chalk on paper, 31.1 x 39.4cm (Private Collection)

tantalising questions about the nature of landscape, history and design.

Turner had another distinguished and enthusiastic Yorkshire patron, Walter Fawkes of Farnley Hall near Otley, whom he visited regularly from 1808 until 1824. Artist and patron became great friends, and Turner invited Fawkes to choose drawings in his sketchbooks that he would then create as highly finished watercolours, as well as painting an extensive collection of interior views of Farnley Hall. However, it was the landscape of lower Wharfedale that captivated him. Freed from the grounds of Harewood he roamed its wildness, taking in the drama of the changing Yorkshire weather as storm clouds rolled across the sky and the watery sun fought to pierce the greyness. Turner's memory of such scenes stayed with him to animate the quick sketches made at the time long after the experience. In 1810 he was staying at Farnley and witnessed a violent snowstorm raging across the valley. According to Fawkes' son, Hawkesworth, he turned to him and said, 'There, Hawkey, in two years you will see this again, and call it Hannibal crossing the Alps.' The immense oil on canvas **Snow Storm: Hannibal and his Army crossing the Alps**, was indeed painted and exhibited at the Royal Academy of Arts in London in 1812. It is one of Turner's most ravishing and disturbing works, the sky a vortex of black and orange beneath which Hannibal's soldiers struggle for their lives. His creative imagination and unparalleled technical skills transform a memory of a Yorkshire blizzard into a maelstrom of terror, the setting for one of the most famous scenes in ancient warfare.

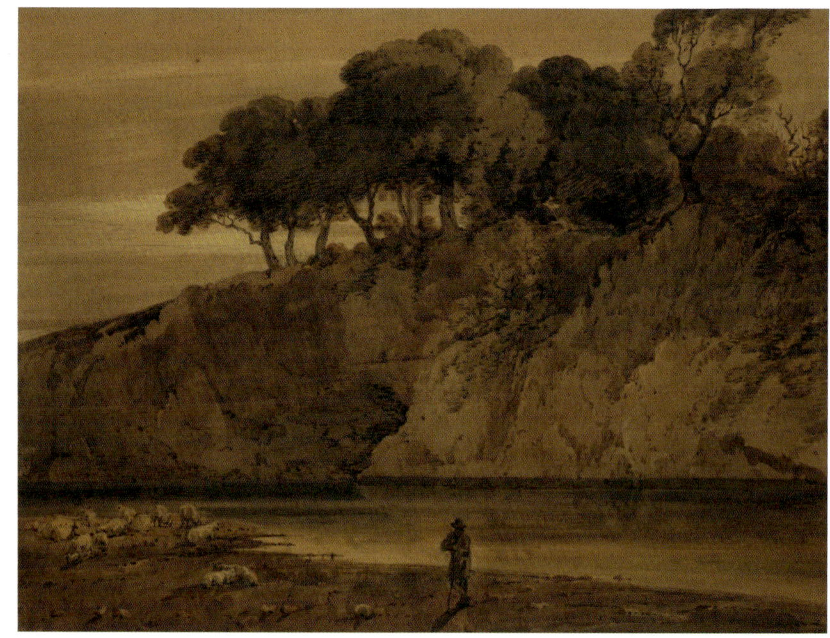

As the eighteenth century rolled over into the nineteenth, the notion of Yorkshire as a dark rocky place populated by unfriendly peasants gradually changed as artists were increasingly drawn to the picturesque sites and a perceived romanticism of the landscape. Thanks to the rapid development of printmaking, many more people were able to see the work of Turner and others in engraved form in books of large plate illustrations, such as Turner's *Picturesque Views in England and Wales*, and tourism was born. At the same time, industrial growth led to the expansion of towns into cities and the ravaging of landscapes as mass industrialisation took its toll. The natural landscape became an ever more precious thing as rural economies were displaced and Turner's Yorkshire farm labourers gravitated towards jobs in mines, mills and factories. Few came to Yorkshire before Turner, but many came after him, seeking out the numerous places that he had visited, drawn and painted. Turner's Yorkshire tours took in too many locations to mention here, but certain ones became places of pilgrimage for generations of artists, and tourists, to come.

Bolton Abbey is one of Yorkshire's best known and loved picturesque places, with the ruined abbey sitting on the banks of the Wharfe; the surrounding Bolton Woods, sliced in two upstream by the fearsome, foaming Strid, and Barden Tower, originally a medieval hunting lodge but a ruin by the seventeenth century, just a walk away along the river.

Thomas Girtin, 1775 - 1802. *On the Wharfe by Bolton Priory* (c. 1798). Watercolour over pencil, 47 x 61.6cm (© Victoria and Albert Museum, London.)

Opposite: J M W Turner, 1755 - 1851. *Snow Storm, Hannibal and his Army crossing the Alps* (exhibited 1812). Oil on canvas, 146 x 237.5cm (Turner Bequest, 1856 – Tate)

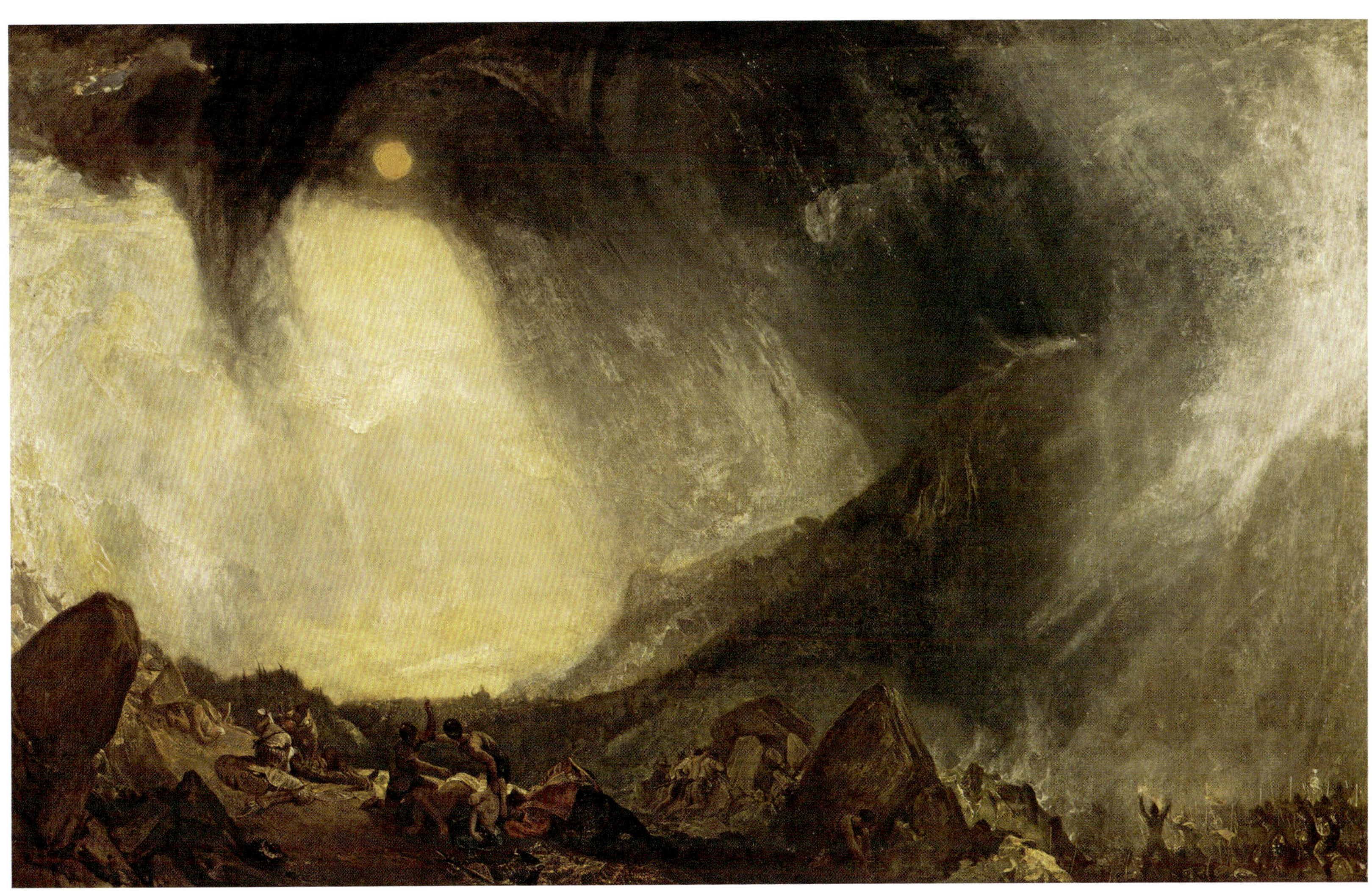

Turner made several visits to Bolton Abbey and produced a number of views, and the painting he made in about 1825, now in the Lady Lever Art Gallery and formerly owned by John Ruskin, is one of his most exquisite. It was also well-known as one of the plates in *Picturesque Views in England and Wales*, the ambitious book project that preoccupied the artist from 1824 until 1838. Turner made the study for this work on a visit to Yorkshire in about 1815. The colour is brighter and stronger than in his earlier views of Bolton Abbey, the influence of the stronger light he had encountered in Italy, but there are elements of the work that we first saw in the Harewood pictures made seventeen years earlier; the ruined building pushed to the margins of the view, the focus on the landscape and the exaggeration of the scale, so that the river bank becomes as high as the Alps. Ruskin hung this painting on his bedroom wall at Brantwood and we know from his writing that he studied it in different lights every morning when he awoke.

Thomas Girtin was born in the same year as Turner in similarly humble circumstances, the son of a Southwark brush maker. Girtin too began his career as topographical watercolourist, he made his own tour of the north and he too had Yorkshire patrons, including Viscount Lascelles, and spent much time at Harewood. The poignant difference between the two men was that Girtin died tragically young at the age of twenty-seven in 1802, but in his short life he produced some of the most beautiful and accomplished paintings and drawings of Yorkshire in British art. So much so that Turner is reputed to have declared, 'If Tom Girtin had lived, I would have starved.' Girtin depicted Bolton Abbey from a number of different viewpoints. In 1798 he painted a view of the bluff opposite the Abbey, thus cutting the picturesque ruin out of the scene altogether. Whereas Turner, in the work treasured by Ruskin, had painted this riverbank as though it were a mountain, Girtin here achieves monumentality by a different route with his heightened sensitivity to the spiritual aspect of nature and the atmosphere with which he endows the subject. In 1800 he painted the east end of Bolton Abbey from across the river in more conventional mode, and then the stepping stones across the Wharfe, again excluding the Abbey altogether from the scene, an indication of just how groundbreaking his work was at this early stage in his sadly truncated career.

The English landscape, having been considered a subject in fine art inferior to the grander history pictures and allegorical themes, grew in popularity in the nineteenth century. Romantic ideas about nature in literature, such as the poetry of Wordsworth and Coleridge, took a grip on painting. Once Turner had broken new ground by exhibiting his paintings with appropriate verse alongside; now it was the norm. The Pre Raphaelites, principally Millais, Rossetti and Holman Hunt, formed their Brotherhood in 1848 in reaction against the far reaching influence of

Opposite: John William Inchbold, 1830 - 1888. *At Bolton: The White Doe of Rylstone* (1855). Oil on wood panel, 68.6 x 50.8cm (Leeds Museums and Galleries)

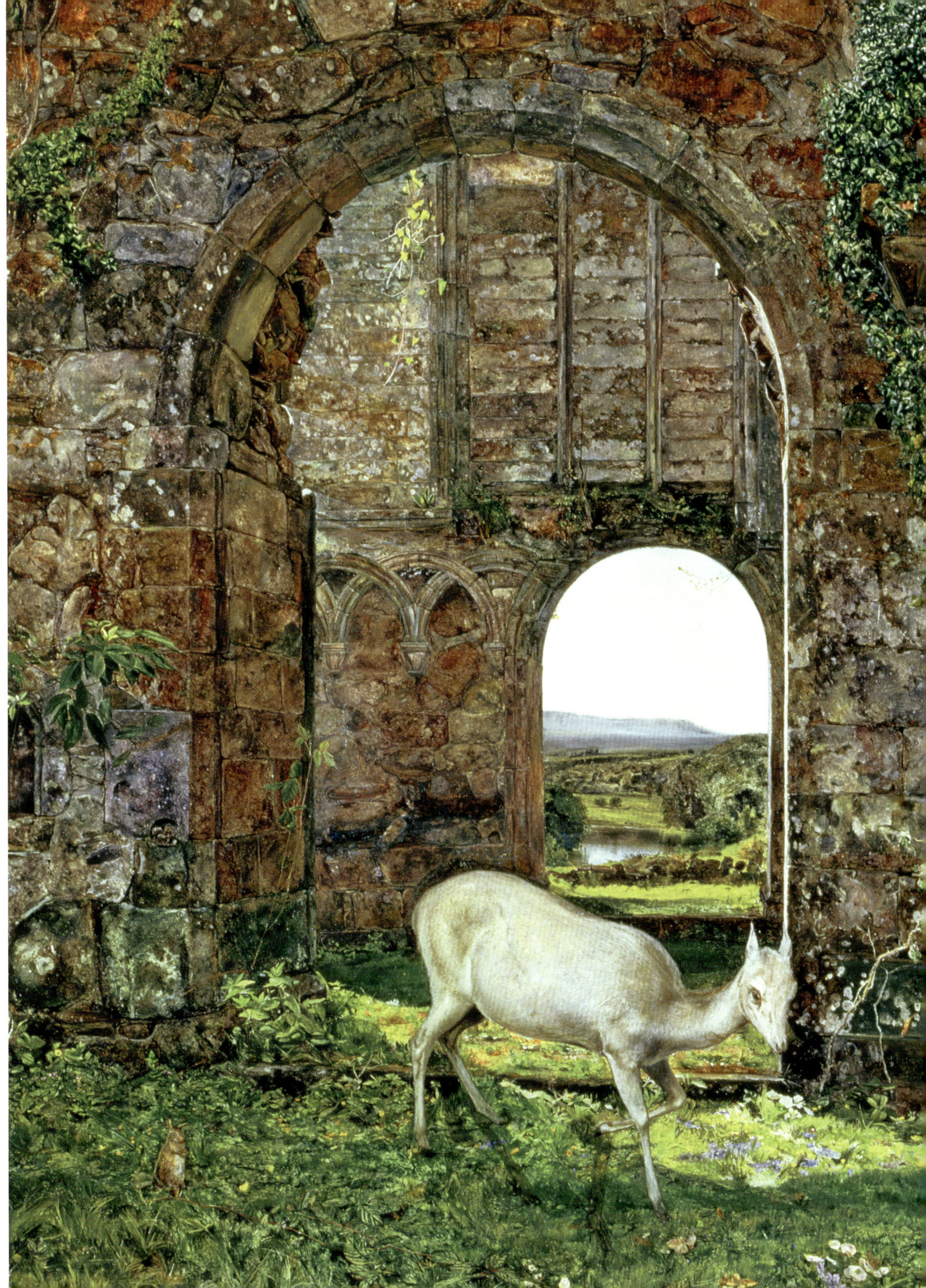

'Joshua Sploshua Reynolds' as they called him. They felt that English art was drowning in brown paint and dullness and called for 'truth to nature' in painting and a return to the pure colouring of early Renaissance art. A new school of Pre Raphaelite landscape painting developed with followers from far and wide. John William Inchbold was born in Leeds, the son of the owner and editor of the *Intelligencer* newspaper. Inchbold studied at the Royal Academy and came to know Ruskin. In **At Bolton, the White Doe at Rylstone** one can see the elaboration of foreground detail that defined the Pre Raphaelite style and drew Ruskin's admiration. Inchbold's painting illustrates William Wordsworth's last lyrical ballad, a poem of the same title. The painting has an obvious parallel in Holman Hunt's *The Scapegoat*, since the white doe is also emblematic of a suffering Christ. This time the setting of Bolton Abbey is significant not just for its picturesque appeal but also for its religious symbolism. We are enclosed by the abbey with just a distant view of the landscape through the archway, our eyes are drawn to the sprigs of wildflowers in the grass and lichen growing on the ancient stone.

Inchbold spent much of his career abroad but in 1857 he was still in Leeds, a contemporary of Atkinson Grimshaw, the self-taught artist who was to become the 'painter of moonlight' and one of the first Victorian artists to take everyday urban life as his subject. Grimshaw's early works of the mid 1860s have often been described as Pre Raphaelite. Inevitably, it has been suggested that Inchbold may have been Grimshaw's mentor, but there is little evidence to back this up. Nor is there anything to support the view that Grimshaw had connections to Ruskin or any of the other Pre Raphaelite artists. Drawing was the backbone of the style and yet Grimshaw does not appear to have used drawing as an academic discipline, instead producing only rough working sketches. Nonetheless, Grimshaw's early paintings of Wharfedale views, such as **Ghyll Beck, Barden, Early Spring**, 1867 undeniably possess Pre Raphaelite qualities. Ingleborough from under White Scar is heroically conceived and truly Pre Raphaelite, possibly even painted on the spot. The view is taken from Ingleborough Common at the start of the path that climbs up to Ingleborough itself, the second highest mountain in Yorkshire, capturing the cold bleakness of the wintry landscape.

Grimshaw is one of Yorkshire's most admired painters, a hard-working artist who never belonged to the London world of art but had many devoted collectors in his native county throughout his lifetime; Walter Battle of Harrogate, for example, owned over eighty of Grimshaw's works. Grimshaw's popularity waned rapidly after his death in 1893, one of the many Victorian casualties of changes in artistic taste, and it was not until the early 1960s that his pictures began to attract interest once more, with the revival in popularity of Victorian art. In 1979 a major show curated by Alex Robertson at Leeds Art Gallery, which travelled to Liverpool and

Atkinson Grimshaw, 1836 - 1893. *Ghyll Beck, Barden, Early spring* (1867). Oil on board, 76.2 x 63.5cm (Private Collection)

OVER: Atkinson Grimshaw, 1836 - 1893. *Ingleborough from under White Scar* (1868). Oil on canvas, 72 x 91.5cm. (Bradford Museums and Galleries)

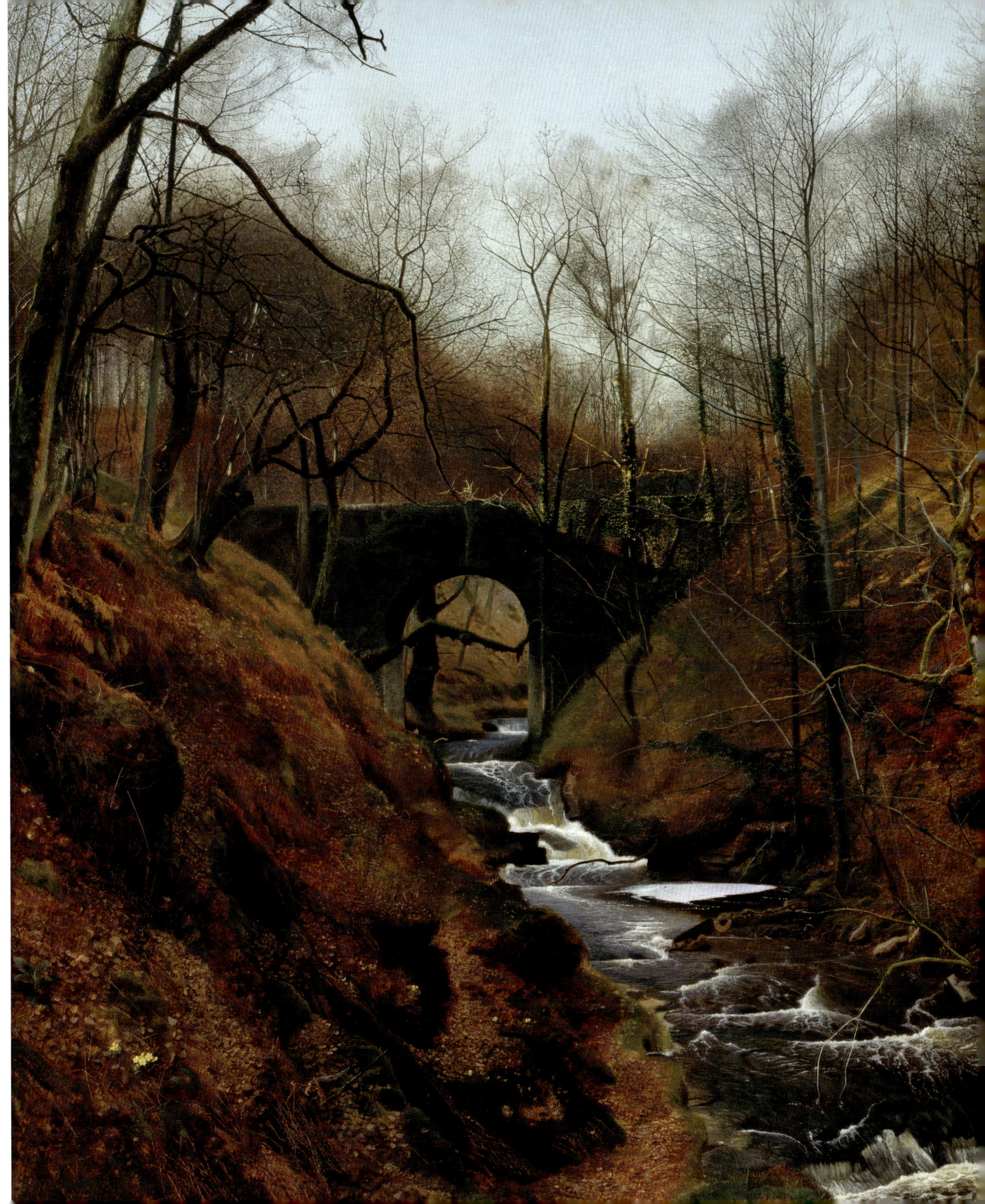

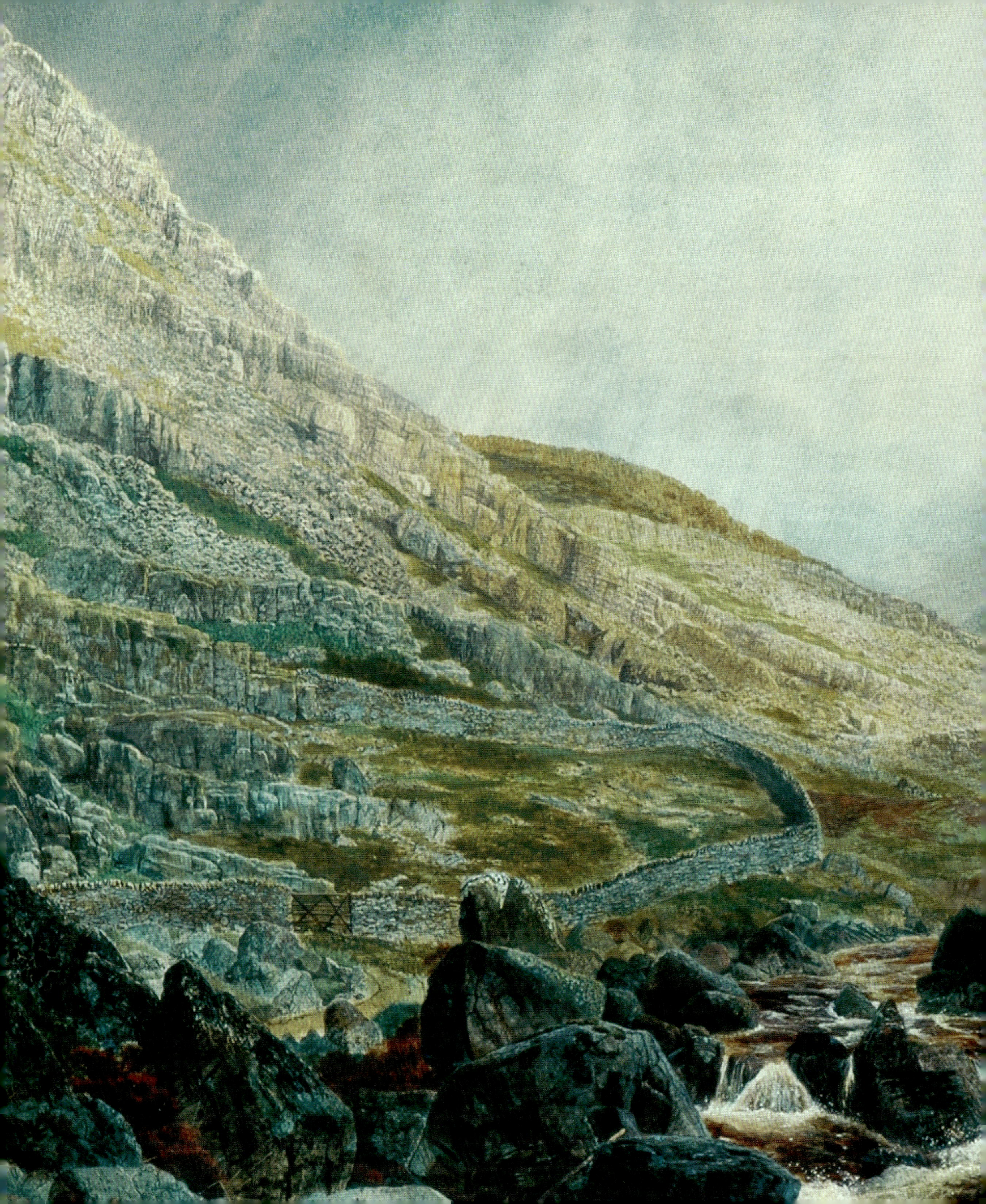

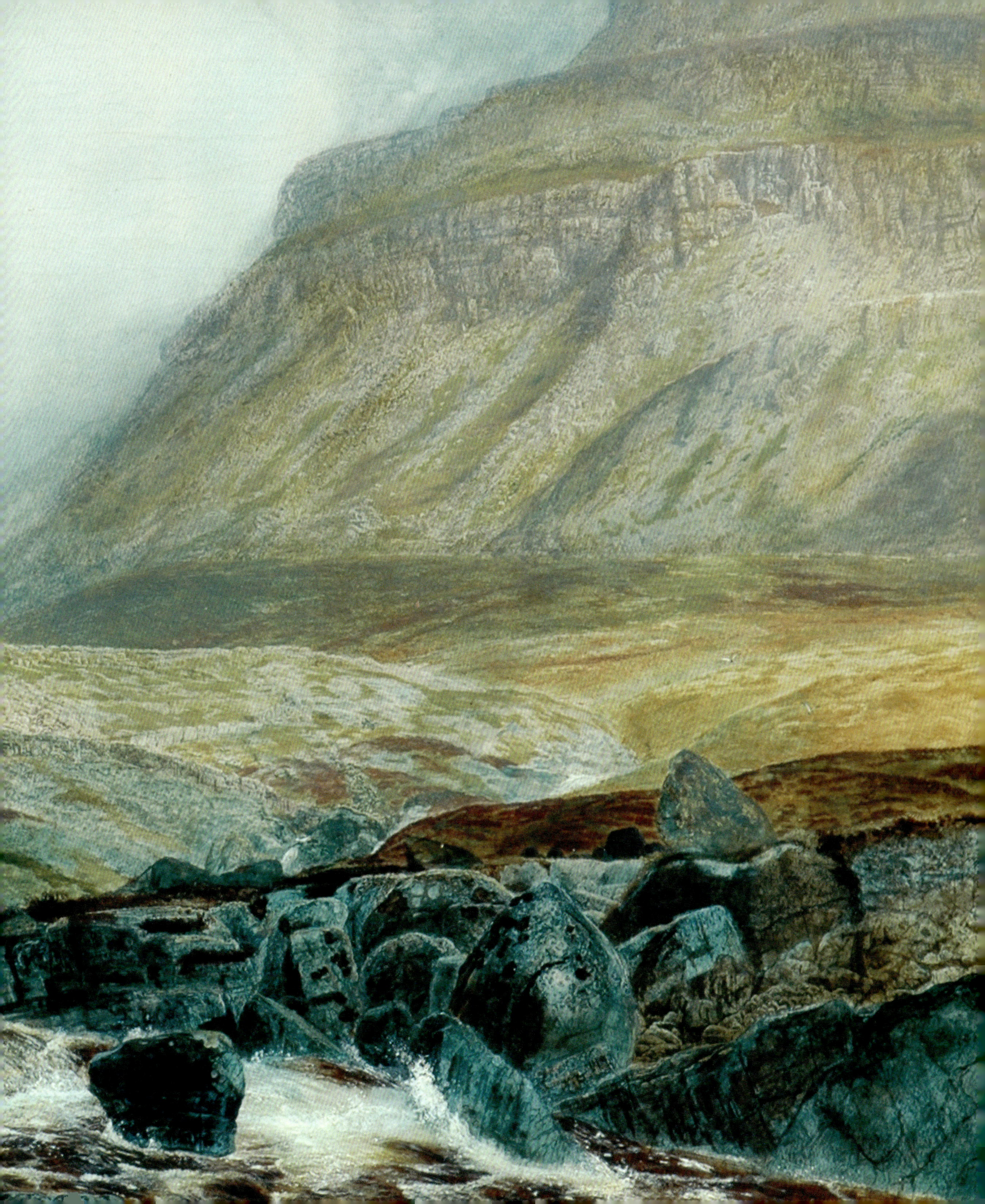

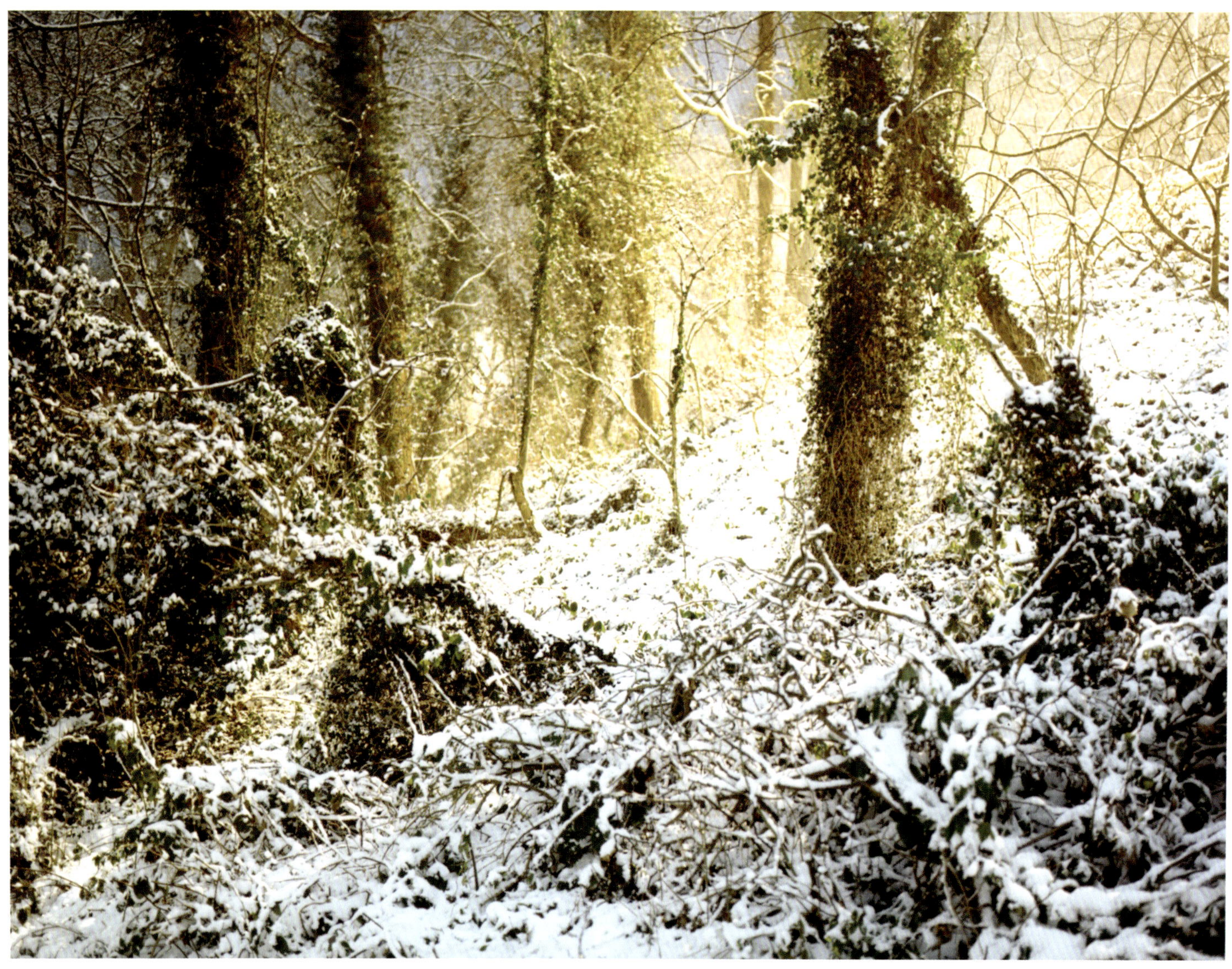

Southampton, brought him firmly back into the public eye. In 2011 Grimshaw's art was given its first significant public gallery show of the twenty-first century at the Mercer Art Gallery, Harrogate, where it attracted record-breaking numbers of visitors, and the Guildhall Art Gallery in the City of London. Bradford photographer Liza Dracup, renowned for the Pre Raphaelite colour of her landscape photographs and her ability to capture the magical and often eerie atmosphere created by the effects of moonlight, was invited to make new work in response to Grimshaw's paintings. Working at night time, she uses her medium format camera as a creative tool to track the landscape, using available light from ambient sources both natural and artificial. In **St Ives (Snow), Yorkshire**, 2010, with the constant waxing and waning of the moon,

Liza Dracup, b. 1968. *St Ives (Snow), Yorkshire* (2010). 80 x 105cm, print (Mercer Art Gallery, Harrogate Borough Council)

transient car headlamps and the glow of streetlights she depicts a Grimshaw inspired view of a local wood that goes beyond reproducing what the eye can see.

Most of the artists discussed so far were visitors to Yorkshire, for whom the landscape had an otherness, a wildness even, that was foreign to them. But for some artists, Yorkshire is their birthplace, their perpetual home and the subject of their art. The painter Katharine Holmes is the third generation of a family of women artists to live in the village of Malham in the Yorkshire Dales, still in the house where her mother and grandmother lived before her. Katharine has a lifelong knowledge of the landscape of Malhamdale. One of the things that makes her work so striking is that she works consistently in the open air in all weathers; not just making small sketches – although she produces many drawings – but working directly in oil onto canvas or in watercolour, gouache, ink onto large sheets of paper that become torn by the wind at the edges. Back in her studio, she may bring home grasses and pebbles to observe at close quarters, continuing to work on a piece combining her plein-air observations with finely tuned memory. The art critic Lynne Green in her essay *Katharine Holmes: The Poetry of Landscape* in the exhibition catalogue for *A Malham Family of Painters* at the Stanley and Audrey Burton Gallery, University of Leeds in 2009 writes, 'I have come to recognise in the painter Katharine Holmes a parallel engagement, motivated by a poetic sensibility as well as an acute sensitivity to both landscape and the natural forces that shape it… [she] explores the dramatic landscape of the Dales in order to embody in paint her visual, emotional and spiritual responses to it… her work provides us with a painterly equivalent of what Wordsworth would have understood as the sublime.' Like Turner, Holmes is enthralled by the effects of light and weather, thus each of her paintings is clearly defined by a sense of the season. She gives her paintings titles such as *On Boss Moor, an Overcast Day* or *The Days beginning to lengthen*. In this artist's work we truly find the inheritance of Turner, in her sensibility to light and atmosphere, and with this Holmes has the freedom of the twenty-first century woman artist. In Turner's time she would not have been allowed to be an artist at all; in the late nineteenth century she could have had a formal art education, but social convention would not easily have allowed her to roam the Dales alone. In Katharine we find an artist who fully exploits her freedom, not tied to patrons as Turner and Girtin were, but with a license to roam and paint.

Constance Pearson, Katharine's grandmother, actually enjoyed an unusual freedom for her generation that enabled her to pursue her painting career. Constance was born into a large Quaker family in Leeds, the daughter of a grocer. She won a scholarship to Leeds School of Art in 1906 and studied full-time with Jacob Kramer, Fred Lawson and others, and met and married Sidney John Pearson who became a

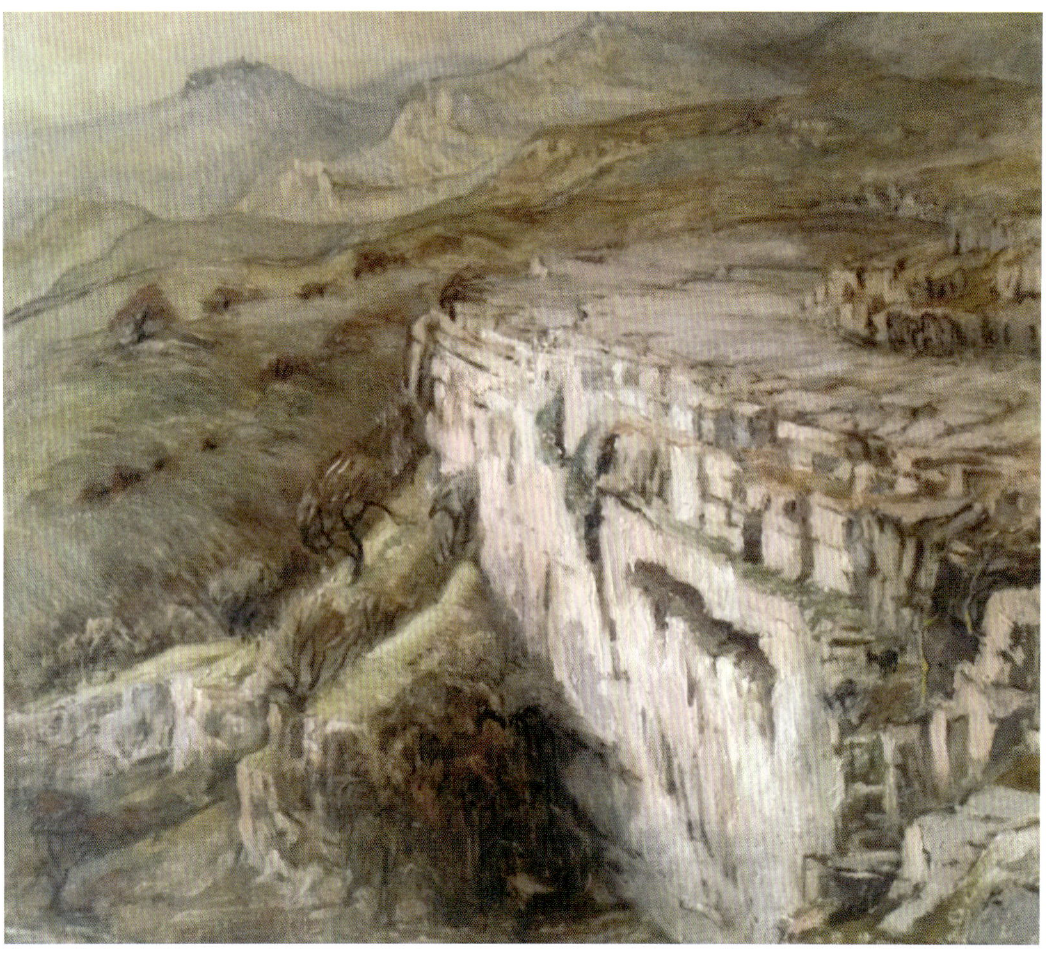

schoolteacher in Bradford. Whilst Sidney taught at Bradford Grammar School, ever the supportive husband he encouraged Constance to go away for the week to her rented studio at Bolton Abbey and he would join her at the weekends. Both went on many painting excursions to Runswick Bay and Staithes where colonies of artists gathered. When Sidney retired from teaching in the 1940s they moved to High Barn Cottage in Malham, the home that has passed down through the generations. Constance painted obsessively all of her life. Her chosen media was watercolour or oils and her subject matter was the world that surrounded her; not only the landscape but village scenes populated by friends and neighbours, pots of wildflowers and local farmers at work. Her paintings of the 1940s and 1950s recorded many aspects of the Dales way of life that not soon after disappeared forever. Famously, these disappearing farming traditions were recorded from a more social historical viewpoint in the illustrations of Marie Hartley, who worked with Ella Pontefract and Joan Ingilby for books such as *The Yorkshire Dales*, first published in 1956.

Constance Pearson, 1886 - 1970. *Malham Cove* (undated). Oil on canvas, 87 x 97cm (Estate of the Artist)

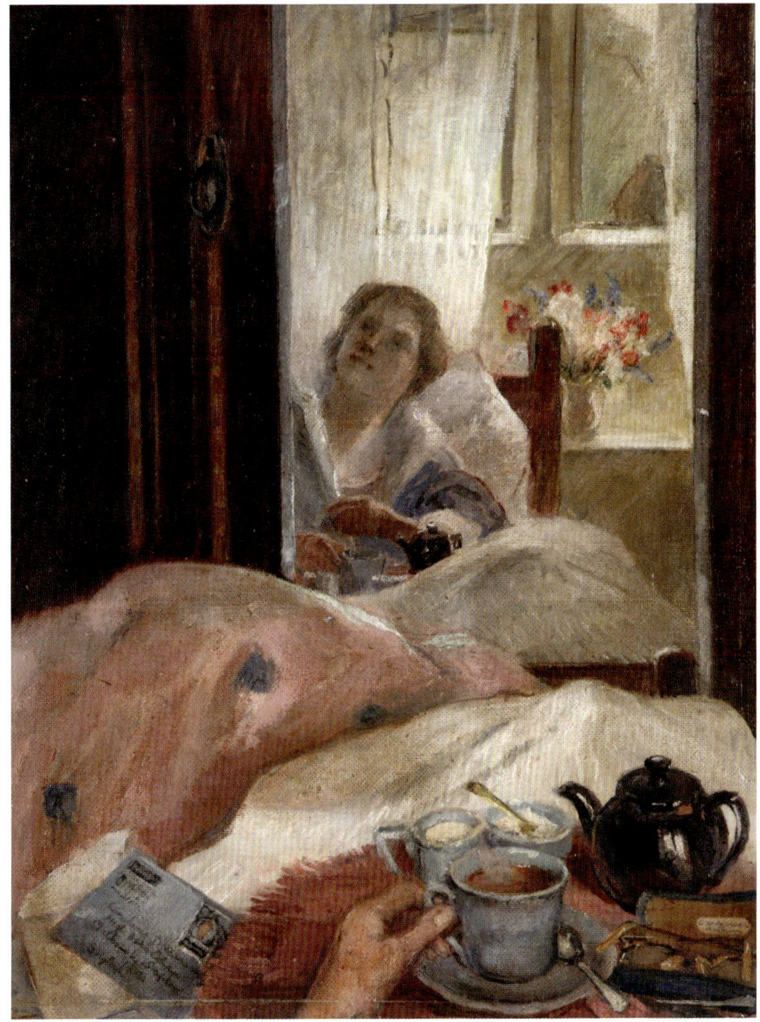

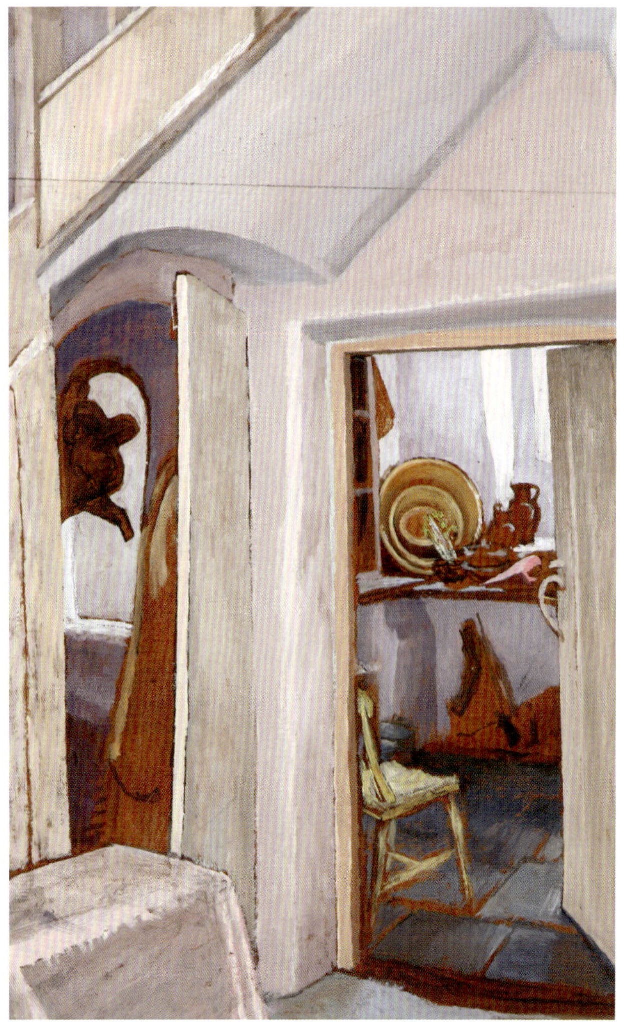

Constance's third child Philippa unsurprisingly followed in her artist parents' footsteps by going to Bradford Art School. Philippa first of all worked as an occupational therapist and then trained as a primary school teacher of art and English at Bretton Hall College, Wakefield. When Philippa married Edward Holmes in 1957, an engineer who came to work in the Dales and lodged at High Barn Cottage, she gave up teaching and became a full-time housewife. Constance, after Sidney's death, lived at the cottage in Malham with her two unmarried sisters, and as they grew older and more infirm, Philippa moved back in with her family to look after them. Her life was taken up with domestic responsibilities, but that did not deter her from painting and drawing. Indeed, she made the house itself and everyday family life the subject for her art, depicting family scenes, corners of the house and even the view from the window on a rainy Dales day. These three women artists each in their own way capture

Left: Constance Pearson, 1886 - 1970. *Morning Tea* (early 1950s), 66 x 49.8cm, oil on hardboard (Estate of the Artist)

Right: Philippa Pearson, 1921 - 1999. *The Pantry at High Barn* (c. 1995), 50 x 40cm, oil on board (Estate of the Artist)

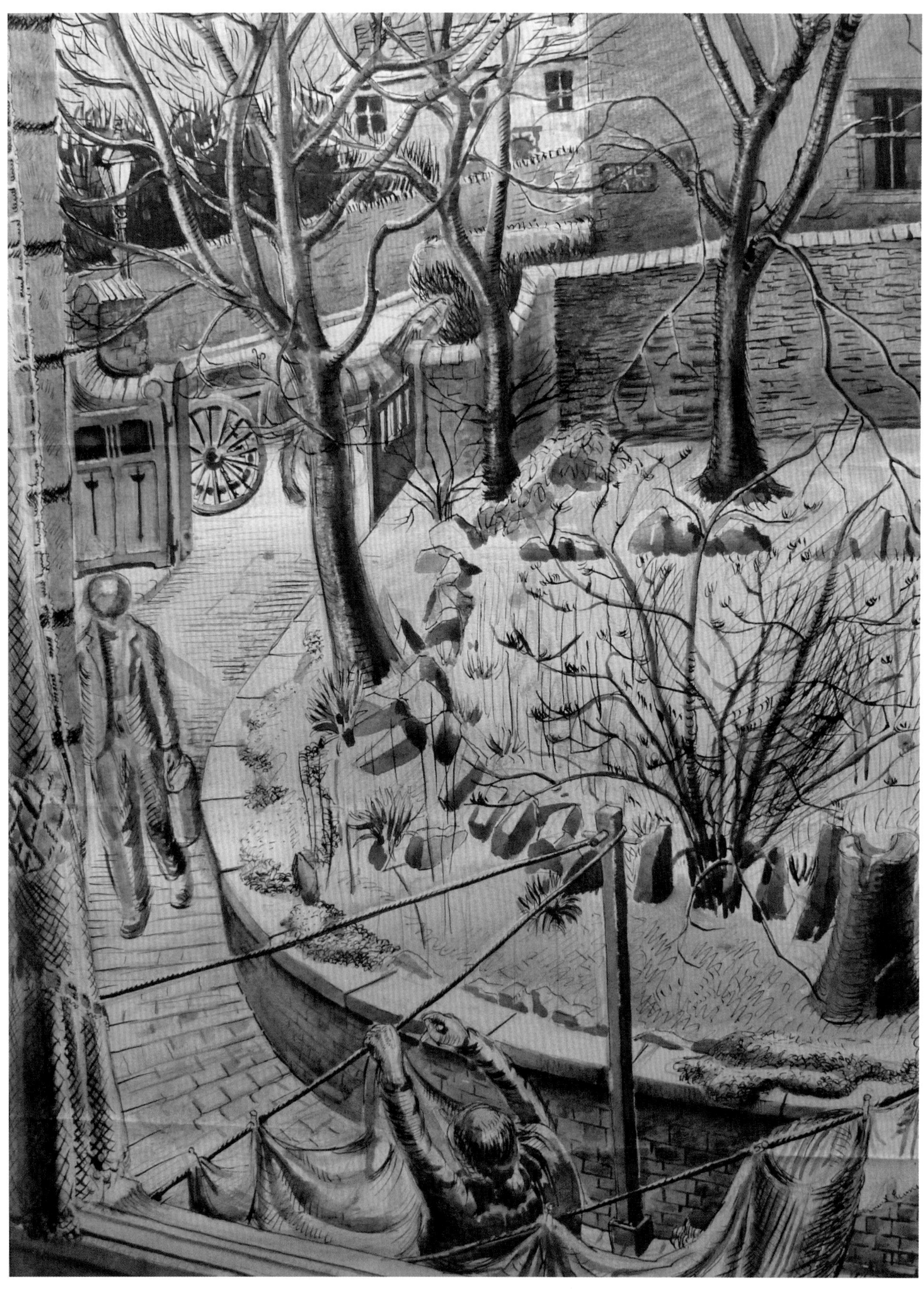

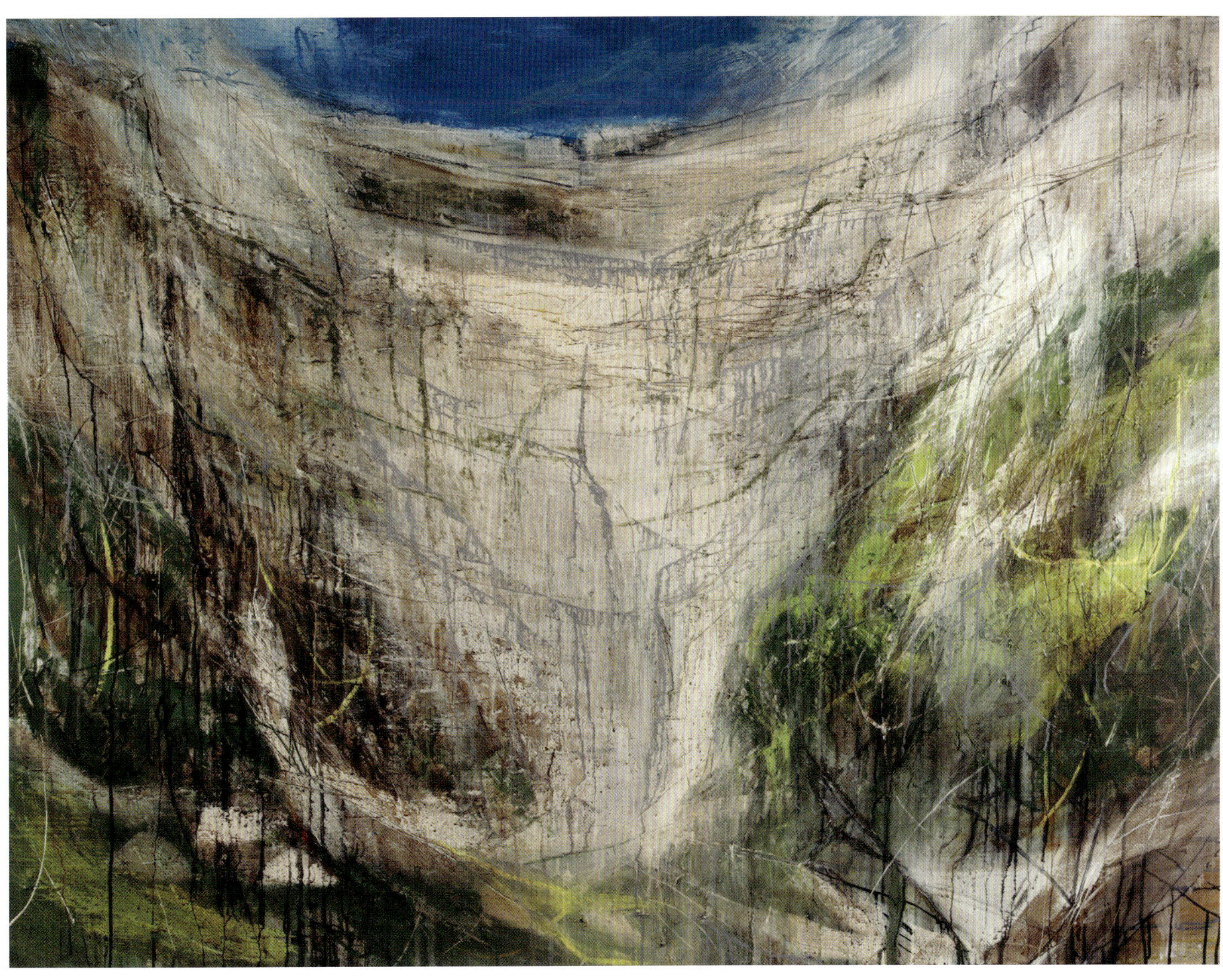

Katharine Holmes, b. 1962. *Malham Limestone*, 2010-11, 150 x 200cm, oil on canvas (courtesy of the Artist)

Opposite: Philippa Pearson, 1921 - 1999. *Bringing in the milk* (c. 1940), 51.6 x 34.5cm, ink and wash (Estate of the Artist)

a powerful sense of Yorkshire. Constance and Philippa lived in different places around the country at various points in their lives and Katharine is extremely well travelled, having worked in Europe, Africa and Japan, yet for all of them Yorkshire, its landscape and its people, is at the very centre of their art.

Fountains Abbey near Ripon is Britain's largest monastic ruin and most complete Cistercian abbey, now a World Heritage site. The outstanding beauty of the ruins and their setting has attracted artists for centuries, including both Turner and Girtin. Turner made drawings and paintings of Fountains from every angle, the most stunning of which is arguably **The Dormitory and Transept of Fountain's Abbey – Evening,** first exhibited in 1798. Girtin perched on a stone coffin in the presbytery

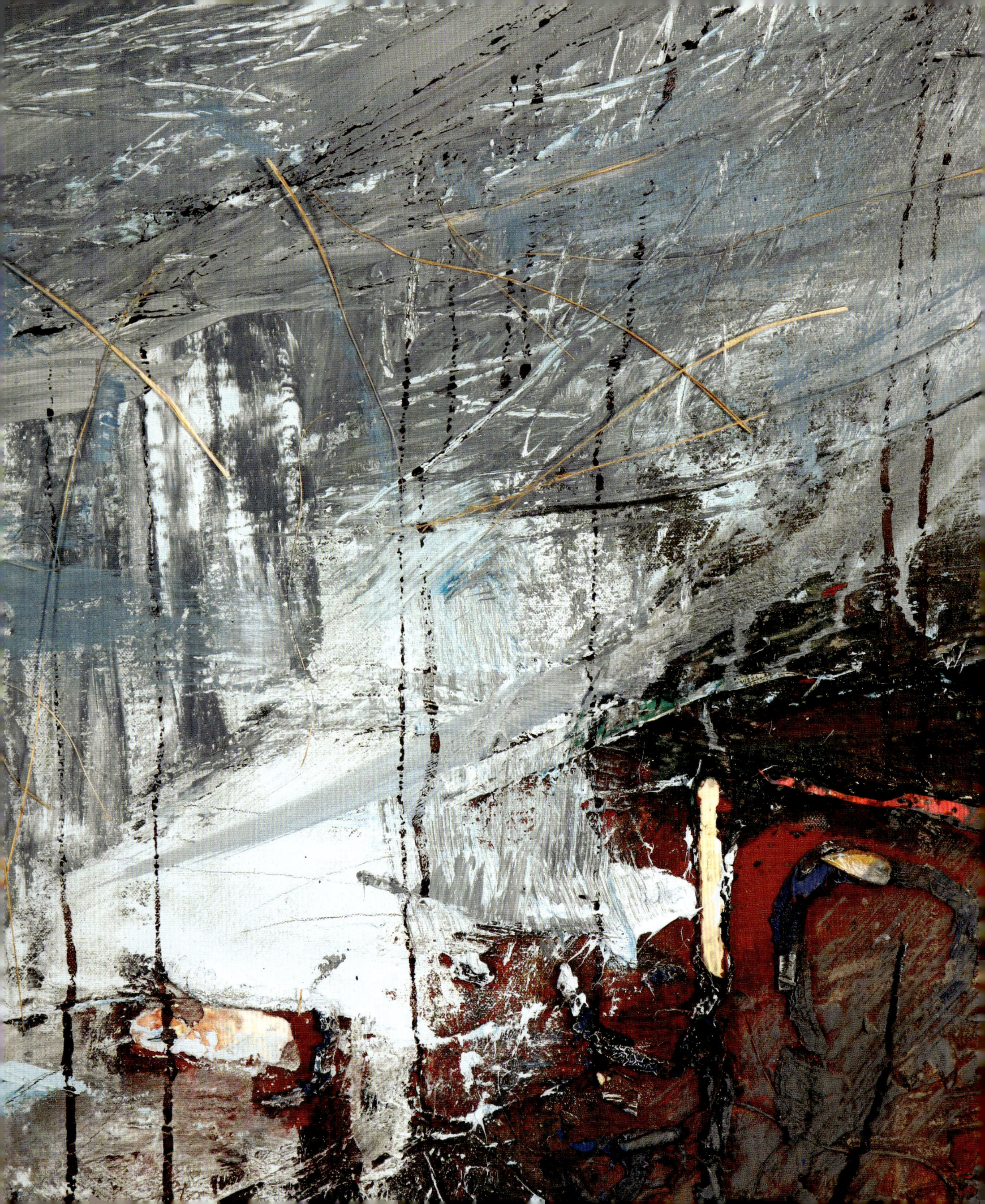

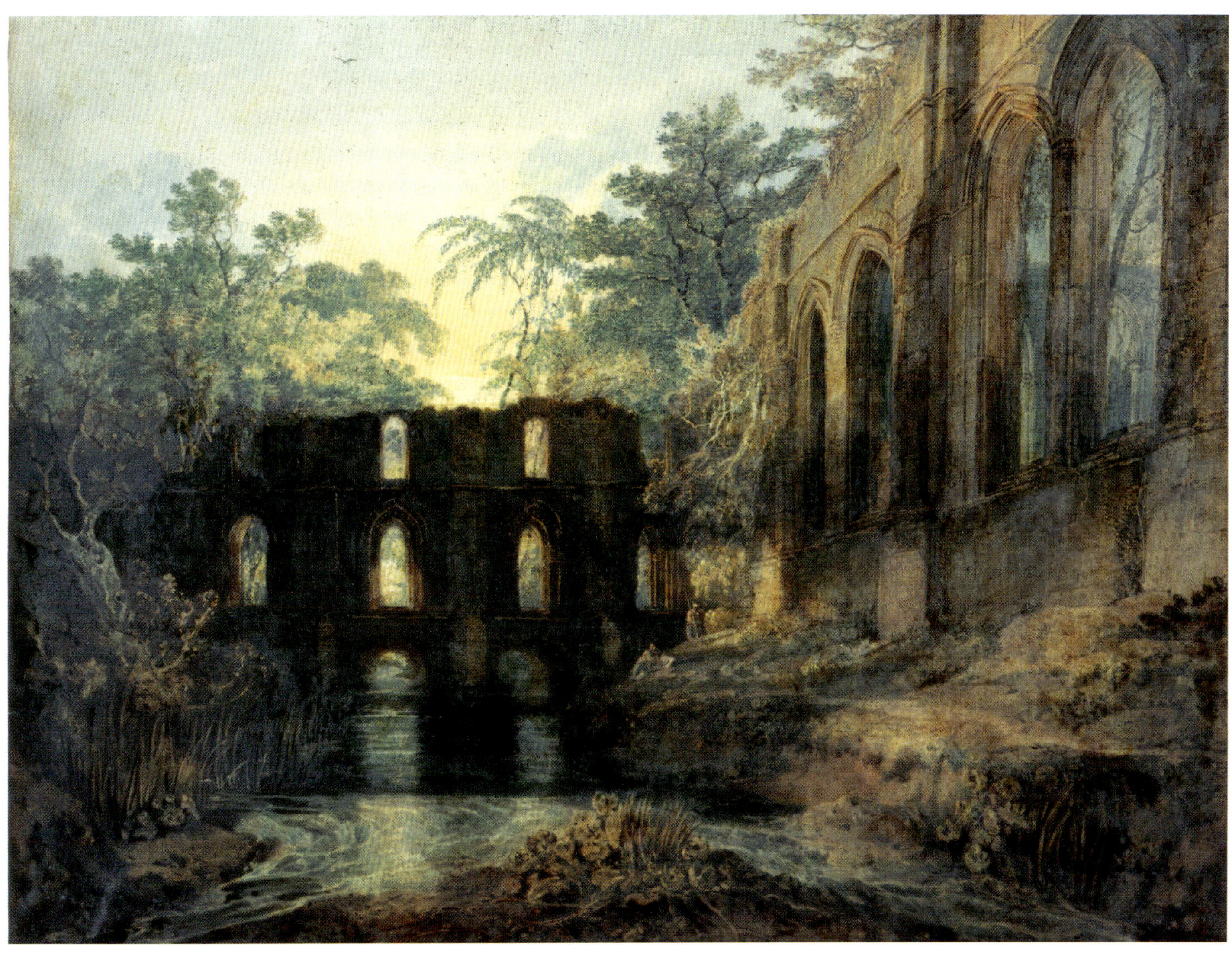

J M W Turner, 1755 - 1851. *The Dormitory and Transept of Fountains Abbey – Evening* (c. 1798). Watercolour on paper, 45.6 x 61cm (York Art Gallery, York Museums Trust)

Opposite: Katharine Holmes, b. 1962. Detail from *Living in a Limestone Landscape, 2009*, 100 x 120cm, oil on canvas (courtesy of the Artist)

to get his viewpoint for his large watercolour of the great east window. More modern artists have approached the subject in different ways, some very much in the tradition of Turner, others less so. Walter Bernard Evans was a long-lived and prolific landscape artist, and from 1887 he and his wife Mary Ann lived in Harrogate. They both came from families of artists and engravers, and Mary Ann's brother Frederick Hollyer was a pioneer in the use of photography for reproducing works of art. Evans made a good living from his Harrogate base, making numerous paintings of Yorkshire abbeys in the summer while Mary Ann organised his finances and their social and domestic life. She kept a diary of their everyday life, which includes some rather scathing comments about Harrogate town

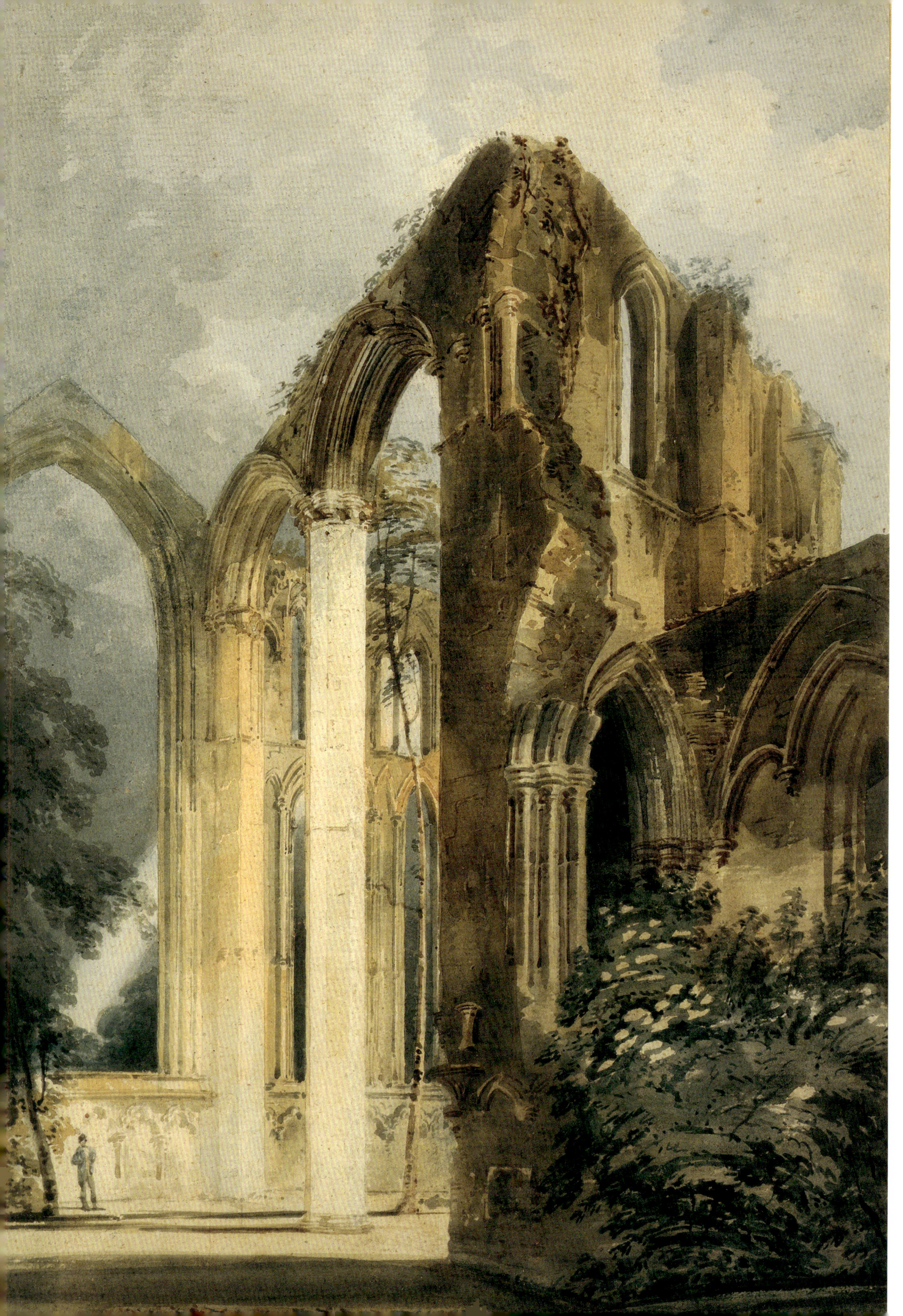

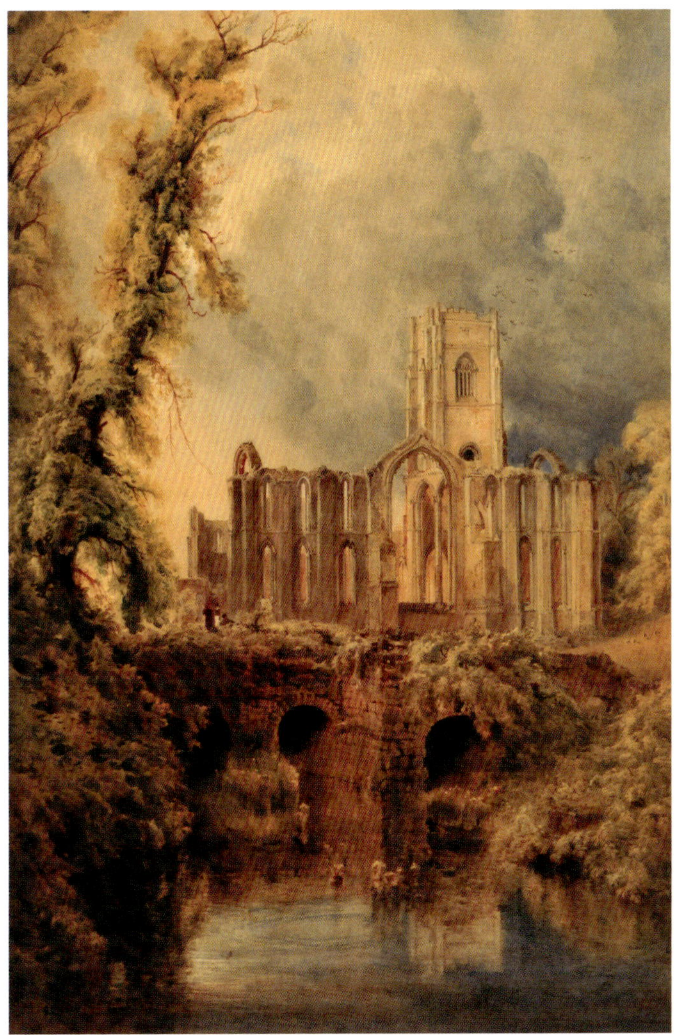

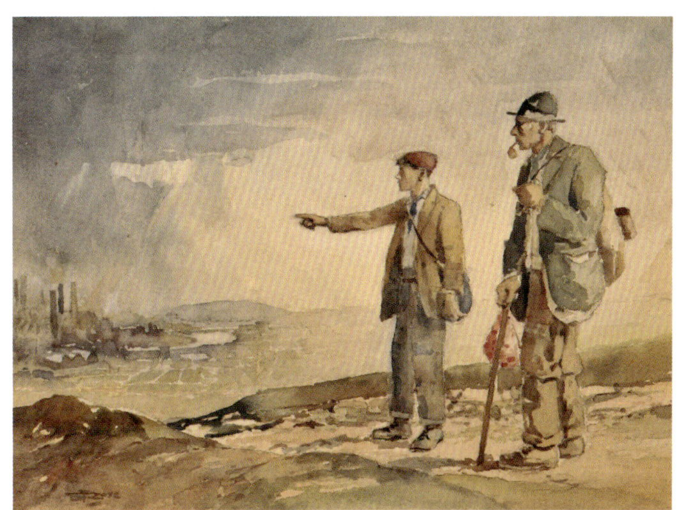

Left: Walter Bernard Evans, 1843 - 1922. *Fountains Abbey* (late 1880s). Watercolour, 101 x 68.8cm (Mercer Art Gallery, Harrogate Borough Council)

Right: David Rose, 1871 - 1964. *Nidderdale Landscape* (c. 1929-1935). Watercolour, 18 x 26cm (Mercer Art Gallery, Harrogate Borough Council)

Opposite: Thomas Girtin, 1775 - 1802. *Fountains Abbey, the great east window from the presbytery* (c. 1799). Watercolour on paper, 46.4 x 32.1cm (Museums Sheffield)

and its visitors and many complaints about the overbearing smell of the sulphur wells. The Evans' winters were spent on the French Riviera, where Walter painted Mediterranean scenes and Mary Ann wrote biting comments about the French in her journal. Evans worked very much in the conventional manner of the later nineteenth century, often painting in watercolour and gouache on a large scale, then framing the works in elaborate gilded frames so that they resembled oil paintings in the Victorian fashion. Evans' view of **Fountains Abbey** shows a familiarity with the engravings of Turner's views of Fountains. A century later the artist Laurie Marr, a pupil of David Bomberg, found his sense of Fountains Abbey in quite a different way, with the vigorous charcoal lines of his drawing.

Fountains Abbey is close to the cathedral city of Ripon built at the confluence of two streams of the River Ure, the Laver and the Skell. Ripon Cathedral, the great expanse of the Market Square and the streets of historic buildings that wind around the dominating bulk of the cathedral have drawn many artists; so too has the surrounding area of North Yorkshire. Travelling southeast from Ripon there is the openness of Nidderdale, an official Area of Outstanding Natural Beauty, with

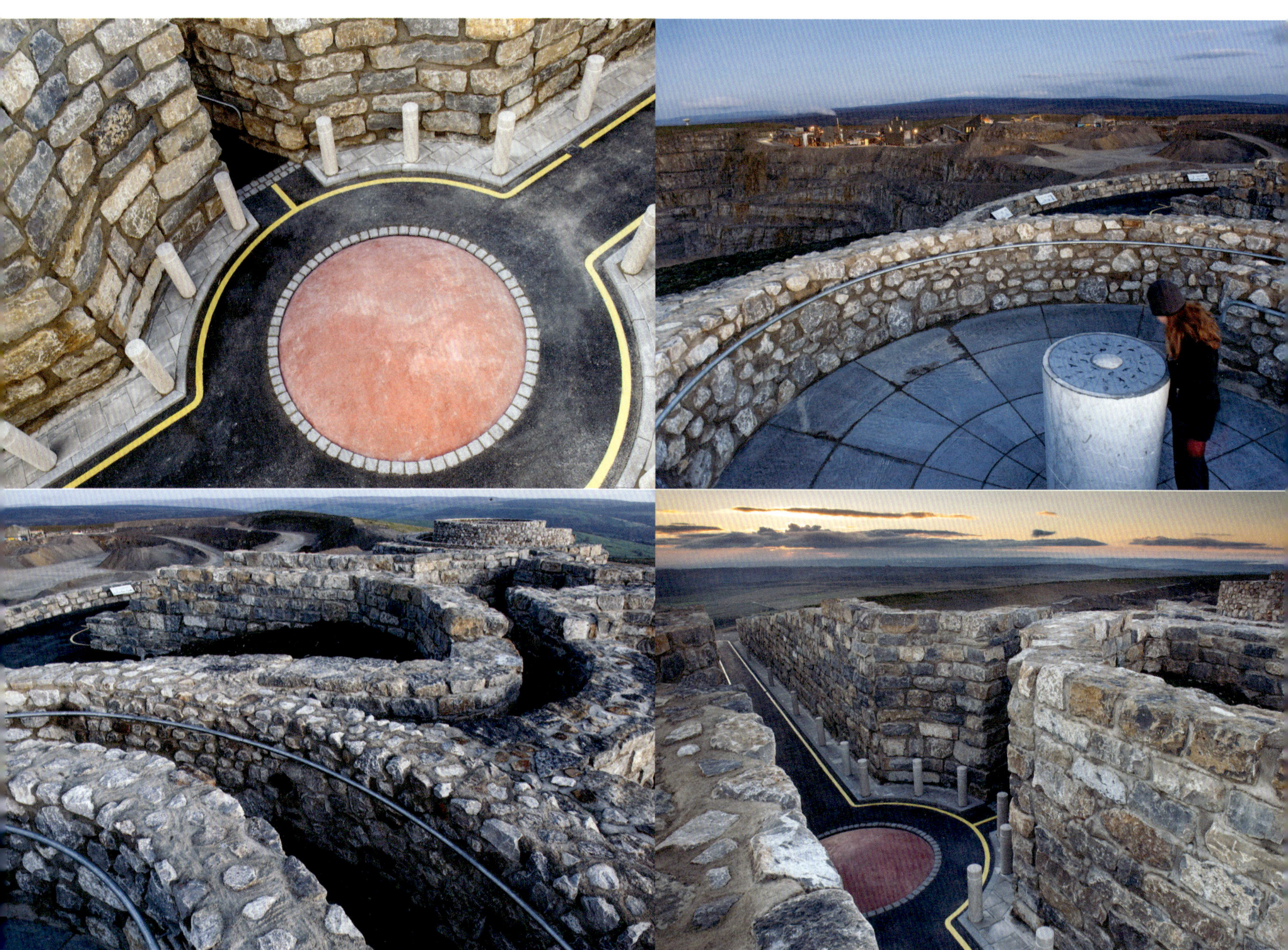

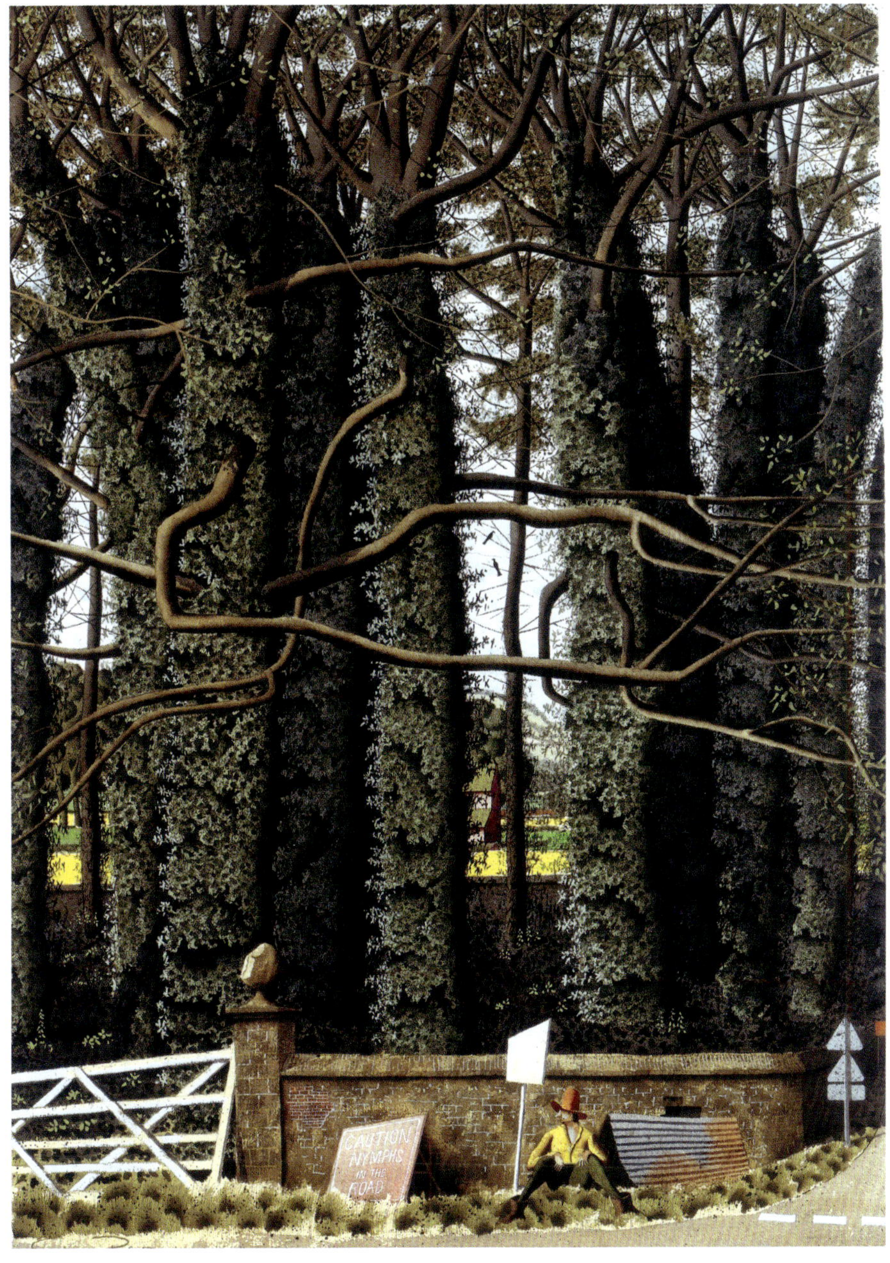

Simon Palmer, b. 1957. *Dryad and his nymphs* (2005). Watercolour and gouache, 94 x 64.5cm (JHW Fine Art)

Opposite: Andrew Sabin, b. 1958. *Coldstones Cut*. Landscape sculpture. (Nidderdale Visual Arts)

the small town of Pateley Bridge at its apex, a place with its own contemporary artistic community, and at the top of the valley the Scar House reservoir. The reservoir was built in the 1920s and a village of 1,250 people settled there for the time it took to build the Nidderdale dam. Among them was the engineer David Rose, an artist manqué who found time to produce numerous drawings and watercolours of the landscape in all its seasons and the teams of workmen labouring on the dam. In 2010 Nidderdale became home to the biggest landscape sculpture in Yorkshire, **Coldstones Cut** created by the artist Andrew Sabin and built at a height of 1,375 feet above sea level. The sculpture works as an array of platforms from which visitors can view the spectacular working quarry on one side and all around them the great rolling shapes of Nidderdale.

Heading out of Ripon to the northwest, the road leads to the genteel market towns of Masham, Leyburn and Bedale, taking in one of Yorkshire's smallest and most entrancing ruins, Jervaulx Abbey. Nikolaus Pevsner writing in *The Buildings of England* in 1966 describes the privately owned abbey ruins as 'well looked after… they have avoided that smoothness which characterizes ruins kept by the Ministry of Public Buildings and Works. Instead there is a wild variety of wildflowers.' Nearby lives the artist Simon Palmer whose highly finished watercolour and gouache paintings are the product, in his own words, of 'the territory of imagination'. This territory finds its physical roots in the landscape that surrounds his home, richly textured and structured around the soaring perpendiculars of exquisitely rendered trees. In Palmer's work the human presence is there, but it lingers around the

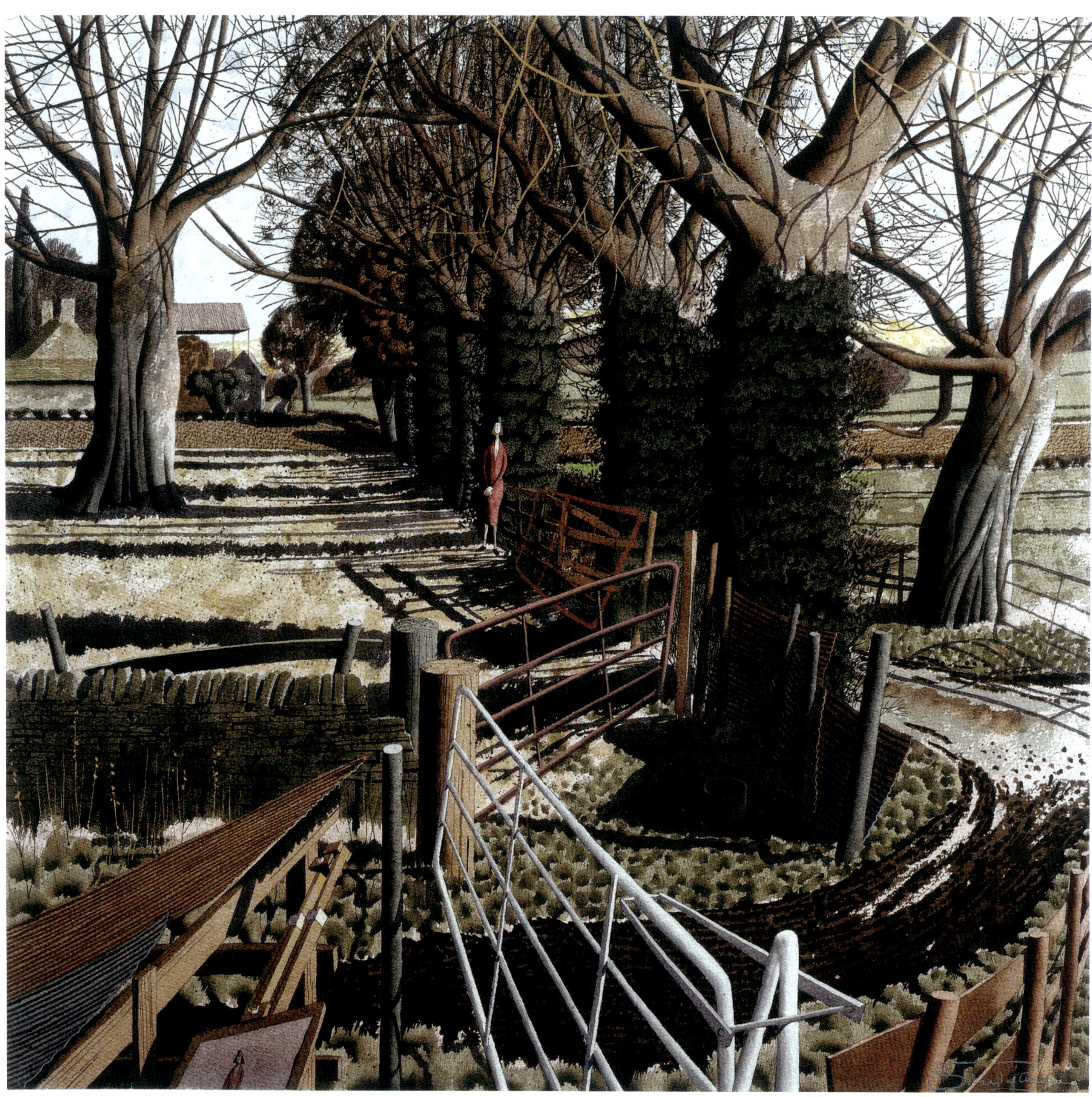

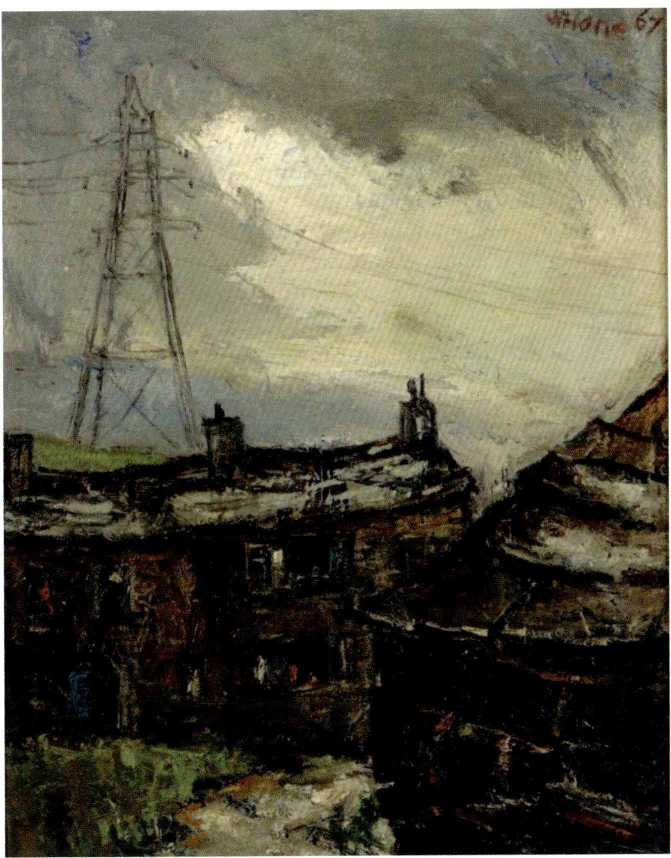

edges, often partially hidden by the trees themselves, which seem to have the more human character. Much has been written about Palmer's place in a line of English landscape tradition, starting with his near namesake Samuel Palmer, tracking through the twentieth century taking in John Piper, Stanley Spencer, the Nash brothers, Eric Ravilious and more. Although he often pays homage to these influences in his work, Palmer's art is not nostalgic. It is a contemporary countryside that informs his vision: a place with corrugated iron sheds, disintegrating barns, glaring road signs and estate agents' boards. There are no cars, though, driving along the twisting lanes, no planes overhead. Classical mythology often intervenes, producing such diverting titles as *The Undocumented Flight of Icarus* or *The Return of Odysseus*. Disturbing texts sometimes creep into the scene, such as a road sign reading 'Caution Nymphs in the Road'. The quirky snippets of implied narrative do not however distract us from the work of art as a whole. There is above all a sense in Palmer's landscapes of an artist's sheer joy in the process of making art. In his own words, 'there is a fundamental pleasure, the illusion of creating three dimensional forms and shapes on a flat piece of paper – a pleasure that I am yet to tire of.'

The Yorkshire Ridings were established as the boundaries of local government in 1889. The West Riding was colossal, encompassing 7,169 square metres, stretching from Sheffield in the south to Sedbergh in the north and from Slaidburn in the west to Adlingfleet in the east. Then eighty-five years later in 1974 it was abolished and Yorkshire, adding bits on and taking other bits away around the edges, was reorganised. Older Yorkshire people have not recovered from this desecration, and talk still of the North, the East and the West Ridings. The inhabitants of the East Riding were so outraged by their loss and assimilation into Humberside that they campaigned for over twenty years to have the name reinstated in 1996. The West Ridingers simply ignored the whole thing. The polymath Herbert Whone – musician, writer, painter and photographer – in 1974 published his book *The Essential West Riding*, a collection of his black and white photographs of his own most loved parts of the West Riding with accompanying extracts from appropriate texts. The specific views that he chose concentrated on Bradford, Leeds and surrounding towns and villages - Keighley, Bingley, Huddersfield, Halifax, Hebden Bridge and Haworth – with quotes from the novels of the Brontës, J B

Herbert Whone, 1925 - 2011. *Pennine Landscape* (c. 1967). Oil on canvas, 67.7 x 54.5cm (Mercer Art Gallery, Harrogate Borough Council)

Opposite: Simon Palmer, b. 1957. *The Last Portrait of Penelope Plain* (2004). Watercolour and gouache, 59 x 59.5cm (JHW Fine Art)

Priestley, and Phyllis Bentley, articles from the *Huddersfield Examiner*, old mining ballads and Yorkshire dialect poetry. Whone's take on the West Riding is irredeemably dour, indeed J B Priestley takes him up on this in his foreword for the book: 'Just as people elsewhere often pretend to be more sensitive than they really are, West Riding types often pretend to be far less sensitive, and may be artists at heart when they are almost giving a performance as wool buyers. And here I might add that the number of artists, writers, musicians, actors, my native city of Bradford has produced is *astounding*... Mr Whone does tend to support the legend that the West Riding is a grim place with people not largely given to enjoying themselves... [whereas] I am now almost famous for grumbling and yet enjoying myself, and this makes me a fairly typical West Riding man.'

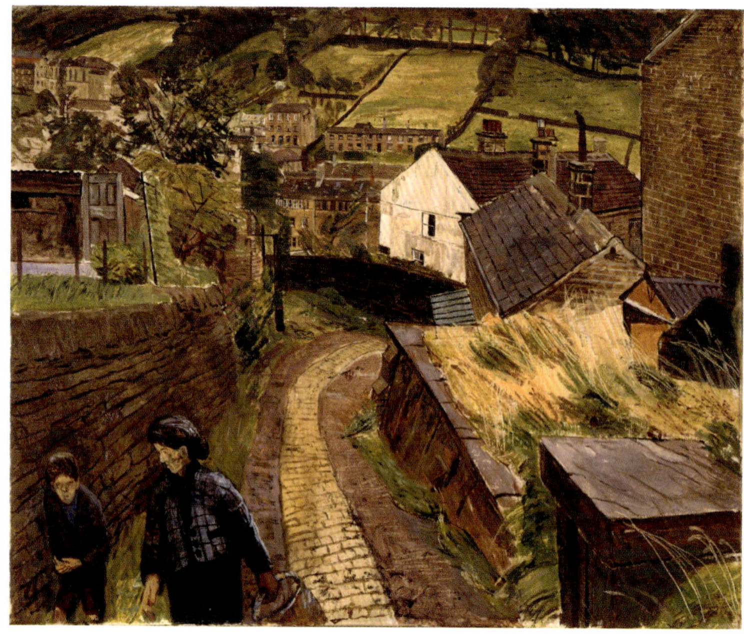

Whone came back to live in the West Riding in 1964 having given up a highly successful career as violinist with the Scottish National Orchestra in Glasgow to move into teaching music at Huddersfield Polytechnic. Not only did this next extremely productive stage in his creative life lead to the publication of several influential books on playing the violin, but also his paintings of the Pennine landscape. Executed in thick impasto with a muted colour range of browns and greens, Whone's oil paintings captured the quintessential ruggedness of this harsh landscape. Others were attracted to this landscape for its strong character. Carel Weight, for example, in his painting **The Road out of Holmfirth** depicts an aspect of the town that remains unchanged today. The narrow cobbled road is Goose Green, which for two hundred years was the main thoroughfare to the nearby villages of Nabb, Damhouse, Ward Place and Cartworth Moor. Weight captures the enclosing atmosphere of the landscape, the vertiginous hills studded with terraces of weavers' cottages sweeping upwards into the background to obliterate the sky and fill the canvas, whilst in the foreground the steep road out of the town rears up to meet the viewer, the figures of a woman and a boy disappearing into the bottom left corner. This painting has Weight's characteristic eerie feeling to it, which is exuded by the huddled figure of the boy who looks up worriedly at the viewer.

Carel Weight, 1908 - 1997. *The Road out of Holmfirth* (1984). Oil on canvas, 50.7 x 61cm (Kirklees Collection, Huddersfield Art Gallery)

The literary landscape of Yorkshire has no more famous location than Haworth, home of the Brontës. The family came to live at Haworth Parsonage when Patrick Brontë was made Perpetual Curate in 1820 –

Opposite: John Bradley, 1786 - 1843. *View of Keighley* (1839). Oil on canvas, 68.6 x 96.5cm (Bradford Museums and Art Galleries)

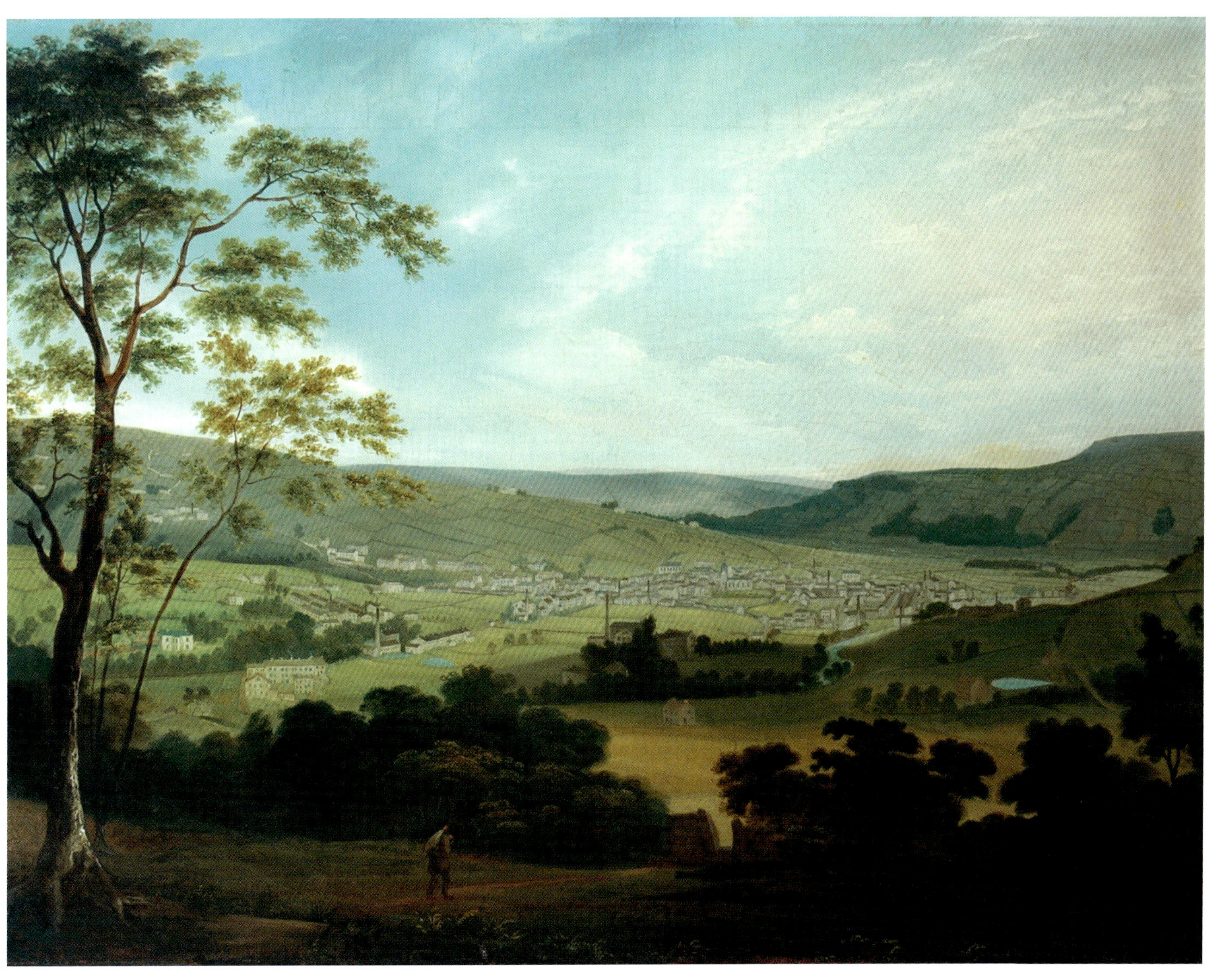

Patrick, his wife Maria, and their six children, Maria, Elizabeth, Charlotte, Branwell, Emily and Anne. The Brontës' story is well known, with their own life histories as poignant and gripping as Charlotte's *Jane Eyre*, Emily's *Wuthering Heights* and Anne's *The Tenant of Wildfell Hall*. Mrs Brontë died soon after the arrival in Haworth, followed by her two oldest daughters Maria and Elizabeth in 1825. Branwell Brontë, the only boy and the child for whom Patrick had the greatest ambitions, squandered his talents with drugs and drink and died aged thirty-one in 1848, followed just a few months later by the death of Emily. Anne Brontë died in Scarborough in May 1849, where poor Charlotte had her last sibling buried at St Mary's church overlooking the sea. Charlotte herself lived long enough to enjoy a little of the fame that her novels brought her, adding *Villette* and *Shirley* to her publications. Much against her father's wishes, in 1854 she married his curate Arthur Bell Nicholls, only to die in the early stages of pregnancy less than a year later. Even in Charlotte's own lifetime, visitors beat a path to her door at the Parsonage, laying the foundations of a tourism industry that has continued to grow for over one hundred and fifty years, with the Parsonage becoming a museum as long ago as 1928. But what was the area like in the Brontës' day, before it came to be dominated by its literary associations?

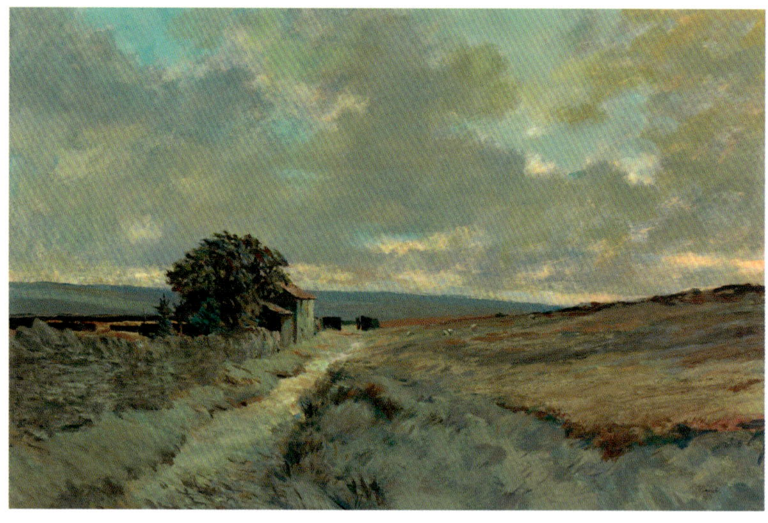

Joseph Pighills, 1902 - 1984. *Far Westfield, Haworth Moor*. Oil on board, 59.5 x 86.5cm (Bradford Museums and Art Galleries)

In 1839, Keighley artist John Bradley painted a panoramic view of his growing hometown, looking across Airedale in the direction of Haworth. The clusters of mills and cottages tumbling down the hillsides are painted in a sketchy manner, as though the artist considered them to be a blemish on a landscape that he has portrayed in classical fashion. The foreground is painted with a dark Claudian palette and the view is framed on one side with an elegant tree and lush vegetation on the other. A traveller makes his way along a path that leads to the middle-ground and the distant view beyond, thus linking the three classical planes of the landscape. Bradley is also distinguished by the fact that Mr Brontë engaged him to teach his children to draw, with an eye on Branwell's prospects as an artist. In the year this picture was painted the Brontës were all occupied with trying to make a living, in all cases not very successfully. Emily left her post as a teacher at Miss Patchett's school at Law Hill after only six months; Branwell came home in May having failed in his attempts to become a portrait painter in Bradford; Charlotte went to be a governess near Skipton but lasted just two months there and Anne left her position as a governess with the Inghams at Mirfield. Nonetheless, they all continued to draw and paint at home.

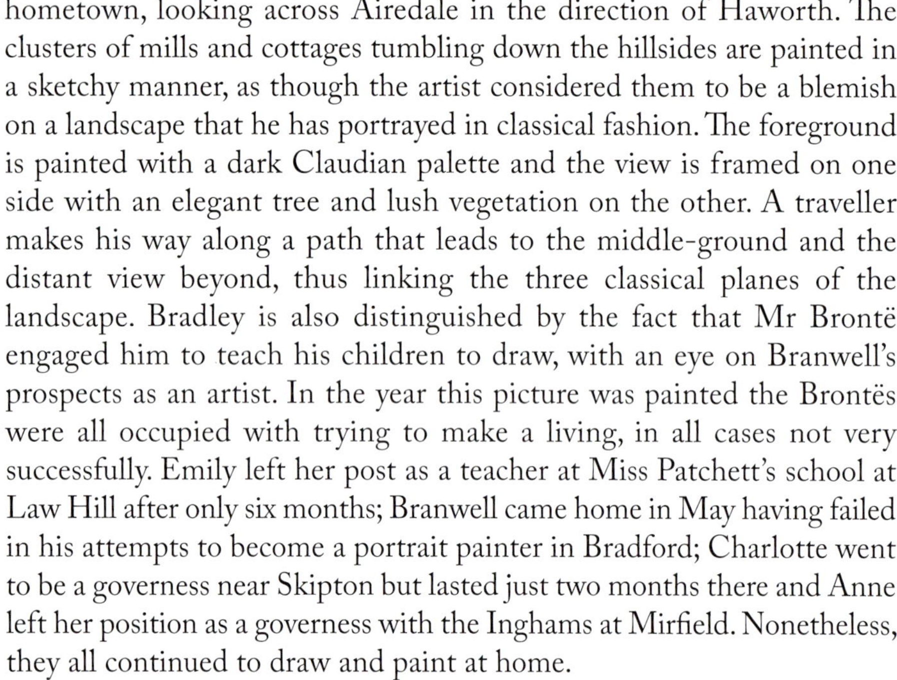

The landscape that is now generally known as 'Brontë country' has attracted many artists since the Brontës found fame with their extraordinary novels, and continues to do so today, with contemporary artists such as Cornelia Parker, Su Blackwell, Sam Taylor-Wood, Charlotte Cory and Paula Rego making installations, prints and photographs for display in the Parsonage. Those who have been absorbed by the natural landscape include local artist Joseph Pighills, who did not begin to paint until his retirement from the woollen mills and had no artistic training. His paintings, such as **Far Westfield, Haworth Moor**

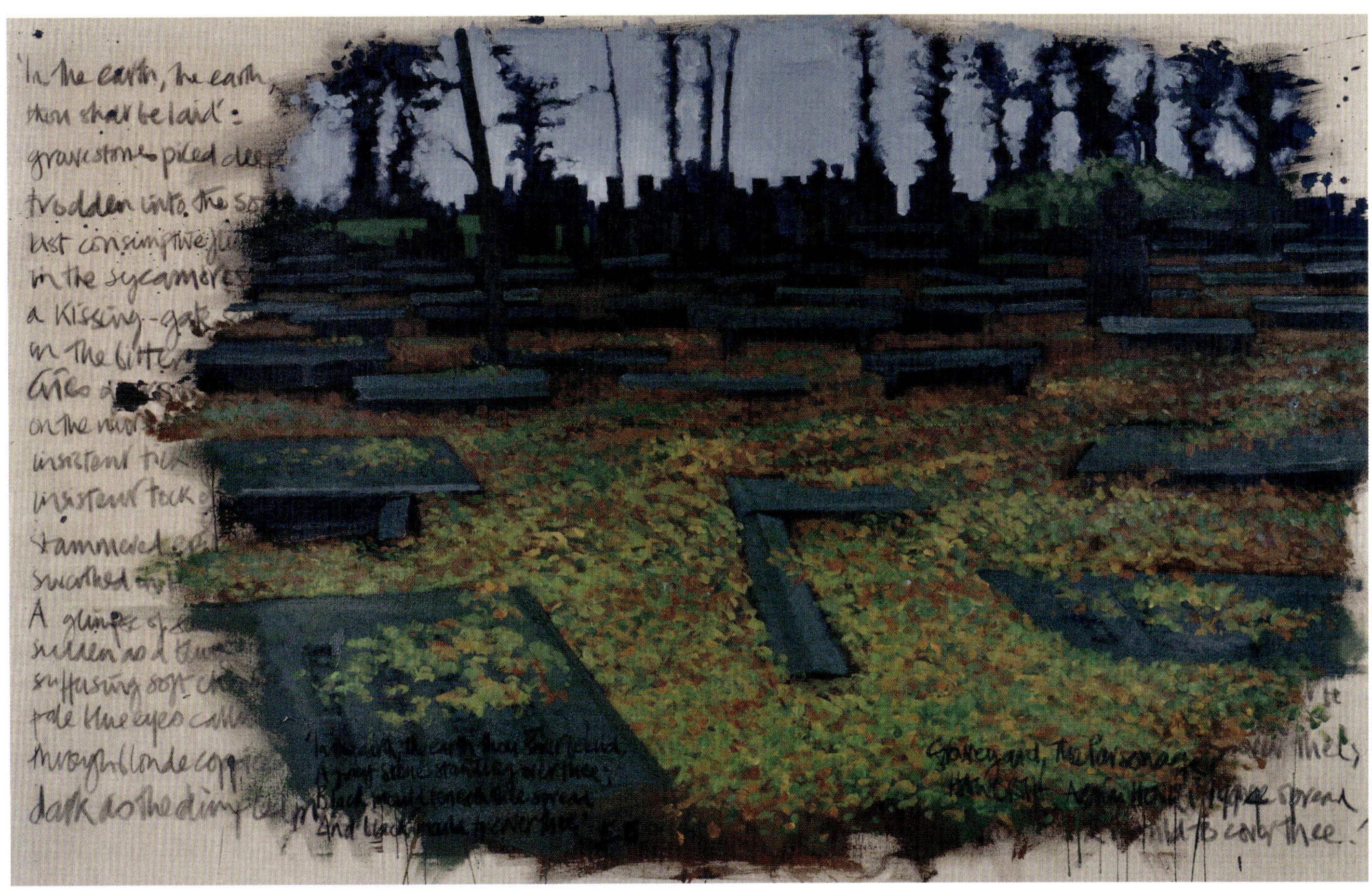

Adrian Henri, 1932 - 2000. *Graveyard, The Parsonage, Haworth* (1994). Acrylic on canvas, 112 x 182cm (Private Collection)

won admiration and Yorkshire collectors, including the politician Sir Denis Healey, for his interpretation of the open moors and the huge brooding skies that look down on them. The journalistic photographer Bill Brandt imbued all of his work with a sense of the artistic. He was drawn to Haworth to create a portfolio of work that captured in stark black and white imagery the spirit of the place. The Liverpool poet and painter Adrian Henri was invited to the Brontë Parsonage Museum for a week-long poetry residency in the atmospheric gloom of late autumn of 1994. Henri worked in the children's bedroom overlooking the graveyard and became increasingly fascinated with the view. For Henri the discovery that Haworth in the Brontës' lifetime had one of the highest death rates in Britain formed an idea for new work. The villagers drank bad water from a well fed by a spring that ran through the graveyard, which gave the artist the disturbing idea of the graveyard feeding itself. This inspired a number of sketches and paintings, including **Graveyard, The Parsonage, Haworth**, 1994. Bare canvas surrounds Henri's image of the tombstones appearing to sink into a bed of fallen leaves, inscribed with lines from a poem by Emily Brontë: 'In the earth, the earth thou shalt be laid / A grey stone standing over thee / Black mould beneath thee spread /And black mould to cover thee.'

Henry Moore, one of the greatest of all modern sculptors, was born in Castleford in Yorkshire, the son of a miner. Although his sculptures are interpretations of the human figure his work as a whole is concerned with the relationship between the landscape and humanity, and it was the Yorkshire landscape that first inspired him. Moore's family was not at all artistic, but he formed an ambition to be a sculptor from a young age, when a teacher at his congregational chapel Sunday school talked to the class about Michelangelo. The first sculpture Moore saw was the Gothic carvings on Saint Oswald's Church at Methley near where he lived, but his true sense of sculpture he found in the landscape that surrounded him. There was not only Adel Crag in Leeds and Brimham Rocks in Nidderdale but also the slag heaps that towered over the mining villages, in Moore's imagination looking like mountains or pyramids.

After serving in the First World War as a gunner at the Western Front, Moore returned to Yorkshire and trained as a teacher, but his interest in art stayed with him and he was awarded a scholarship to Leeds College of Art to study sculpture, the only student to do so. From there he went on to the Royal College of Art in London where he struggled to conform to the traditional ideas then current in his chosen art. It was the 1920s, the era of Cubism, Epstein and Brancusi, none of which was popular at the Royal College, so Moore went in search of other inspiration, which he found in the Primitive art in the British Museum. Moore remained as a teacher at the RCA but was constantly met with prejudice for his interest in abstract form. In 1928 his first exhibition caused controversy. Although his subject was the classical female figure and his technique was superb, people were offended by what they saw as the sexual nature of his female figure. Moore's belief was that 'Art is the expression of imagination and not the imitation of life', and his Yorkshire determination helped him to face down his critics and hang on to his vision. In fact, in some ways Moore belonged to a long Romantic landscape tradition in English art because of his passion for the landscape. It was his practice to work outdoors so that he could see his sculpture against the sky and work with the changing effects of light. There is a monumental quality to all of his art that links as much to the overwhelming presence of the slag heaps around Moore's Castleford childhood home as it does to the new abstract movement in modern art in which Moore played such an immensely significant role. Today Moore's work can be seen to particularly good advantage sited carefully within the landscape at the Yorkshire Sculpture Park near Wakefield. The undulating hills and distant views of surrounding countryside offer different settings appropriate to individual sculptures and the space in which to view such monumental works as **Draped seated woman, 1957-58.**

Henry Moore, 1898 - 1986. *Draped seated woman* (1957-58). Bronze (Yorkshire Sculpture Park)

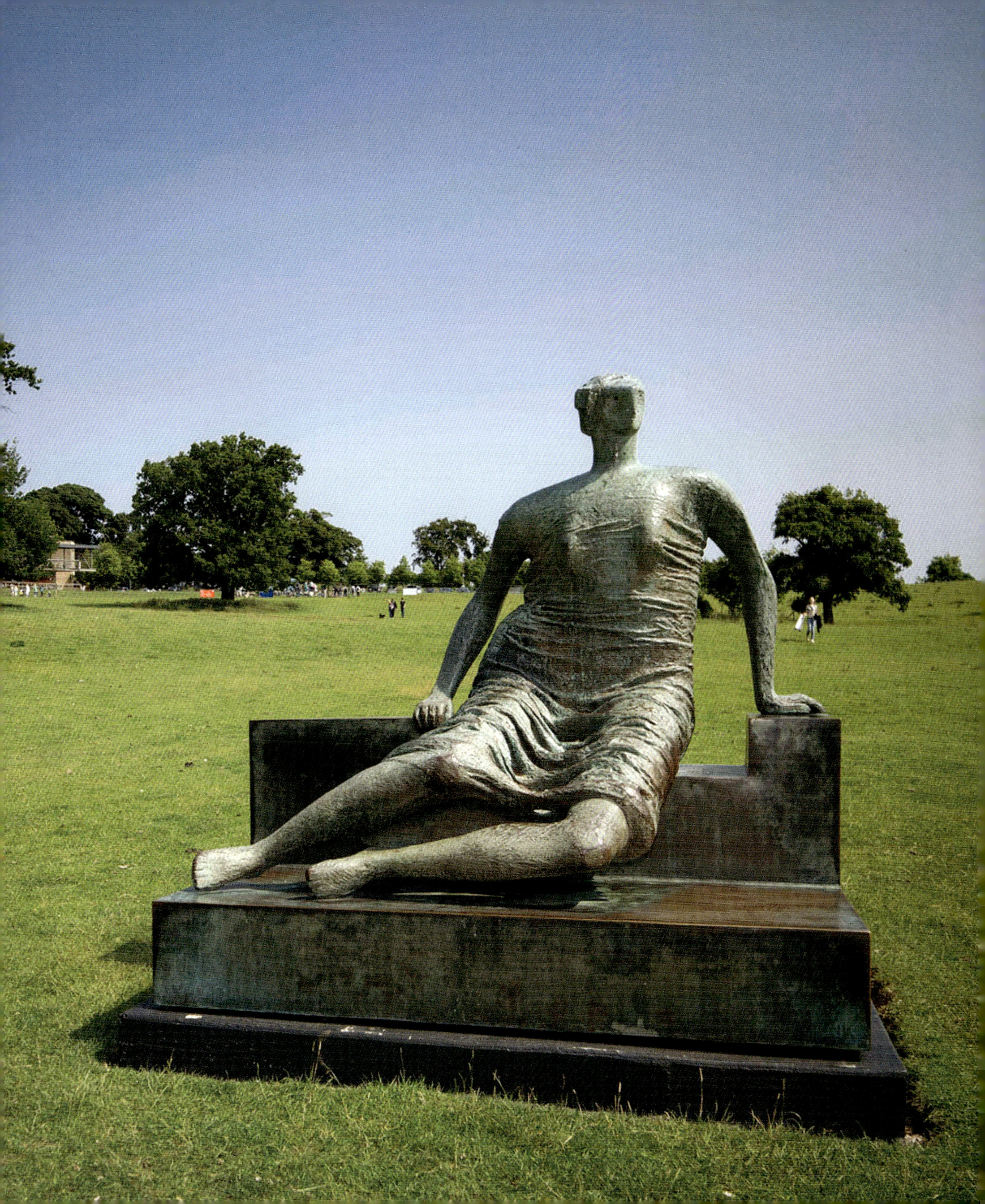

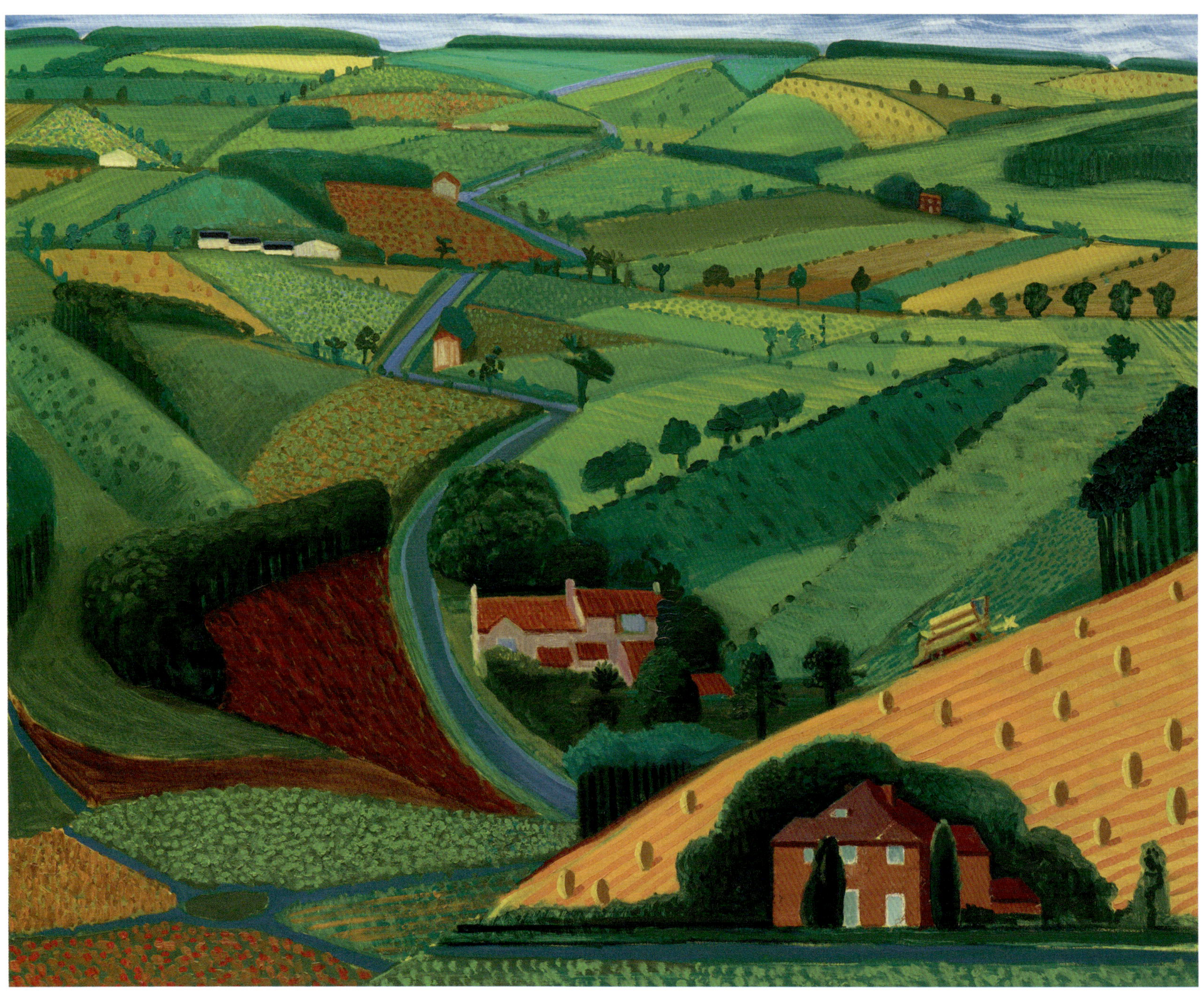

David Hockney (b. 1937). *The Road across the Wolds* (1997). Oil on canvas, 121.9 x 152.4cm

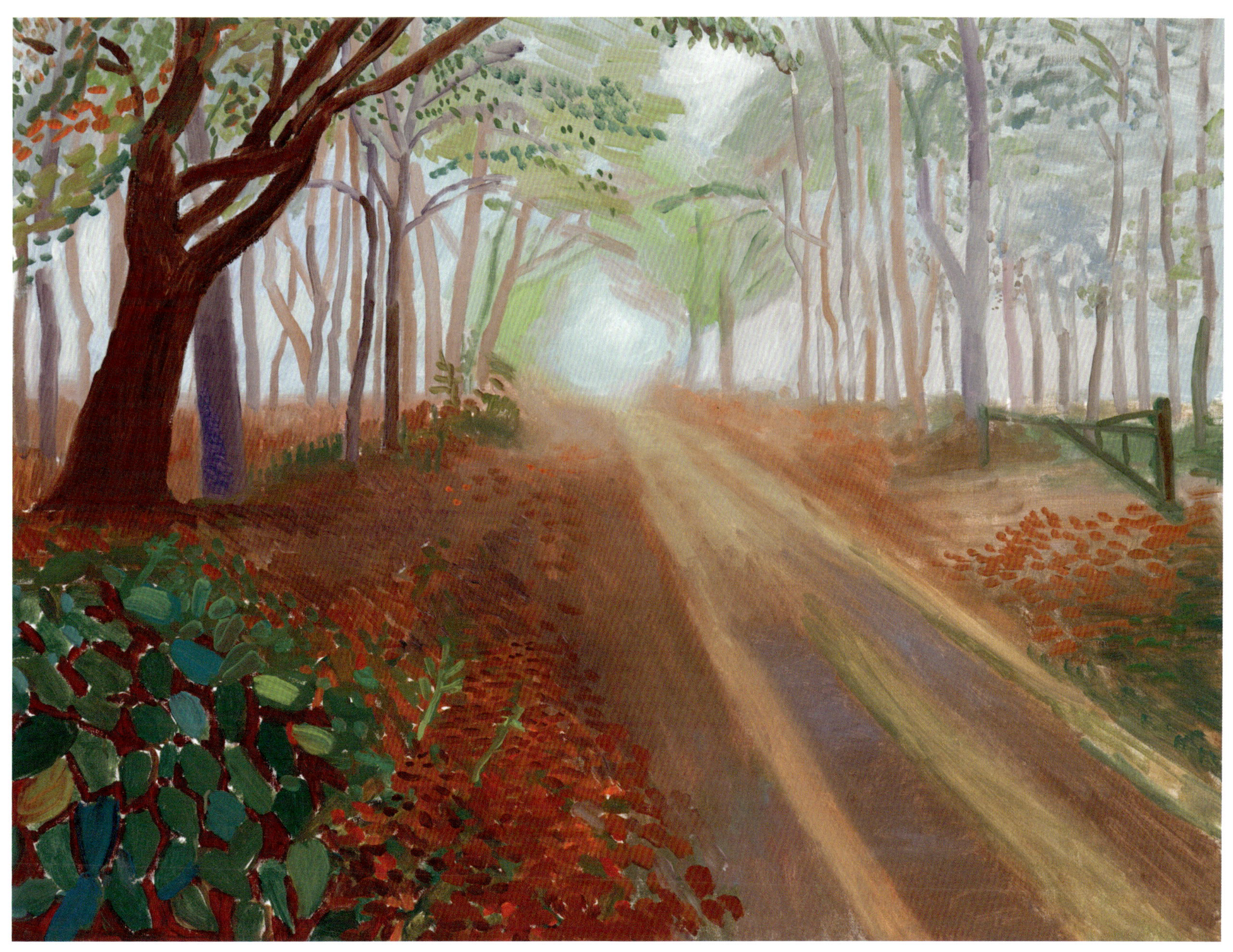

David Hockney (b. 1937). *Woldgate Mist* (November 2005). Oil on canvas, 91.4 x 121.9cm

Photo Credit: Richard Schmidt

David Hockney is England's most famous contemporary artist. He was born in Bradford where he went to art school, then he went on to the Royal College of Art where he belonged to a new generation of young British Pop artists in the early 1960s. Hockney is an artist of great versatility – a painter, printmaker, photographer, filmmaker and stage designer – and throughout his career he has continued to experiment in all of these different art forms. Photography has always captivated him and he has constantly adopted new technology as a creative tool, in recent years in his seventies producing iPad landscape and portrait drawings. Indeed, Hockney's art can be described as a continuous exploration of the visual world. Energy and curiosity spur him on in his creativity, for example in his book *Secret Knowledge*, an analysis of the technology of mirrors, drawing aids and the *camera obscura* that was used by artists since the Renaissance. Hockney's work is all about looking at nature, exploring space, line and colour, and his subject matter, it could be said, is the story of his own life. In 1964, having barely made it a subject for his early paintings, Hockney left Yorkshire behind to live in Los Angeles. There he found the world that he wanted for himself both as a young gay man and as an artist, painting huge bright blue skies and the white splash on the surface of a swimming pool in flat acrylics. Glamorous young men peopled his paintings, as did new American admirers and collectors, attracted to the work that made him internationally famous. One could not imagine that he would ever want to return to Yorkshire, but, as has often been said, Yorkshiremen, and women, always go home in the end.

Hockney was sixty when he returned to spend more time in Yorkshire in 1997. It was his love for an old friend who was dying that inspired him to start to paint the Yorkshire landscape. He chose east Yorkshire, an area of which he had fond childhood memories of working on a farm there, and it was the place where his beloved mother Laura had moved to live, in Bridlington, for the last years of her life. East Yorkshire, with its flat plains and curving Wolds, is little known and few artists have been tempted to work there. Indeed, the obscurity of this part of Yorkshire and its lack of a market for tourism was a strong element in its attraction for Hockney. Since 2005 Hockney has produced a massive group of landscape works in paint, film and new media that depict Yorkshire as it has never been seen before. In the 1950s, a student in Bradford, Hockney painted a small view of this same landscape in heavy impasto dark greens and browns. Over fifty years later the landscape in Hockney's paintings has erupted into a blaze of colour. The winding roads, bordered by trees, hedges and grass verges studded with wild flowers, are transformed by patches of bright yellow sunlight and purple shadows cast by the vibrant greenery of the trees arching over the road. Hockney paints out of doors in all weathers, capturing the changing seasons with variations of his palette, but never dispensing with shades of purple, aquamarine and

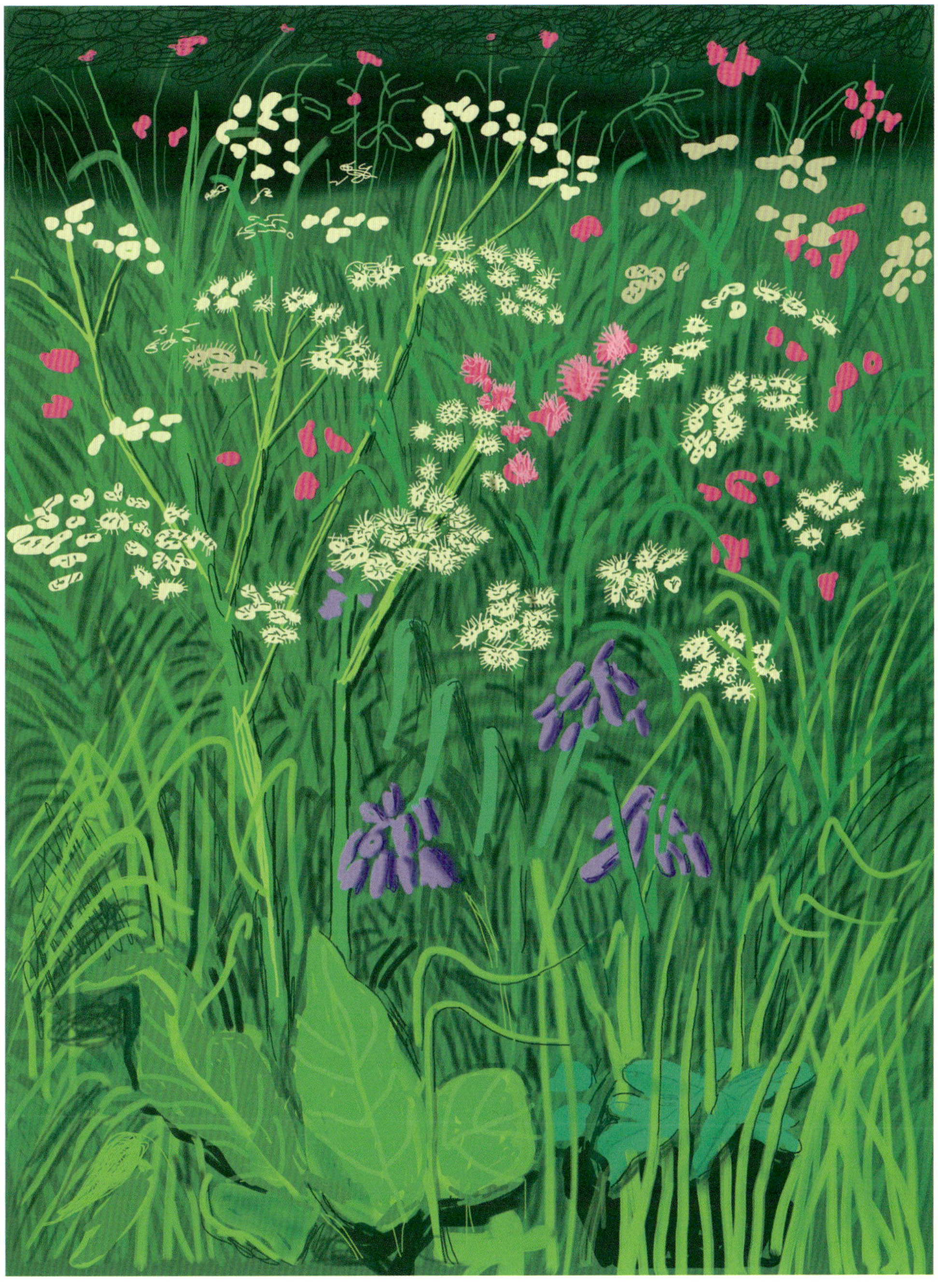

vermilion even in deepest darkest winter. In order to give a sense of the panorama in front of him he sometimes works on large canvases made up of multiple sections, a method of composition that is also used in a film he made of the changing seasons. When he was not painting on this large scale, the artist made rapid sketches on his iPhone.

In 2012 a decade's worth of Hockney's landscape work was shown in the exhibition *A Bigger Picture* at the Royal Academy of Arts in London, touring on to Bilbao and Cologne. The London exhibition was the most visited in the Royal Academy's history and the work drew massive critical attention. Hockney had at last come home to Yorkshire to create a new vision of a little known part of this vast county, which, for over two hundred years, had welcomed so many outstanding landscape artists to explore its beauty and its diversity.

David Hockney (b. 1937). *The Arrival of Spring in Woldgate, East Yorkshire in 2011 (twenty-eleven)* (119.44 17 May). iPad drawing on paper, 67.3 x 50.2cm © David Hockney

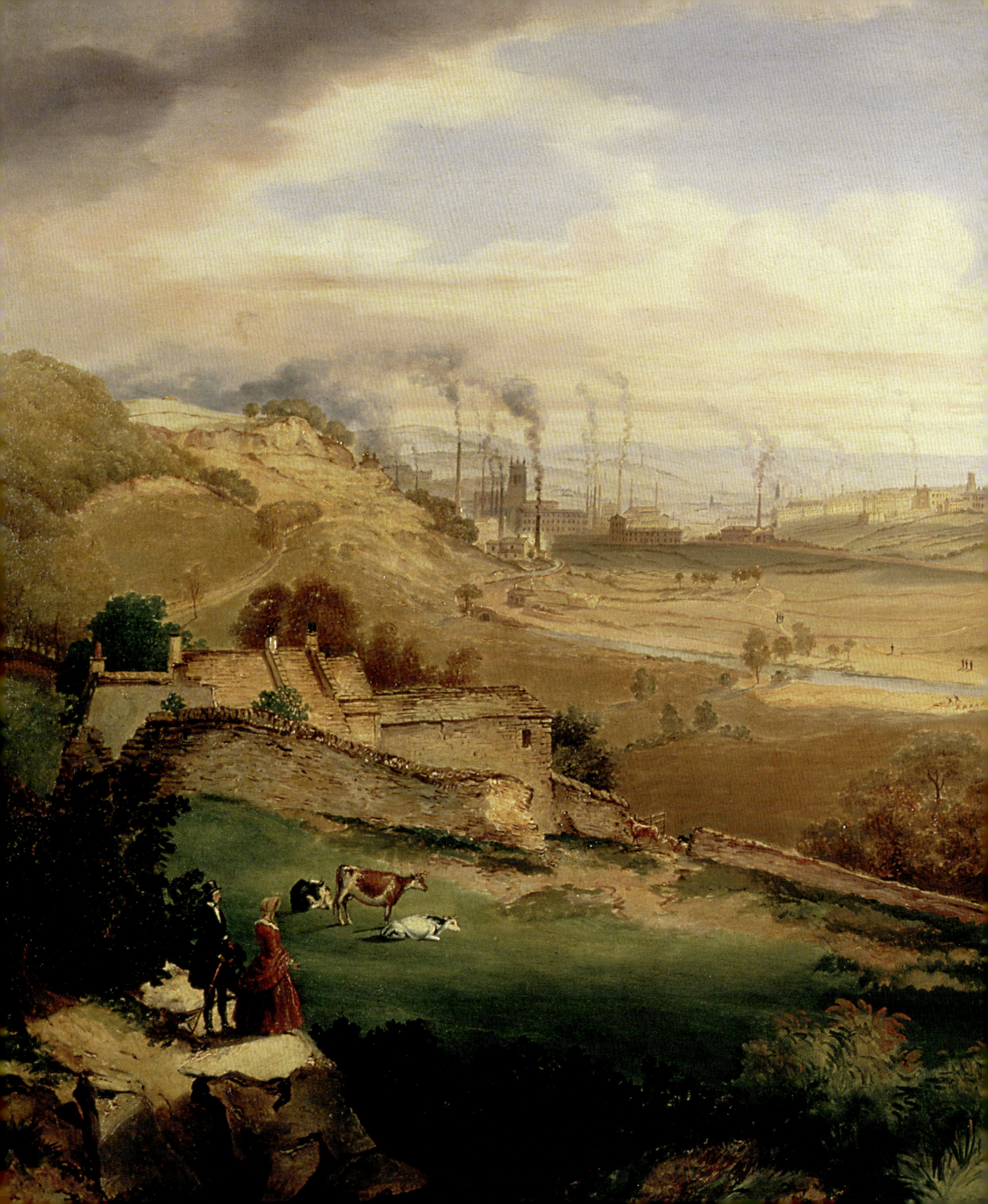

3. City and Industry

William Cowen, 1791 - 1864.
Detail of *View of Bradford* (1849).
Oil on canvas, 71 x 141.5cm
(Bradford Museums and Art Galleries)

In 1849 William Cowen painted a **View of Bradford** that records the point in time when the new industrial cities of Yorkshire increasingly and inevitably encroached upon the landscape. The view is framed in the classical manner with arching trees on one side and on the other a promontory of rock from which a well-dressed couple gaze upon the valley spread out in front of them. Their daughters meanwhile play with their dogs in the field beneath the trees. The foreground is contrasted with the middle ground in the usual manner, with the colours warming from green to brown, but the distinct detail of the stone wall also acts as a line that separates the old agricultural life of the countryside from the new industry of Bradford. We look beyond the grazing cows and the ramshackle farm buildings onto the brave new world of smoking factory chimneys, the mills and the canal with a white sailed cargo boat. By 1841 there were thirty-eight worsted mills in Bradford town and two-thirds of the country's wool production was processed in Bradford. By 1850, Bradford had become the wool capital of the world with a population of 100,000. Cowen's painting of 1849 therefore romanticises the view by putting an emphasis on the disappearing countryside and playing down the dark satanic mills, thus indicating a sense of nostalgia for a bygone age. Cowen, who was born in Rotherham and became a drawing teacher in Sheffield, also painted views of Rotherham, Sheffield and Huddersfield, all of which have the same classical composition and take the same romantic viewpoint of Yorkshire's massive industrial change in the mid nineteenth century.

Atkinson Grimshaw painted atmospheric moonlit scenes of nineteenth century urban Yorkshire that have captured the imagination of the modern day audience, just as they did with the Victorian gallery goers and collectors from the 1860s until 1893 when he met his untimely death. The young Atkinson had no artistic training; indeed, such an interest was considered time-wasting, foolish and unproductive by his strict Baptist parents Mary Atkinson and father David Grimshaw. His mother supposedly turned off the gas in his room and threw his paints on the fire, so the would-be artist resorted to searching out local book dealers and framers who might have paintings for him to study. In 1852, no doubt at his parents' behest, Grimshaw joined the Great Northern Railway Company as a clerk and seemed set for a career in a major modern business. These were the years when he began to study and practise the art of painting in his spare time. Grimshaw was fortunate in that there was a growing interest in the fine arts in Leeds, with the Northern Society promoting artists of the British School, exhibitions in small private galleries, country house art collections to visit and books and prints to consult in the Leeds Library. In 1858 Grimshaw married his cousin Fanny and their marriage enabled him to leave the family home and gave him the encouragement and support to give up his railway job and embark on a career as an artist around 1861.

Grimshaw rapidly developed towards his own style and technique during the 1860s and by 1870 the artist was able to suggest a much more atmospheric view of the world where mood, poetry and even mystery took hold. From that point on he became 'the painter of moonlight', building up a loyal band of wealthy northern collectors and finding the financial success that he needed to support his growing family. In 1870 he rented Knostrop Old Hall in Leeds, a seventeenth century stone built mansion with great character, which appealed to Grimshaw's sense of living in style. The move to Knostrop in fact saw Grimshaw achieve his most consistent style and to create his immediately recognisable themes, such as the moonlit suburban lane with a mysterious half hidden house and the lone figure of a woman walking along the road, as in **Silver Moonlight**, 1880. The 1870s was Grimshaw's most successful decade. He refined his technique, expanded his subject matter and moved successfully into the London and provincial art markets, represented by Thomas Agnew and Son. Increasingly, his new moonlit landscapes and cityscapes bathed his subjects in an evocative glow that suggested the poetic atmosphere that is the most appealing feature of his work. Grimshaw was a prolific painter and often repeated his most popular subjects in order to keep the money coming in to support his family. Underlying the ups and downs of his career, Grimshaw's family history, although typical of the Victorian age, was profoundly sad. In the first five years of marriage, the couple had four babies who were stillborn or died shortly after birth, and one, Clara, who lived to be twelve. Altogether, they had sixteen children, only six of whom – Arthur, Enid, Louis, Wilfred and twins Lancelot and Elaine – survived into adult life. Moonlit landscapes had been painted since the seventeenth century, but Grimshaw was different: he used it to illuminate the contemporary urban scene, which had changed so much in the previous half century. The everyday realities of modern urban life appealed to him, but there was a general unease in society about this social, economic and visual change in the established order. It was perhaps a sense of regret for the loss of the old world that inspired Grimshaw to make paintings imbued with a sense of poetic nostalgia, thus making them so appealing

Atkinson Grimshaw (1836 - 1893). *Tree Shadows on the Park Wall, Roundhay Park, Leeds* (1872). Oil on card, 55.2 x 44.2cm (Leeds Art Gallery, Leeds Museums and Galleries)

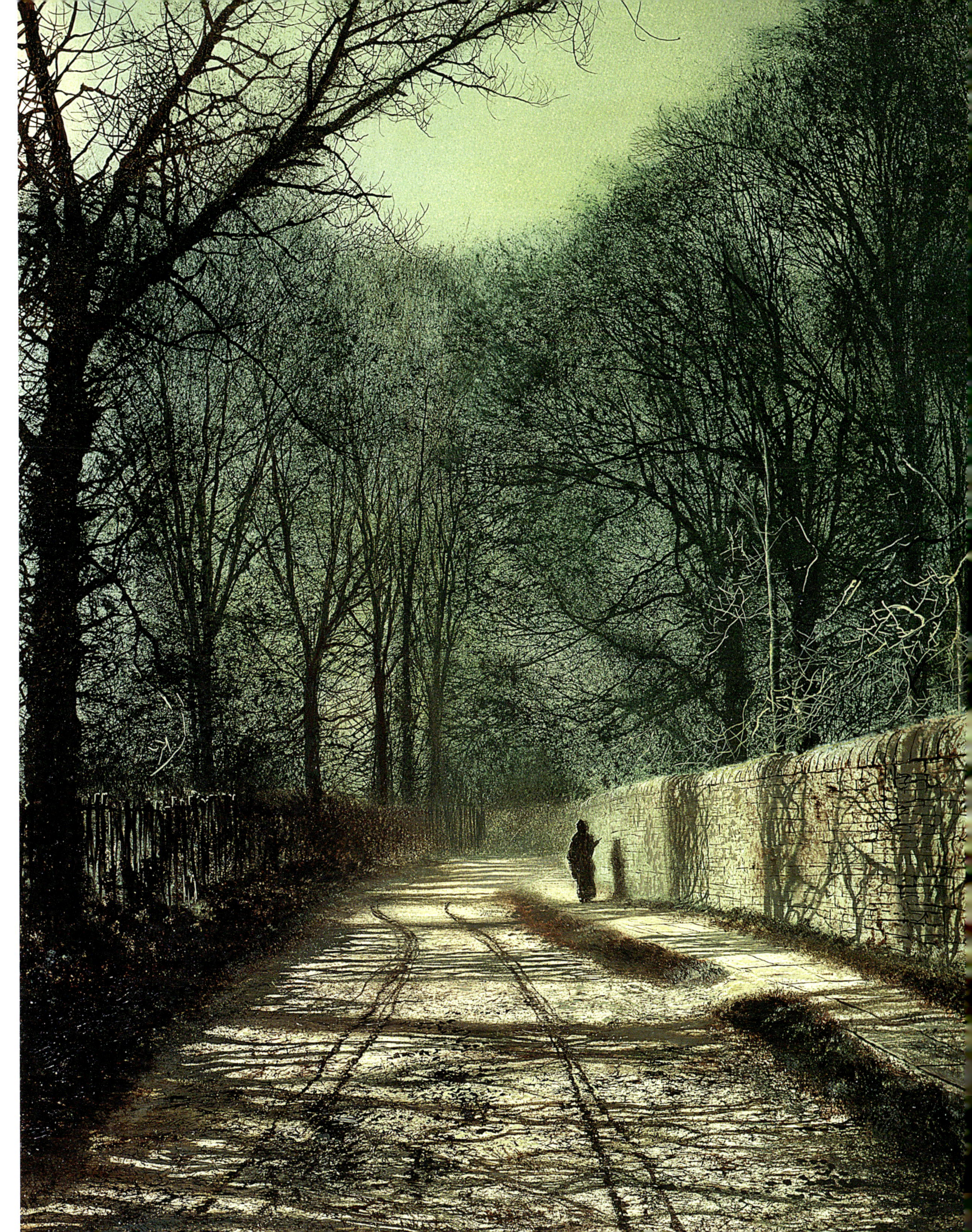

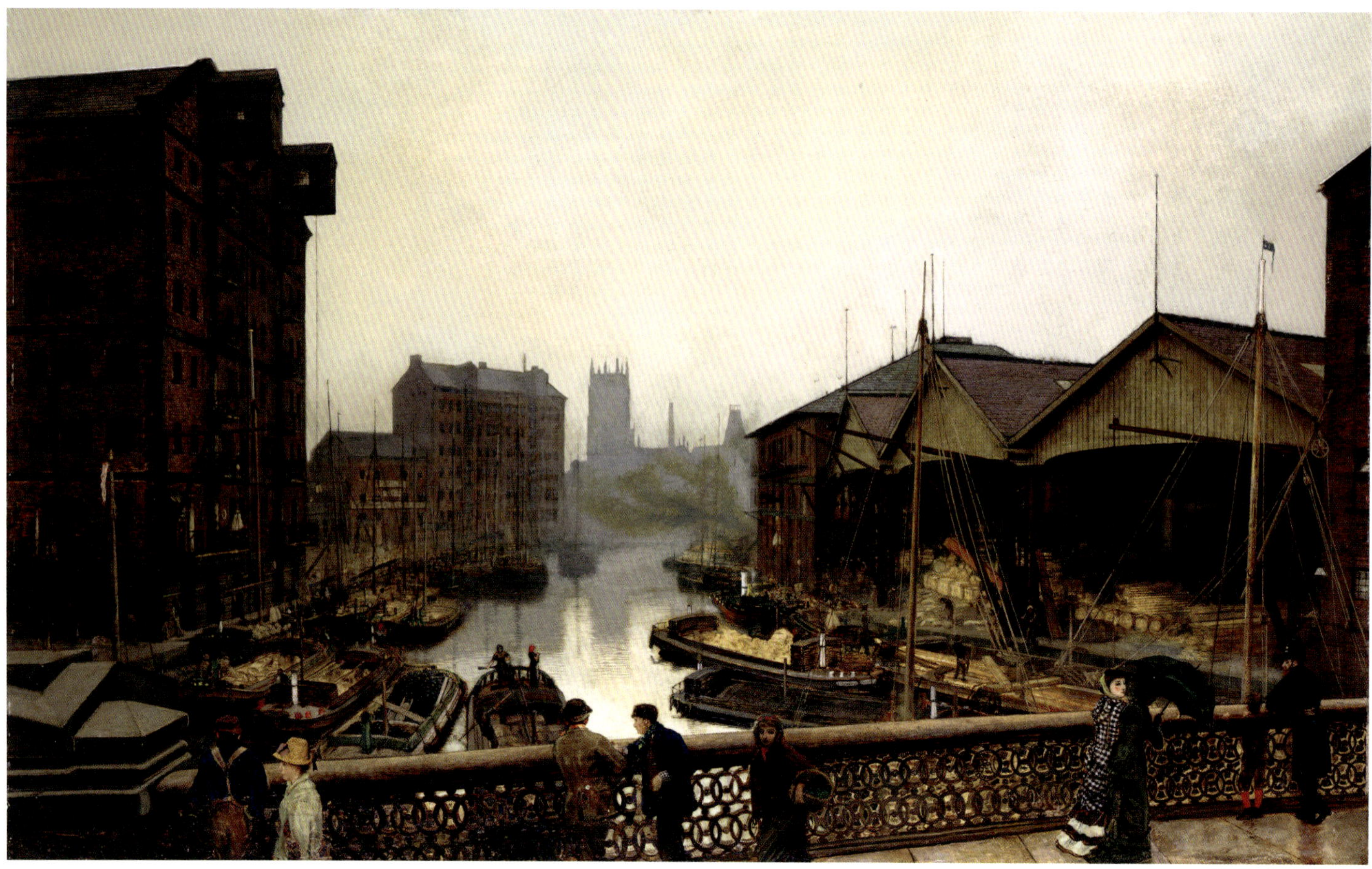

Atkinson Grimshaw (1836 - 1893). *Leeds Bridge* (1880). Oil on canvas, 75 x 121.9cm (Leeds Art Gallery, Leeds Museums and Galleries)

both to his contemporaries and to viewers in the twenty first century. **Tree Shadows on the Park Wall, Roundhay Park, Leeds** is quintessential Grimshaw, with the moonlight filtering through the branches of the trees onto the stone wall and pavement of a Leeds street and its solitary passer-by.

Grimshaw experimented with different subjects throughout his career, including classical scenes in the style of Alma Tadema and portraits of fashionable pretty women in the manner of Tissot, but the urban scene was his main concern. In **Leeds Bridge** he dispenses with the moonlight to depict a rather more social realist image of Leeds life and industry. The viewpoint the artist has taken, with the cropping of the figures ranged across the bridge, is rather like a photograph. What adds to this effect is the way two of the figures appear to acknowledge the viewer's presence: the girl just off-centre in shawls and apron, looks straight at us, whilst the woman in the gaudy black and white dress looks back at us over her shoulder. On the far left, a genteel looking woman walks on obliviously. What is remarkable for the time is that Grimshaw's female figures are as natural a part of the everyday scene as the workmen leaning on the bridge, not mere decorative elements. There is also the rare detail of female manual workers; two barge-women stand in the prow of the vessel just emerging from under the bridge, with one leaning back against the tiller whilst the other looks out across the water, hands busy with her knitting. In this one painting, Grimshaw has contrived to include five women from across the social classes, giving the image a modernity and realism uncommon for the time.

Frank Rutter, who was the modernist curator of Leeds Art Gallery from 1912 to 1917, probably did not have much admiration for Atkinson Grimshaw as he arrived at the gallery when Victorian painting was sinking fast in popularity. **Leeds Bridge** did not enter the Leeds collection until 1927, but had Rutter known it he may have been impressed by the equal representation of women. In 1910 Rutter had actively begun to support women's suffrage, giving sanctuary to suffragettes released from prison under the Cat and Mouse Act, something he continued to do whilst he was in Leeds. Rutter initially had plans to create a modern art collection for Leeds, but had been frustrated in this aim by 'boorish' local councillors. Nonetheless, his curatorship had a significant impact on Leeds Art Gallery. Before he left the city, he co-founded the Leeds Art Collections Fund with Michael Sadler, who was the vice-chancellor of Leeds University and a collector of work by Kandinsky and Gauguin. The Fund, which continues to this day, helped with acquisitions and exhibitions, including a show of Post Impressionism at the Leeds Art Club in June 1913. The discussions there about contemporary art had a significant influence on the thinking of the anarchist, poet and critic Herbert Read who was introduced to modern art by Rutter. In his five years at Leeds, Rutter managed to have an influence on acquisitions of modern art for the collection in spite of the councillors. It was he who encouraged the Camden Town painter Charles Ginner to create a series of paintings of the industrial cities of Yorkshire. The Camden Town artists were a loosely organised London exhibiting group who produced small-scale paintings of the everyday surroundings and pursuits of typically lower middle and working class people. They were less concerned with social history than their desire to make art based on truthful observation and to discover scenes of visual fascination within urban life. Ginner visited Leeds with fellow London artist Harold Gilman for the first time in 1913 and he painted many industrial scenes of Leeds, including **Leeds Canal** in 1914, which was eventually given to the gallery in 1962. The painting demonstrates Ginner's interest in the effects of natural light on the non-naturalistic colours of the industrial city of Leeds.

Yorkshire sat at the heart of the industrial revolution in England. The industries are virtually now all gone, although the evidence exists today in the form of the many industrial museums, historic canals, heritage steam railways and Victorian buildings that make up a large part of the twenty-first century Yorkshire industry of tourism. Leeds, Bradford,

Sheffield, Wakefield, Huddersfield, Halifax and York were once the centres of the clothing, textiles, steel, coal and railway industries. All of these have their artistic heritage, none perhaps more evocative than that of the coal mining industry. Coal mining was punishing work and it made fortunes for the Victorian mine-owners, but it was the backbone of great Yorkshire communities, now all gone. The sculptor Henry Moore was born into the mining community and never worked in it as his father had done, but he did find in the miners themselves the subject for some of his most powerful and moving drawings. Moore was an official war artist in the Second World War and mining was a reserved occupation during wartime. After the artist had completed the Shelter drawings of 1941, his studies of Londoners taking refuge from the Blitz in the underground, he visited the Wheldale Colliery in his hometown of Castleford in West Yorkshire, where he drew the miners underground in 1942, the only drawings he ever made of people at work in non-static poses. Moore was never romantic about the mines and he was at first reluctant to accept the commission, preferring his wartime shelter drawings because they connected with his sculptures of reclining figures. In the British Museum a group of the small sketchbooks that Moore took down the mine with him to make his studies are preserved. He produced other larger scale works such as **Miner Drilling**, which, with his Shelter drawings, are considered to be some of his greatest graphic work. The muscular figure of the miner cramped in the harsh conditions of the mine to drill the coal seam brings the work of Michelangelo to mind, the artist who was the first to influence Moore.

Moore's drawing of the miner drilling now belongs to the National Coal Mining Museum near Wakefield, a proud but poignant repository for the art and artefacts of a now obsolete Yorkshire mining history. The collection includes paintings by Peter Watson who had no connections with the coal industry but he was fascinated by the potential of the industrial landscape. He was commissioned in the 1970s by the South Yorkshire Coal Board to make an artistic record of the pits fated to close, thus shattering the local communities. The artist recalled, 'I was just given completely free rein, there was no health and safety, I would just turn up and be told to help myself, clambering over rail lines and slag heaps. At

Henry Moore (1898 - 1986). *Miner Drilling* (1942). Pencil, wax crayons, coloured crayons, pen and ink and wash on paper, 31.1 x 21.4cm (National Coal Mining Museum for England)

Opposite: Charles Ginner (1878 - 1952). *Leeds Canal* (1914). Oil on canvas, 73.6 x 58.4cm (Leeds Art Gallery, Leeds Museums and Galleries)

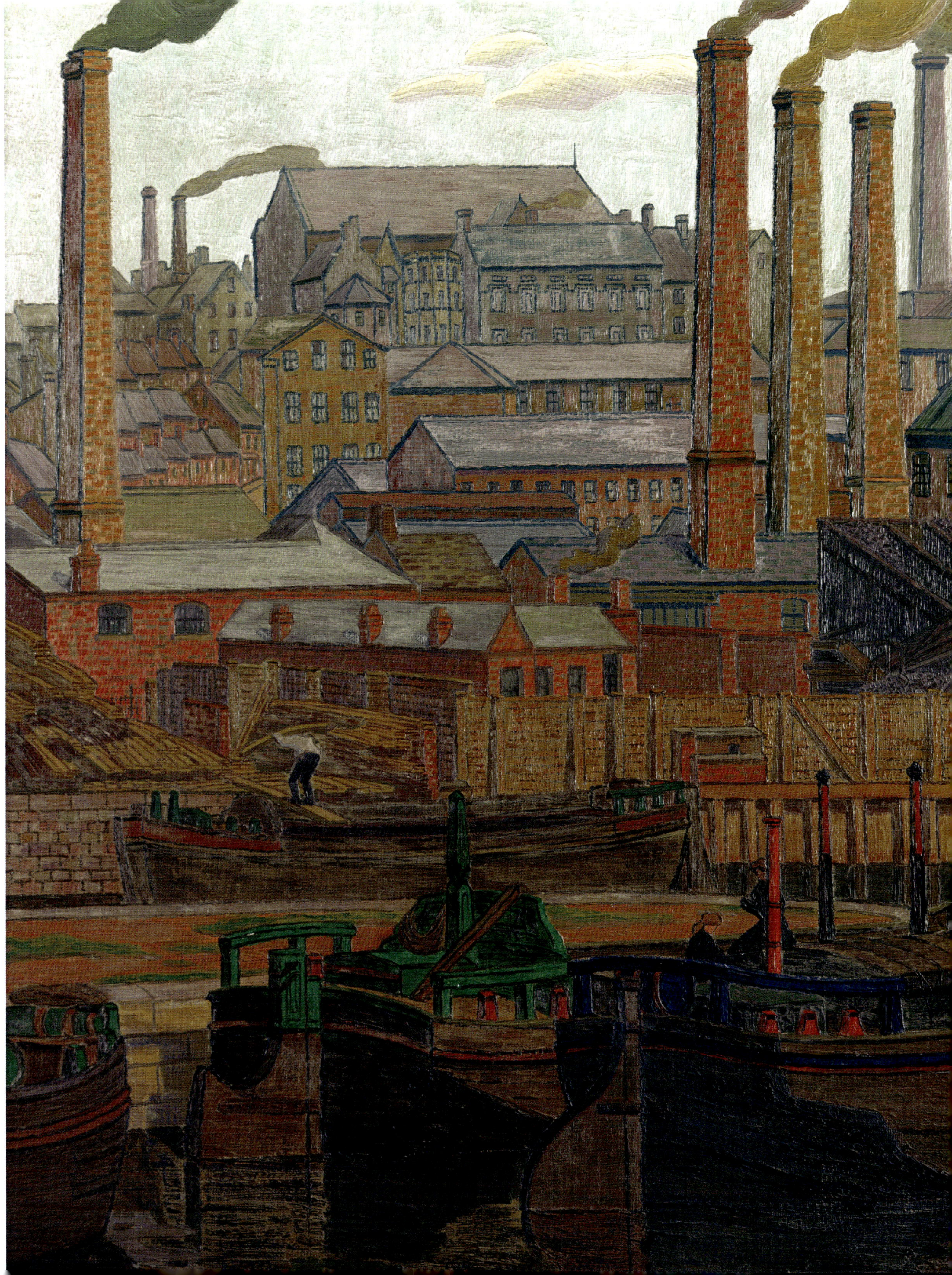

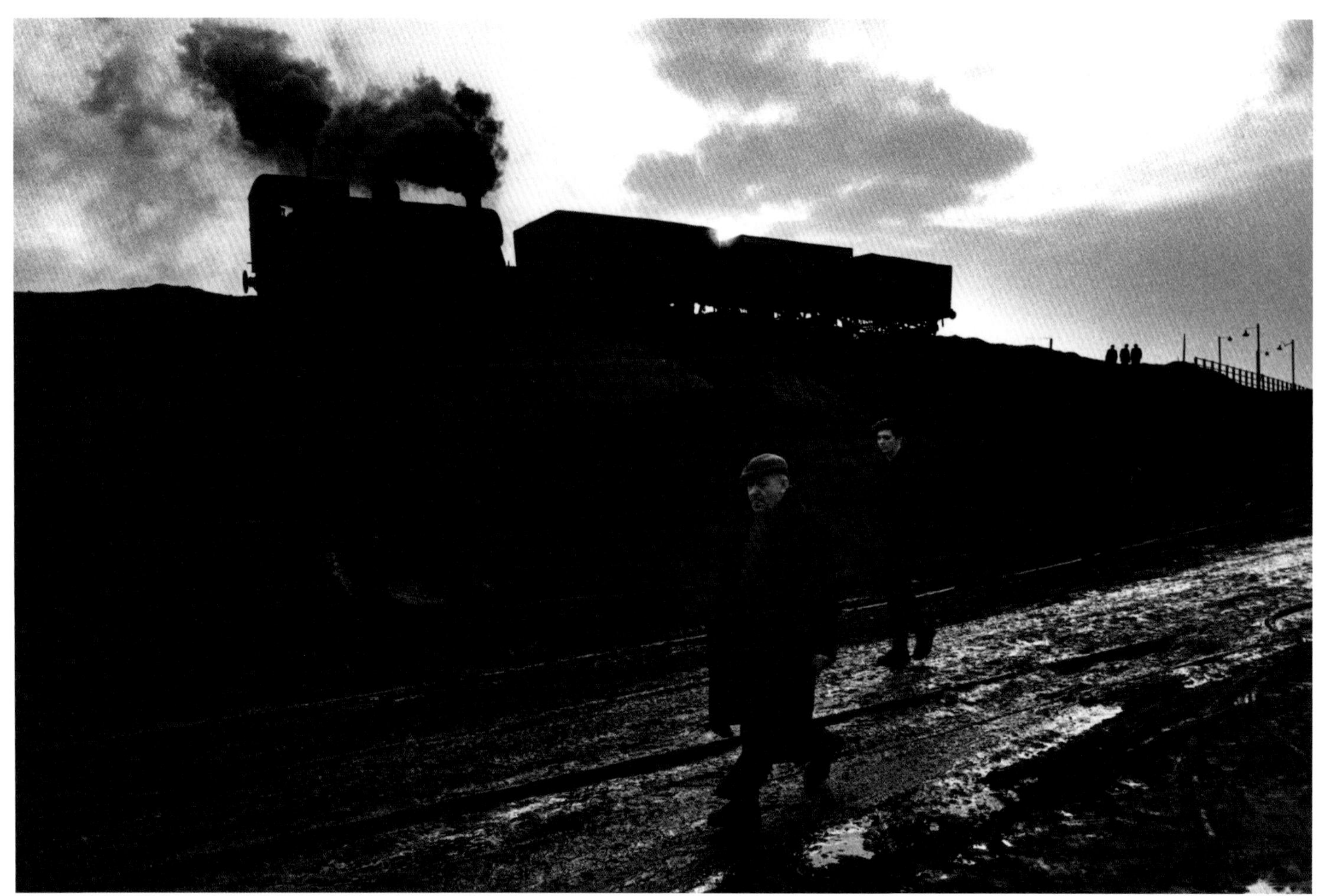

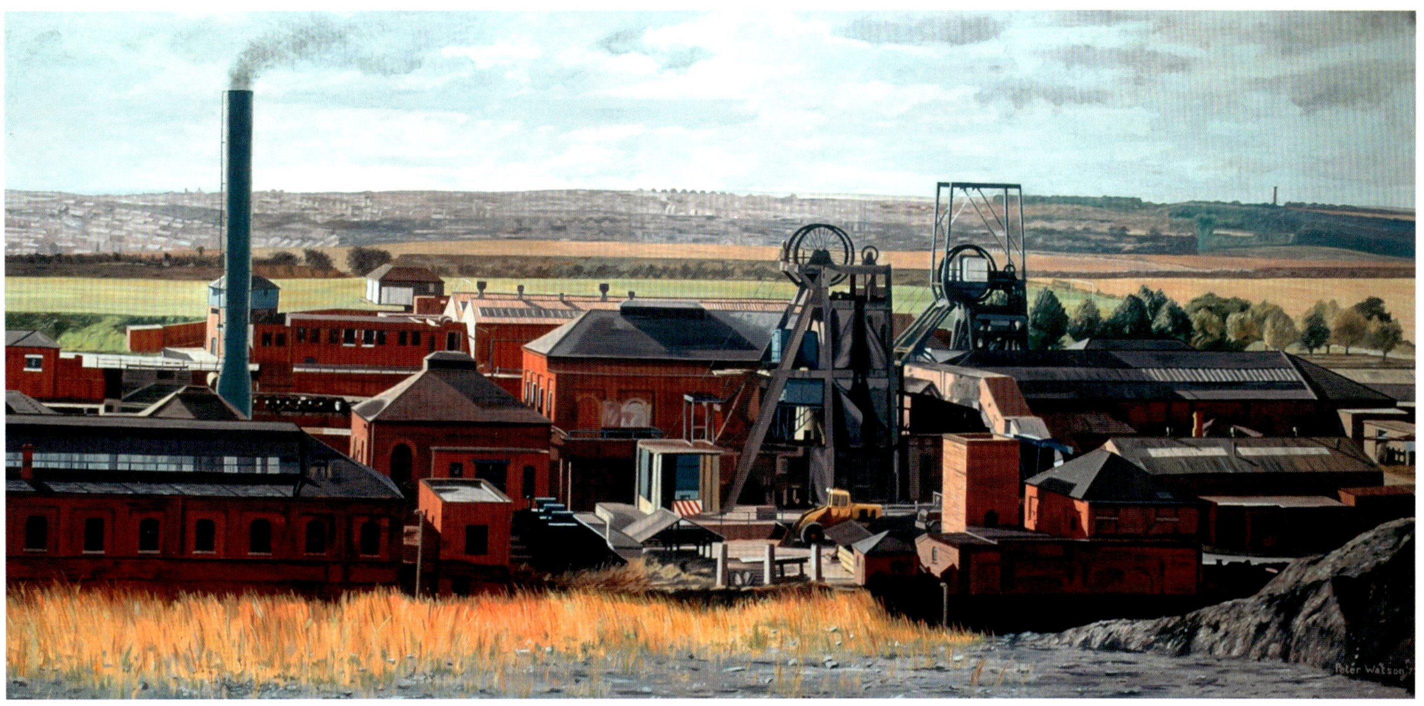

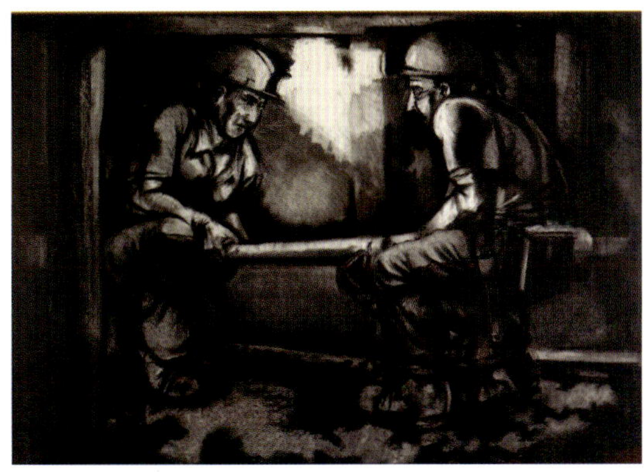

Peter Watson, b. 1952. *New Stubbin Pit* (1977). Acrylic on board, 74 x 150cm (National Coal Mining Museum for England)

Harry Malkin, b. 1951. *Untitled*. Charcoal on paper, 109.2 x 152cm (National Coal Mining Museum for England)

Opposite: Don McCullin, b. 1935. *Yorkshire Miners Go Home, Doncaster* (1963). Photograph. (National Coal Mining Museum for England)

times I would turn up at mines where the manager didn't even know the pit was going to close. I felt like the grim reaper.' Watson's painting of **New Stubbin Pit**, 1977, near Rawmarsh, Rotherham, depicts the mine the year before it closed, surrounded by cornfields, once more bringing industry and countryside together. Don McCullin, the internationally famous war photographer, was also an outsider, a Londoner. Influenced by the work of Bill Brandt, he went to south Yorkshire in the 1960s to capture dark views of the struggling industrial north. Intermittently over the decades, McCullin focused his lens on his own country, revealing the gritty realities and lingering class divisions of post-war England. In works such as **Yorkshire Miners Go Home, Doncaster**, 1963, we can see McCullin's dramatic style already emerging, and the political voice, which consistently spoke for the dispossessed.

Harry Malkin, like Henry Moore, was the son of a miner from Castleford, only instead of pursuing a career in art when young, Malkin followed his father into the pit. Malkin has worked as a sculptor and painter since he was made redundant from the coal industry in 1985 after spending twenty years working on the coal-face at Fryston Colliery. Malkin relates that, 'I have always been a constant drawer and maker. I attended the local schools from primary to senior to leave at the age of fifteen without any significant note other than being a good artist. The thoughts of developing this at this stage was unheard of so upon leaving school in 1966 without any prospects I was tempted into the mining fraternity by my father… While at the mine I would put my creative talents to use in other directions, cutting, fabricating and welding steel as well as assembling and maintaining complex machinery. All of these skills came into use later as a practising artist, particularly as an artist making big pieces in steel, wood and other materials in public places… In 1985 Fryston had promised us seven years more work, but under the harsh re-structuring of the Tory government it closed for Christmas, never to re-open again.' Malkin's charcoal drawing of engineers at work in the mine conveys the awful claustrophobia of the working space, which the artist has described as being like 'crawling underneath a chair and stopping there all day.'

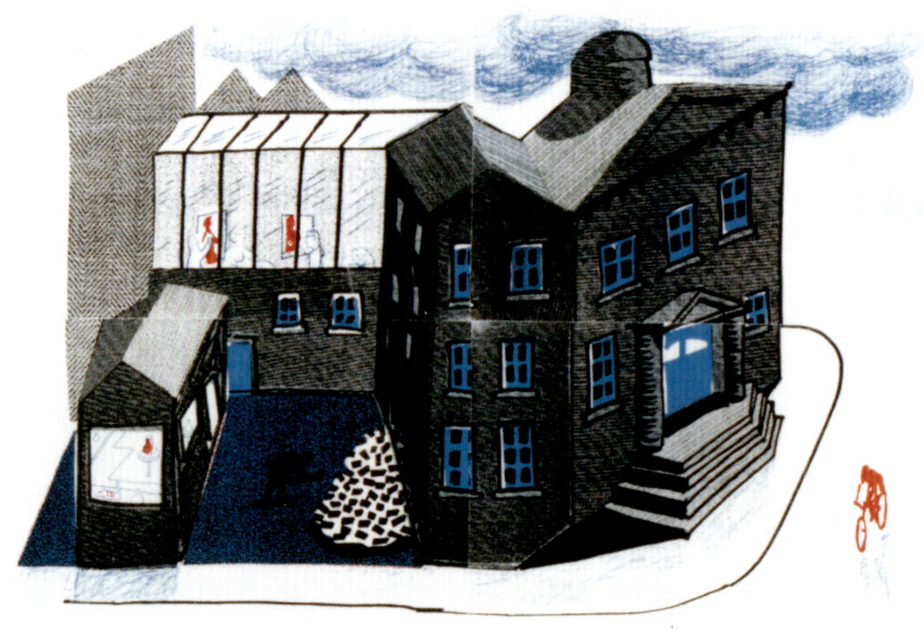

David Hockney was a student at Bradford College of Art in 1956 when he painted a view of **Bolton Junction, Eccleshill**, the place where he grew up. Eccleshill was once the site of many big Victorian mills, some of which survive, most significantly Moorside Mills, which is the Bradford Industrial Museum. No mills are visible in the nineteen-year-old Hockney's vision of his hometown. What we see is a windswept road junction with a figure walking towards us beneath a grey sky. The almost monochrome colour scheme of the painting could not be more different to what was to come less than ten years later when Hockney made his escape to California. Hockney spent most of his time in Los Angeles for the next thirty years, but he came back regularly to Yorkshire for his family and friends. Salts Mill at Saltaire – one of the area's biggest redundant mills - had been converted by Hockney's friends Jonathan and Margaret Silver into a hub for the creative industries with gallery spaces where Hockney has always shown his work. The artist has worked in partnership with his friends there in many ways, including sending from America a huge drawing in sections by fax. In 1989 he produced for display there another piece of Bradford history, a lithograph depicting the College of

David Hockney, b. 1937. *Regional College of Art, Bradford, 1957*, 1989, Home Made Print, Edition: 50, 78 x 108cm
© David Hockney

Opposite: David Hockney, b. 1937. *Bolton Junction, Eccleshill* (1956). Oil on board, 121.9 x 101.6cm
© David Hockney
Bradford Museums and Art Galleries
Photo Credit: Prudence Cuming Associates

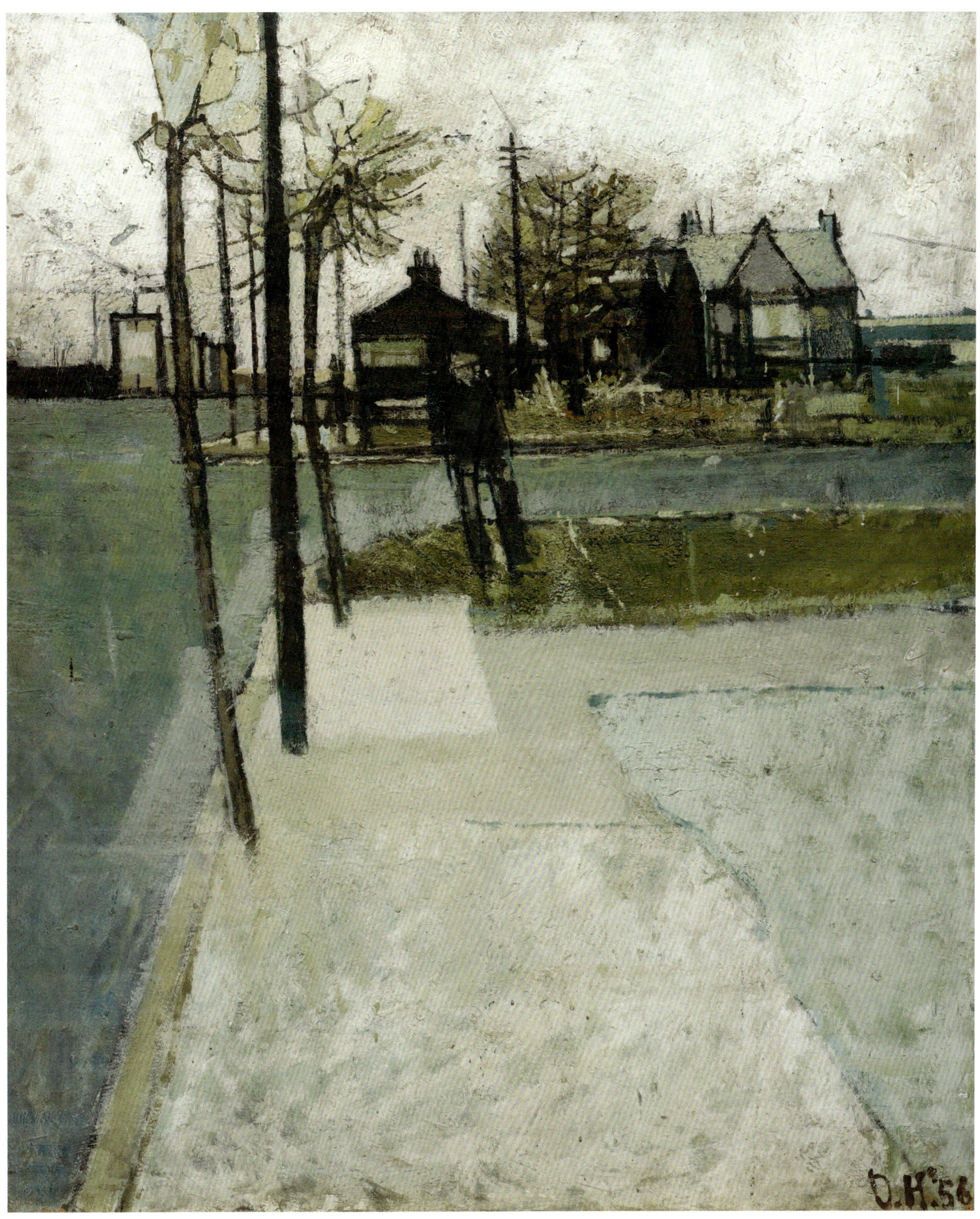

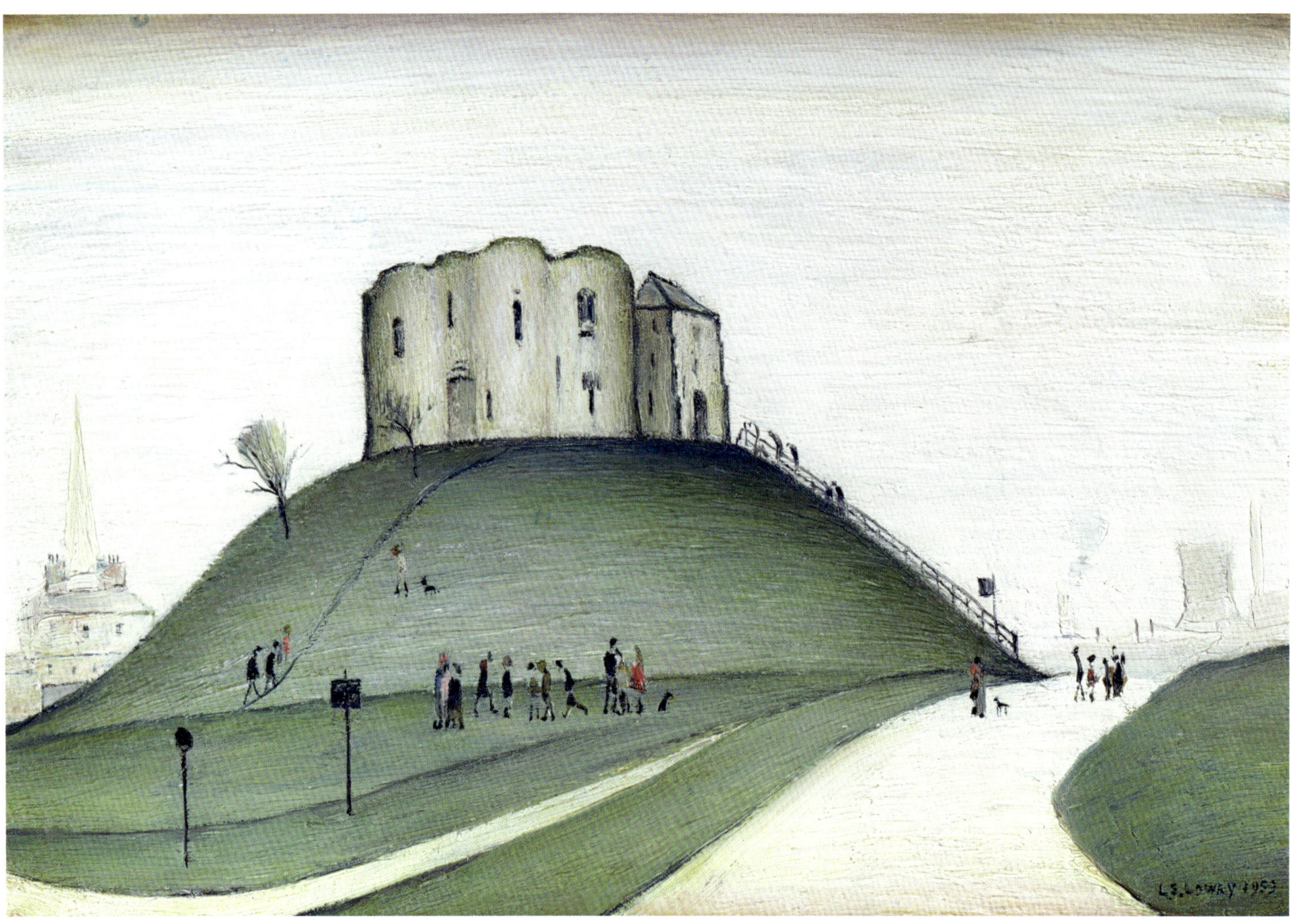

Art in the old Bradford Mechanics Institute. At the time Hockney had a particular interest in space, and here he plays around with the spatial concept of the building so that it can be seen from several angles at once. Through the windows of the new atrium we can see students at work on their easels, whilst in the yard below a single figure appears to be breaking something up into many pieces. A frustrated artist perhaps? Neither of these works by Hockney convey any sense of affection for the city, but they do suggest some of the reasons why he wanted to get away from it.

L S Lowry, on the other hand, loved the big industrial cities of the north. Salford and Manchester were his home territory, but he also travelled further afield, including Yorkshire where he painted Grantley Hall, Ripon, in 1952, **Clifford's Tower, York**, in 1953 and Huddersfield in 1965. The first two of these works were less usual subjects for him. Grantley Hall was for many years an educational training centre with a reputation for running good art classes, and the view of Clifford's Tower was commissioned by the city of York with the funds of the Evelyn

L S Lowry, 1887 - 1976. *Clifford's Tower, York* (1953). Oil on canvas, 35.6 x 50.8cm (York Art Gallery, York Museums Trust)

Opposite: L S Lowry, 1887 - 1976. Detail of *Huddersfield* (1965). Oil on canvas, 59.5 x 75cm (Kirklees Collection, Huddersfield Art Gallery)

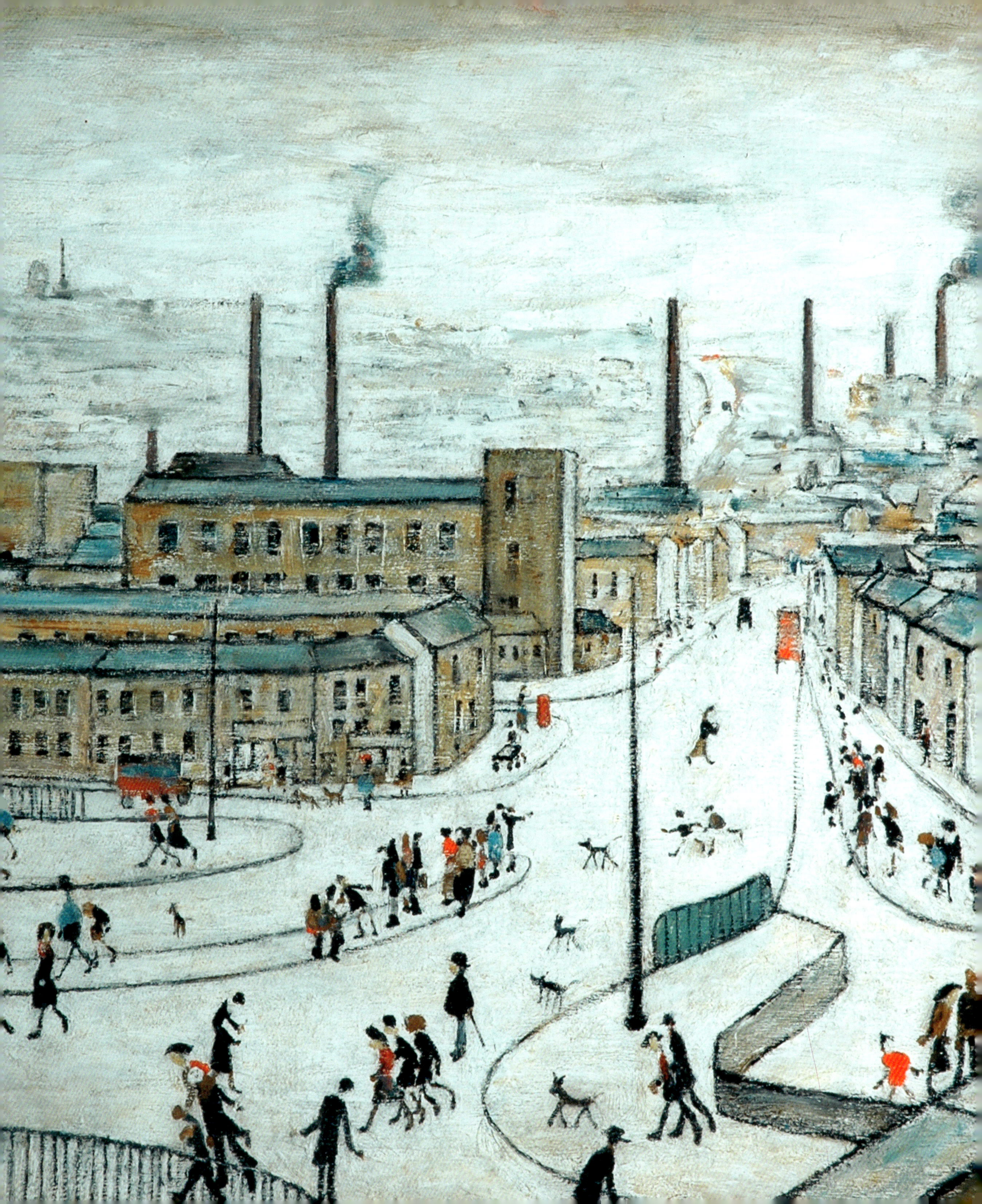

Award, which allowed for the purchase of a view of York by a leading British artist. Although the award only allowed for the purchase of a watercolour Lowry provided an oil painting. Lowry's view of **Huddersfield**, commissioned by the old Huddersfield Corporation, is classic Lowry. The town is viewed looking down Chapel Hill towards Newsome. By 1965 Lowry had moved to Mottram, just over the hill from Holmfirth, and he went to Huddersfield on a regular basis. The smoking mill chimneys track the perspective of the road out to the hills beyond, whilst the foreground is populated by the people, and dogs, of Huddersfield going about their daily business. Lowry habitually used a very basic range of colours - ivory, black, vermilion, Prussian blue, yellow ochre and flake white - which he mixed on his palette and painted onto a white background. Lowry said of his paintings, 'I saw the industrial scene and I was affected by it. I tried to paint it all the time. I tried to paint the industrial scene as best I could. It wasn't easy. Well, a camera could have done the scene straight off.'

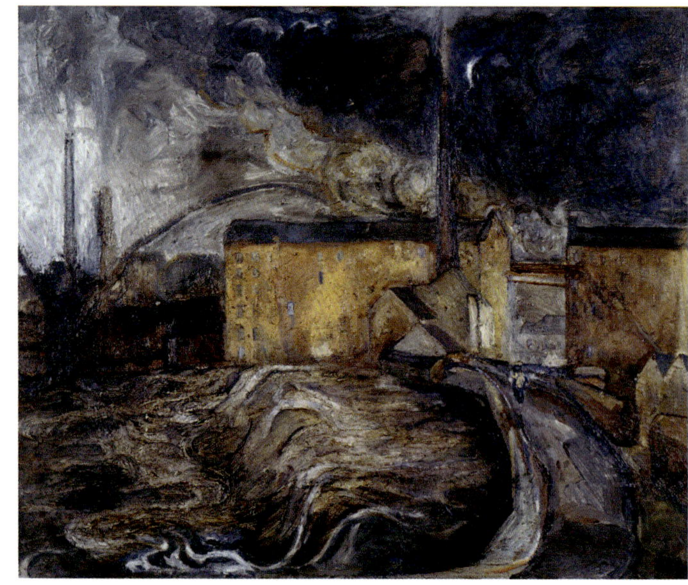

Lowry worked as rent collector but he chose to conceal this fact because he did not want to be thought of as a spare-time painter. He was annoyed to be described as an amateur or primitive painter, remarking 'If people call me a Sunday painter I'm a Sunday painter who paints every day of the week!' His job enabled him to walk all over the city, observing the ebb and flow of people going to and from work, children playing in the street and the everyday incidents that made up the fabric of working class life. He would make quick sketches on the spot on whatever paper he had in his pockets. In the Second World War he experienced the bombing of Manchester then the rebuilding, slum clearances and new housing. Lowry's significance as an artist has often been dismissed, perhaps because of a prejudice against northern artists in England, but his paintings have left us not only with the greatness of one man's individual art but also with an incomparable record of working class life in the twentieth century.

Lowry was extremely generous to other artists, and in 1955 he bought two paintings and a drawing at the Beaux Arts Gallery in Bond Street, London from the very first exhibition of twenty-four year old Cumbrian painter Sheila Fell. The artists were friends for many years and Lowry advised and encouraged Fell and bought twenty of her pictures. Lowry gave Miss Fell, as he called her, a weekly allowance of three pounds and would meet her in Aspatria, her birthplace, where they would go out to the countryside to paint. The landscape of Cumberland was Fell's main

Sheila Fell, 1931 - 1979. *King's Mill, Huddersfield* (1968). Oil on canvas, 63.3 x 76.3cm (Kirklees Collection, Huddersfield Art Gallery)

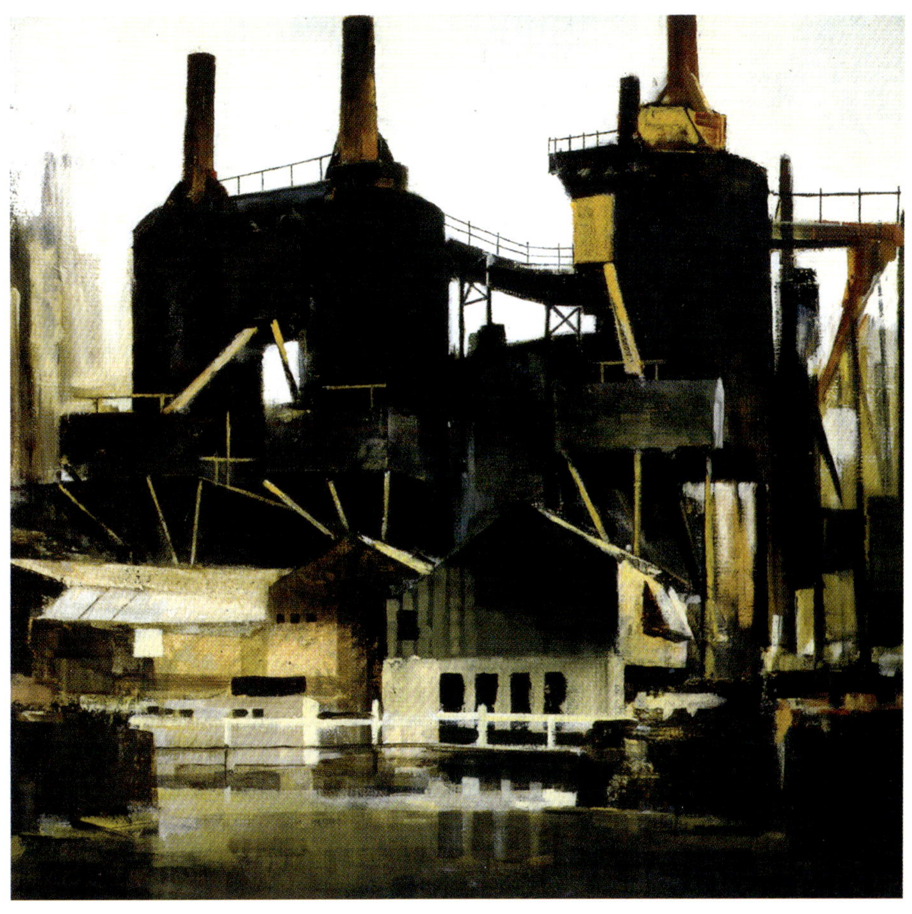

subject, but occasionally she would go elsewhere. In 1968 she was commissioned by the forward thinking Corporation of Huddersfield, perhaps influenced by her mentor, Lowry, to paint a view of the town, **King's Mill, Huddersfield**. Fell depicts the industrial scene as though it were the natural landscape, in sweeping shapes and closely related tones of yellow, grey and brown. Her painter's eye transforms the water in the weir and the clouds above into a maelstrom of paint, and one can detect the influence of both Cézanne and Van Gogh. Famously, talking to Hunter Davies in 1979 for an article in *The Sunday Times*, she said, 'I don't think of myself as a woman artist. Artists are either good or bad. I also intend to live until 104. I've promised myself I will. It's what keeps me going when I worry if I'll ever have time to do all the paintings in my head.' It was not to be. Before the piece went to press she was dead from alcoholic poisoning aged only forty-eight.

Edna Lumb, another outstanding woman artist, was born in Leeds and her artistic ability and determination won her a place at Leeds College of Art. Lumb worked in oils, watercolour, ink and etching, responding to the industrial landscape with the same fervour as Lowry. In the 1960s she

Edna Lumb, 1931 - 1992. *Giggleswick Quarry*. Oil on canvas (Private collection)

became expert at catching machines in motion using a refined watercolour technique and was invited to paint the last great engines of steam power in the mills, railways and mines, recording a vanishing world. For much of her painting career Edna Lumb travelled all over the country in pursuit of her subject – to Bradford for the mills, York for the trains, Liverpool for the old docks. Lumb once turned up at a factory, ready to paint its machinery in action, and wondered why the staff was so unwelcoming, then realised that they had mistaken her for a government inspector.

In 1973 she had a major exhibition at the Bradford Industrial Museum that was reviewed by Angela Croome in *The New Scientist*, in which Lumb's text for the show is quoted: 'We are conditioned by our forefathers to consider industry as something ugly so as to be as far as possible disguised. Through the medium of painting I believe that the excitement I feel about mills… and industrial constructions can enable people to see beauty in the drama of power… Mill chimneys, pit heads, quarries, can be seen as so many sentinels providing the same elegance of composition to the Yorkshire and Lancashire landscape as poplar trees lining the roads of France.' At Giggleswick Quarry in North Yorkshire, for instance, she transforms the dark hulks of the quarry buildings into a veritable Ghormenghast. Wherever she went to paint, arriving with a transit van full of easels and paints, she talked to the workers about the machines they operated. When she painted mills and factories that had long since stopped work she was aware of the people who used to be there, and in her mind conjured up the noise and activity. Lumb at first struggled to find an audience for her art then in the 1970s enjoyed great success with her exhibitions but sadly died when she was barely sixty with so much more to do.

Halifax is one of the most dramatic looking industrial towns of West Yorkshire, set in a huge bowl of a valley. Many artists have depicted Halifax in many different ways. John Piper produced two of the most striking views of the place in a pair of large-scale canvases, **Halifax no 1** and **Halifax no 2** in 1961. Piper was in a way a documenter of the country, but his abstract style cast images of places in a highly distinctive way. In the Second World War he was commissioned to record bomb damage in the cities of England, such as Coventry and Bristol, which he did with drama and astonishing colour combinations. A great friend of Sir Osbert Sitwell, Piper made many visits to Renishaw Hall near Sheffield, where he painted numerous views of the house and its surroundings. Piper enjoyed being the artist guest at stately homes and he made paintings of other great houses in Yorkshire, such as Castle Howard near York and Harewood House, Leeds, but he did not ignore the cities, including Leeds and Sheffield on his journeys. Piper's view of Halifax has the appearance and vivacity of a firework display; he looks down from afar into the night-time valley bowl and captures the glare of street lights, the black silhouette

John Piper (1903 - 1992). *Halifax no 2* (c. 1961). Oil on board, 91.5 x 120.5cm (Calderdale MBC Museums)

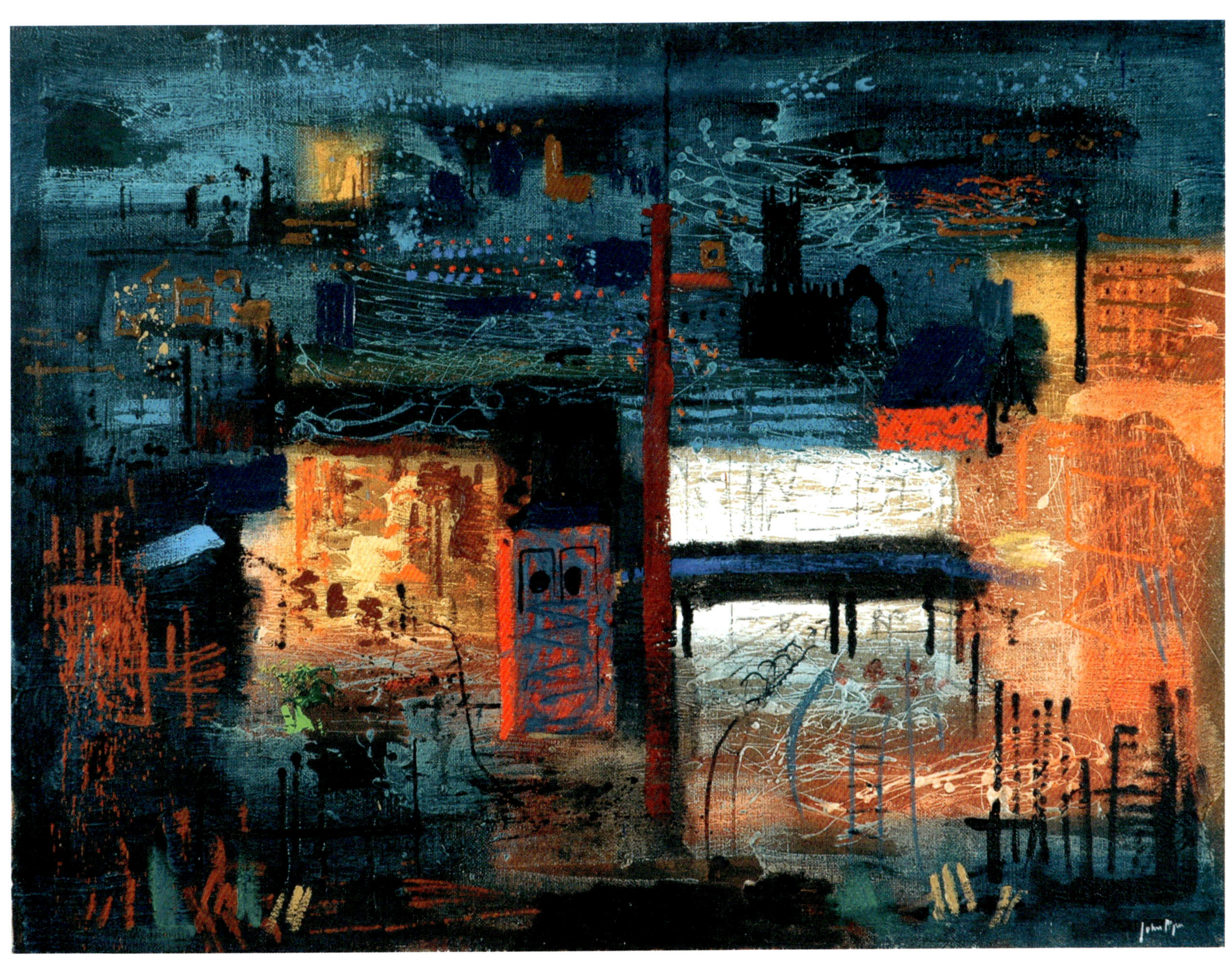

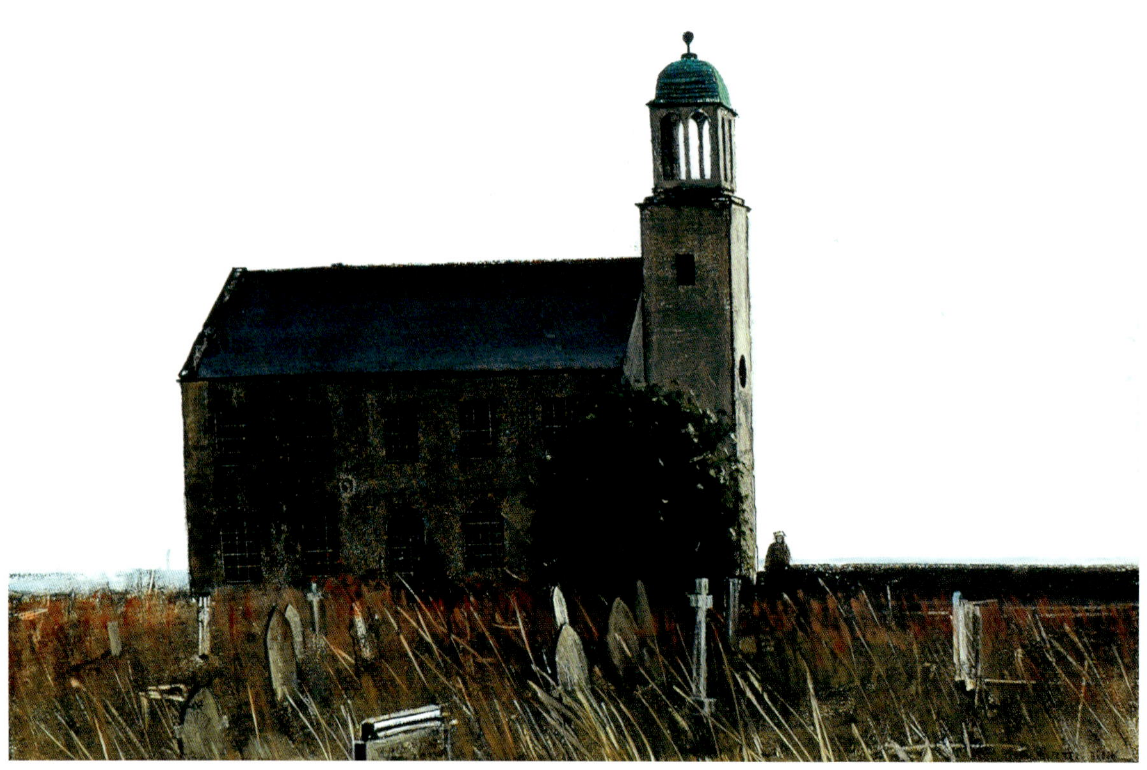

of a church and the inevitable bulk of the mill buildings.

Piper was a great traveller, but some twentieth century artists never liked to stray too far away from their own front door. One of these was the prolific Peter Brook, whose paintings of west Yorkshire can be found in most of the public art collections in the county. Brook did in fact paint many other places, but, as Lancashire was for Lowry, Yorkshire was his first love. Brook's paintings always capture the starkness of Yorkshire towns, which he often preferred to paint in the winter, but at the same time he contrives to inject his own cheerful personality into his pictures. This is perfectly exemplified by one of his Halifax subjects, **Self-portrait with Lightcliffe Old Church, Halifax**, painted in the late 1970s, once owned by Arthur Haigh who was one of Yorkshire's most dedicated art collectors. It has the Spartan looking church with gravestones at every angle surrounding it, then, if one looks very closely, there is the artist, a tiny figure with a flat cap leaning against the church wall.

Yorkshire's industrial towns and cities had so many mighty mill

Peter Brook, 1927 - 2009. *Self -portrait with Lightcliffe Old Church, Halifax* (1970s). Oil on canvas, 50 x 60.5cm (Bradford Museums and Art Galleries)

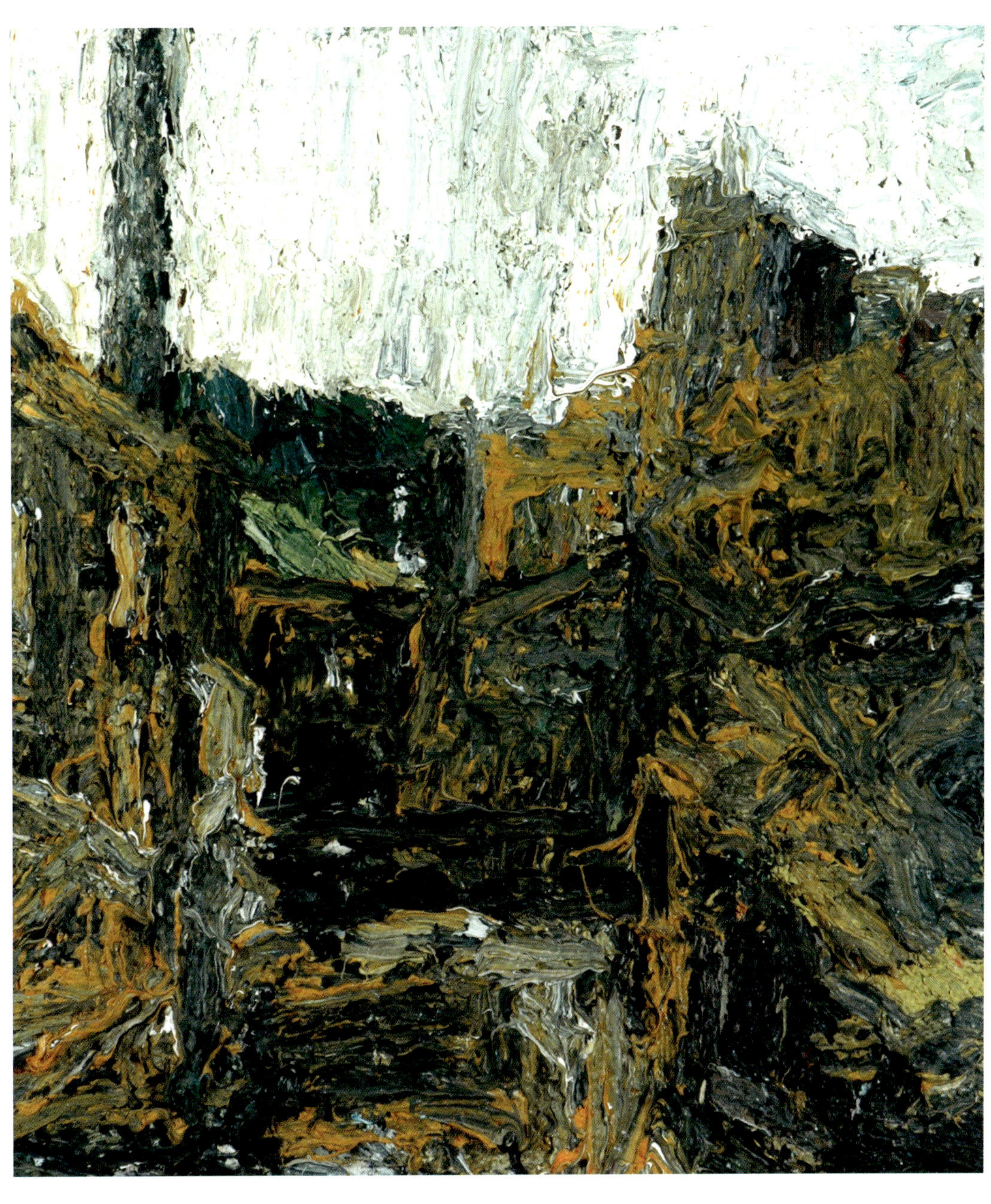

Jake Attree, b. 1950. *Study of Dean Clough from North Bridge* (1999). Oil on board, 39.2 x 30cm (Calderdale MBC Museums)

buildings that it proved impossible to demolish all of them once the manufacturing industries went into fatal decline. Some of the most significant ones survived to become commercial and cultural centres in the new world of the 1980s. Dean Clough Mill in Halifax, overlooked by the Victorian Gothic revival bridge, was built in the 1840s to the 1860s to house Crossley's, at one time the largest carpet factory in the world. In the 1980s it was converted into a centre for largely cultural industry, with gallery space and artists' studios. Jake Attree is one of Dean Clough's coterie of well-known Yorkshire painters and draughtsmen. Attree's **Study**

of Dean Clough from the North Bridge, one of many views he has painted and drawn of the place, captures the maze of humongous stone buildings with his characteristic brown, black and ochre palette applied with thick impasto. This style emerged in the 1970s in Liverpool when Attree was taught by Mike Knowles who had himself been a pupil of Frank Auerbach. As well as this art school education Attree was also inspired by Constable's statement that 'there is no easy way to become a good painter, it can only be obtained by long contemplation and incessant labour'. Thus he chooses to work on layers of paint over and over until the correct balance of form and texture emerges. Then he knows that the painting is finished. Halifax is important to Attree, but it is the city of York where he was born that absorbs most of his attention. Perversely, it is not only the ravishingly beautiful York Minster and the medieval city walls that Attree depicts; the artist is also inclined to study the other side of York, a place with working class housing and modern industry. Baile Hill, off the tourist track, is one such subject. As the writer Lynne Green has pointed out, underlying Attree's work there is a prodigious and scholarly knowledge of art history. From an intense study of the paintings of the Northern Renaissance artist Peter Bruegel, Attree developed his own conviction that the ordinary and commonplace are worthy of being his subject matter.

For centuries, the beautiful city of York has never failed to attract artists to enter its walls. Hull, it has to be said, has not enjoyed so much attention. Built on the River Hull near the mouth of the Humber estuary, now straddled by the magnificent Humber Bridge, this far-flung capital city of east Yorkshire has an introspective character all of its own. Once a prosperous port with its own deep-sea fishing industry, Hull was badly bombed in the Second World War. Much of the city centre was destroyed with over a thousand people killed in air raids, putting it on a par with London and Coventry in the devastation it suffered. The city went into a post-war decline from which it struggled to recover. Nowadays unemployment is high, with many factories and businesses now redundant, but Hull survives, its flat city landscape punctuated by some extraordinarily shaped tall buildings such as the former British Extracting Company silo, built in 1919. Myles Lynley, painter and draughtsman, studied at Harrogate College of Art and Bristol Polytechnic in the 1980s, then he returned to live in east Yorkshire near the Wolds and the Holderness coast. Whilst Hockney has painted the Wolds in lavish colour, Lynley has turned his eye on Hull, making dramatic large-scale charcoal drawings and paintings of both its moribund and working industry. Lynley's view of the great bulk of the silo transforms it into a towering cathedral soaring into the sky with, it could be said, a presence that almost rivals that of York Minster.

Myles Linley, b. 1967. *The British Extracting Company* (2012). Acrylic, charcoal and ink on paper, 110 x 56cm (Courtesy of the Artist)

Myles Linley, b. 1967. *River Hull 1* (2012). Charcoal and ink on paper, 56 x 80cm (Courtesy of the Artist)

Myles Linley, b. 1967. *River Hull 2* (2012). Charcoal and ink on paper, 25 x 52cm (Courtesy of the Artist)

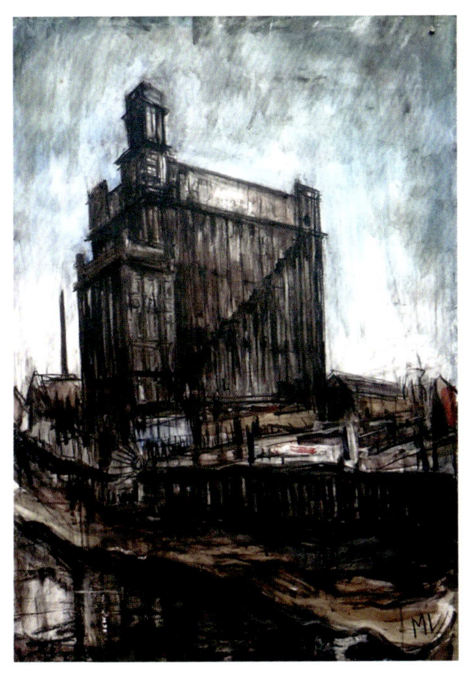
ML

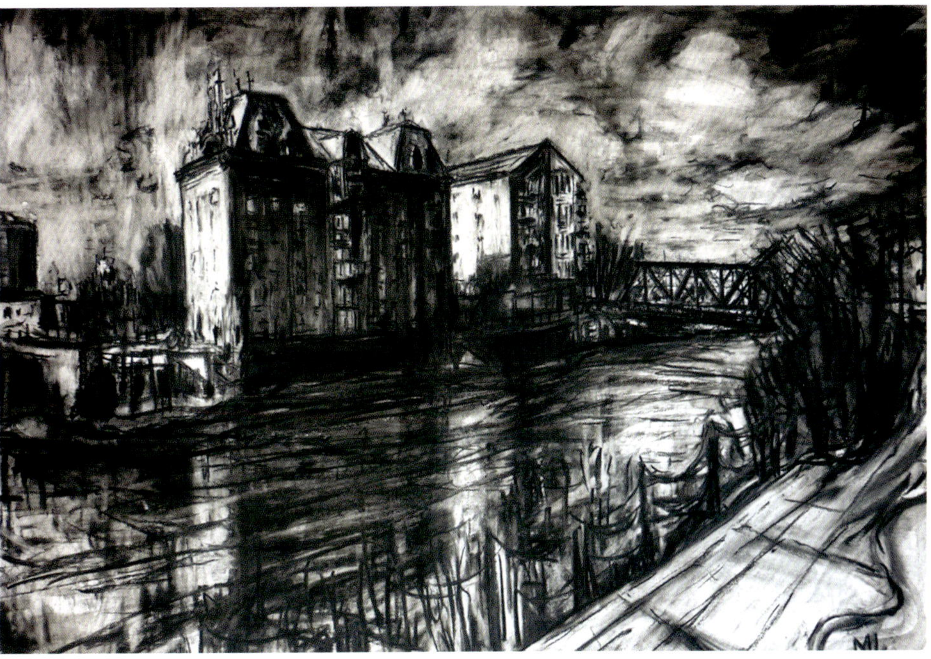
ML

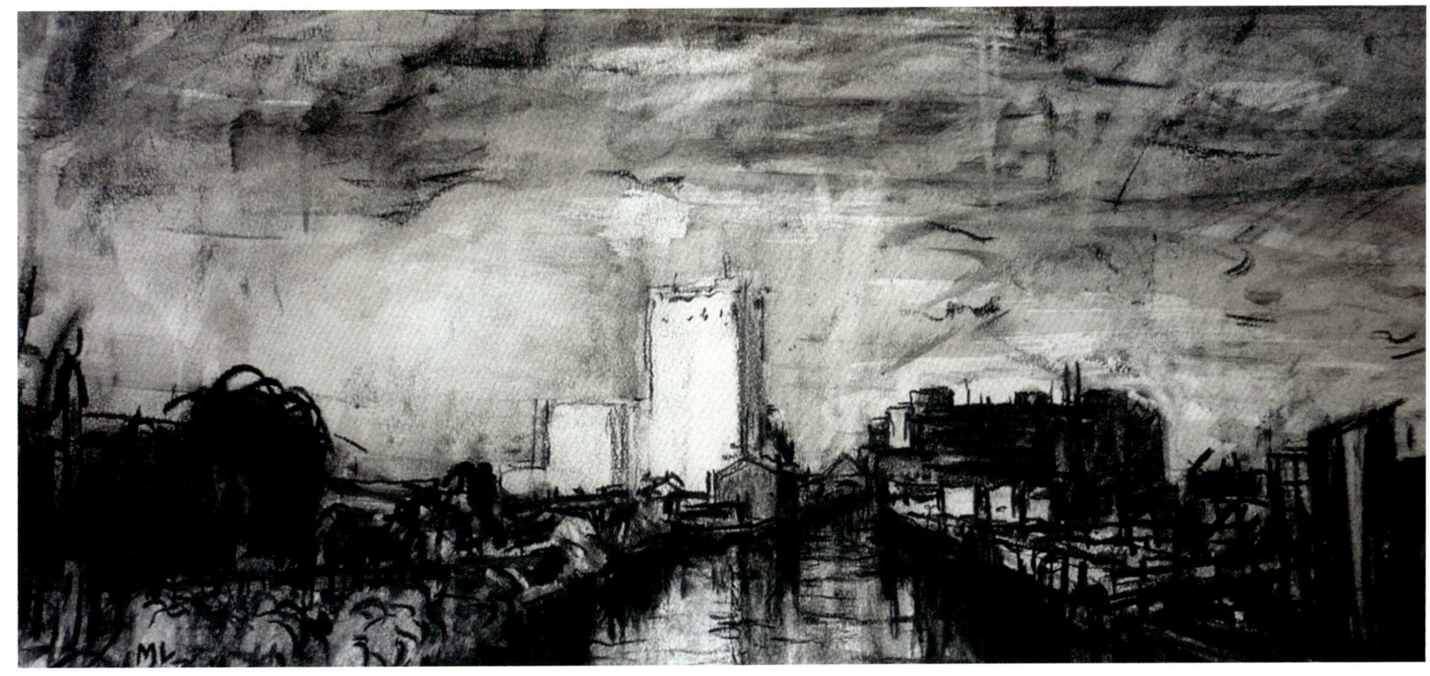
ML

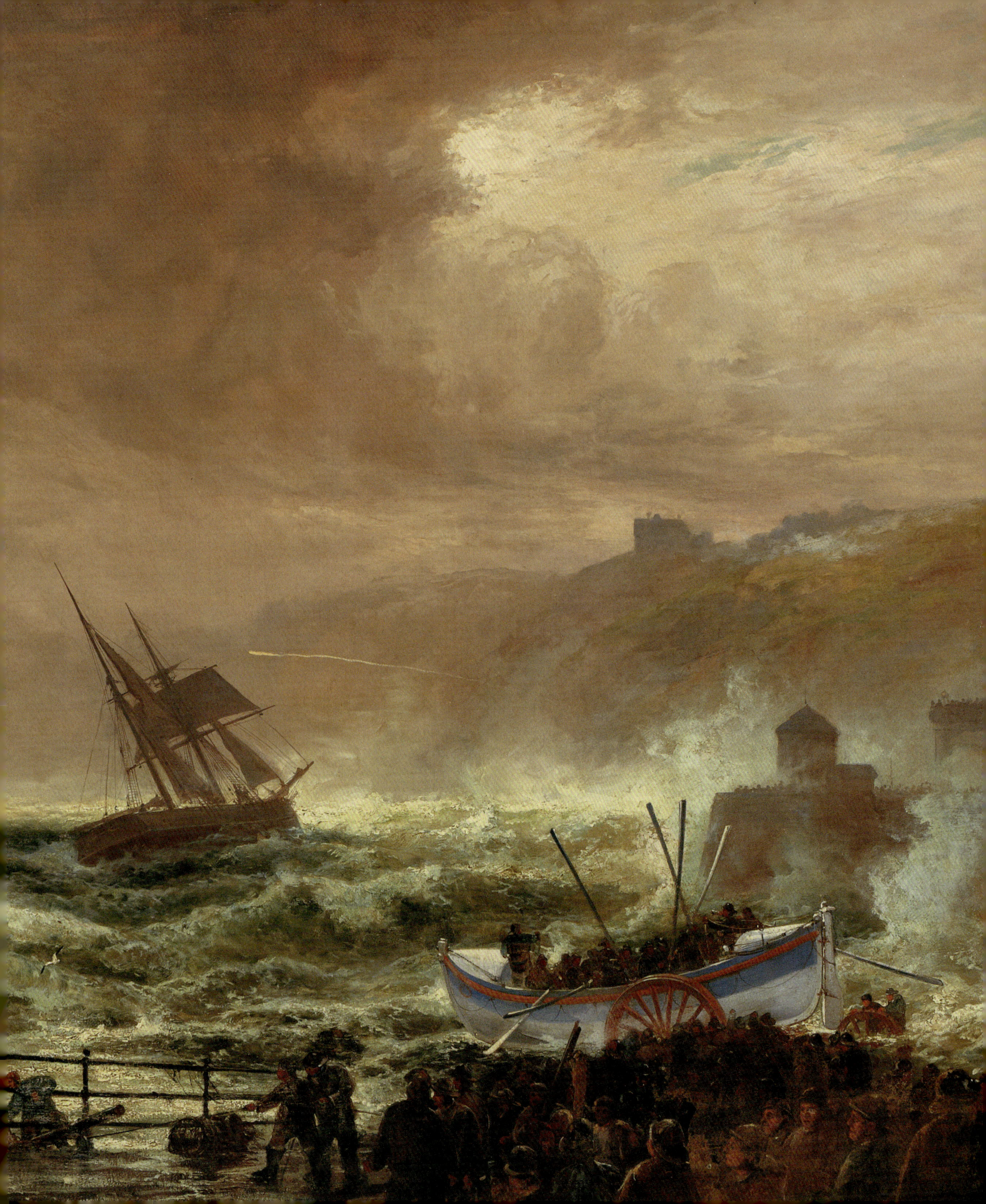

4. The Sea

Yorkshire has a remarkable coastline: rugged, romantic, awe-inspiring, dangerous and rich in its own history. Artists have been attracted by these qualities from the end of the nineteenth century to the present day. The North Sea, and the vast openness of the skies that constantly reflect its ever-changing mood, is the biggest draw in a county so big that some of its inhabitants have a sense of living further away from the sea than anyone else in England.

It is not the sea alone, however, that has provided native and visiting artists with such a wealth of subject matter; there are places along the coast that are atypical, more like Cornish villages, locked between towering cliffs and characterised by the red tiled roofs of the cottages. Until the relatively recent demise of the Yorkshire fishing industry the people of the north east coast fishing villages and towns lived a way of life that was perpetually shrouded in danger and anxiety. Staithes fishermen, for example, left anxious families behind as they set out to sea each day, not knowing whether they would return. Ships were wrecked on the rocks around the coast, challenging the local lifeboat men with dangerous rescues and tragic loss of life. Stories of such dramatic events abounded, such as the momentous rescue on 18 January 1881 when the brig Visitor ran aground at Robin Hood's Bay. The local lifeboat was unseaworthy and the storm was so violent that the lifeboat from Whitby had to be carried overland for six miles to the Bay. This journey went along roads climbing up to five hundred feet and through snowdrifts seven feet deep. Two hundred men, women and children from Whitby, Hawsker and every other place along the way worked to clear the road and eighteen horses towed the boat, while men cleared the way up from Robin Hood's Bay to meet them. The lifeboat was launched just two hours after leaving Whitby and on its second attempt all the crew were rescued.

Robert Ernest Roe painted a group of three paintings, each depicting a different viewpoint of the same sea rescue in the great storm of 1880. Roe specialised in Yorkshire coastal scenes and lived and worked in Scarborough where he had a studio on Huntriss Row from the 1860s to the 1880s. In the first of the group of his paintings the Scarborough lifeboat is being launched below Cliff Bridge to reach the shipwreck off

Robert Ernest Roe, 1852 - 1921. Detail of *Wreck off Spa, showing lifeboat being launched below Cliff Bridge* (1881). Oil on canvas, 99 x 150cm (Scarborough Museums and Art Gallery, Scarborough Museums Trust)

the Spa. Crowds of people throng around to help it on its way while others hang over the harbour wall to watch. At that moment the sun breaks through the clouds, a symbol of hope for the victims. In the larger central picture the lifeboat battles with the waves as the crew row out to the wreck. In the background Cuthbert Brodrick's Grand Hotel is caught by the light of pink and orange clouds, reflected in the turmoil of the water. This painting is flanked on its right by the scene as a rocket shoots a line out towards the wreck so that the crew could be removed one at a time by breeches buoy. Here the view takes in the Grand and the Scarborough Castle, with the colours darkening to emphasise the atmosphere of the dramatic narrative as it plays its way across the three ambitious paintings.

Roe's images of places along the Yorkshire coast, including Staithes and Robin Hood's Bay, take the broader view, encompassing both landscape and sea. Other artists studied the subject in close-up, engaging as much with the local people as they did with the setting. Laura Knight, one of the first British women to be honoured in the twentieth century for her work as an artist, is notable for her early career paintings of everyday life in Staithes, which she first visited in 1897 when she was twenty, then two years later went to live there. Staithes is a fishing village north of Whitby that contrives to be both picturesque and bleak at the same time. It is tucked into a cove between two high cliffs with one steep hill of a road leading down to the harbour and another to the village. The houses are built right up to the edge of the sea, where they are routinely thrashed by storms. Artists had been attracted by the situation and character of the village since the 1880s, and until about 1909 there was a loose kind of colony of artists living there or staying for the summer. The older established artists there included Gilbert Foster, Mark Senior and Fred Jackson all of whom had carved out a new picture-buying public for their kind of contemporary art. These were the northern industrialists who were making a fortune out of mines and factories and who were, ironically, looking for pictures of rural life for their drawing rooms. Artistic life in Staithes helped the local economy, with people willing to pose for much needed small amounts of money, or else they got on with their daily lives, unperturbed by the watchers.

The Staithes artists, some of who had studied in Paris, absorbed the influence of French Realism and Impressionism. They shared in the practice of painting in the open air, benefiting in summer from the long days and the twilight effects. There was an abundance of subject matter to sketch and paint: the boats being dragged in and out of the sea, the catch being unloaded and the figures of the women laden down with heavy baskets of mussels. But there was also an underlying harshness to the place in which Knight claimed that she began to be the artist she wanted to be. '… It was there I found myself and what I might do. The life and place were what I yearned for – the freedom, the austerity, the

Robert Ernest Roe, 1852 - 1921. *Wreck below the Grand Hotel* (1881). Oil on canvas, 121.9 x 243.8cm (Scarborough Museums and Art Gallery, Scarborough Museums Trust)

Robert Ernest Roe, 1852 - 1921. *Wreck off Spa with crowd on sands* (1881). Oil on canvas, 123 x 210cm (Scarborough Museums and Art Gallery, Scarborough Museums Trust)

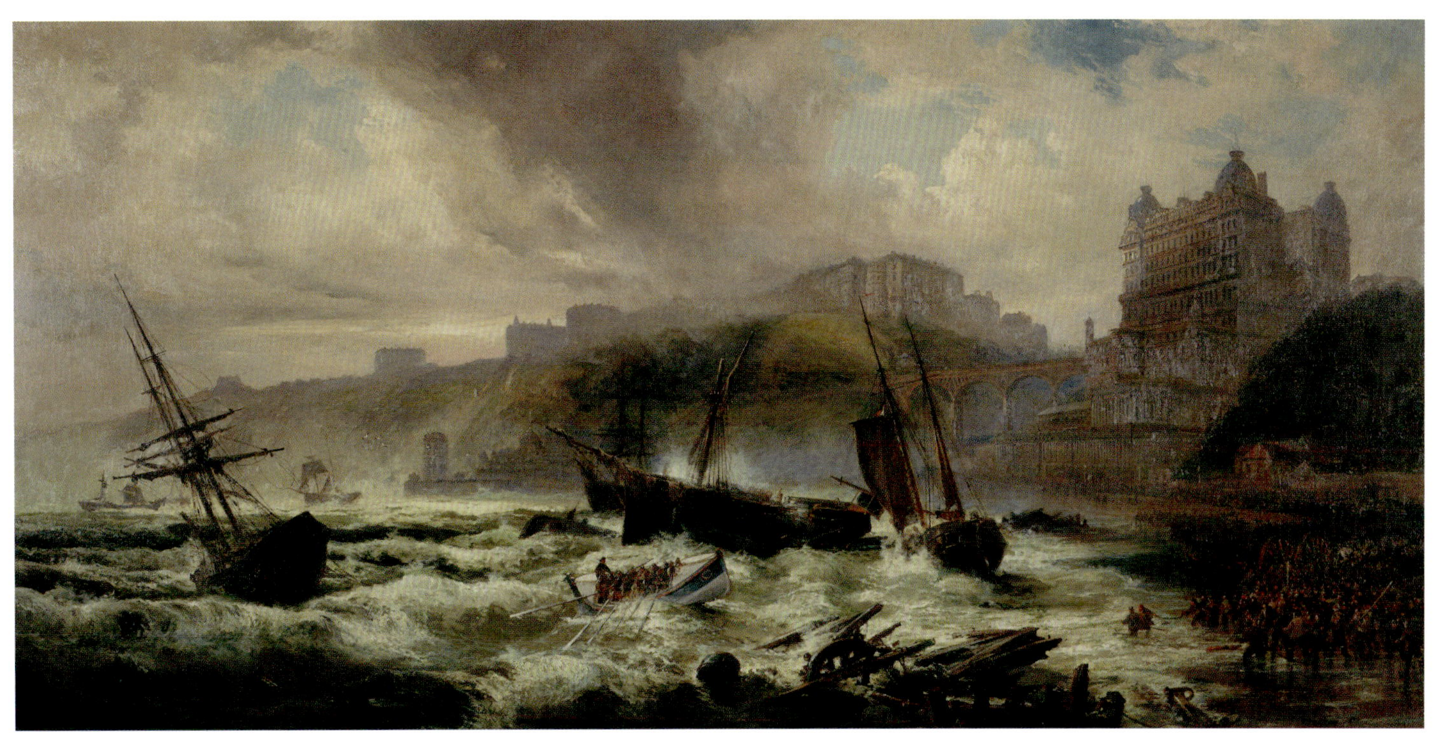

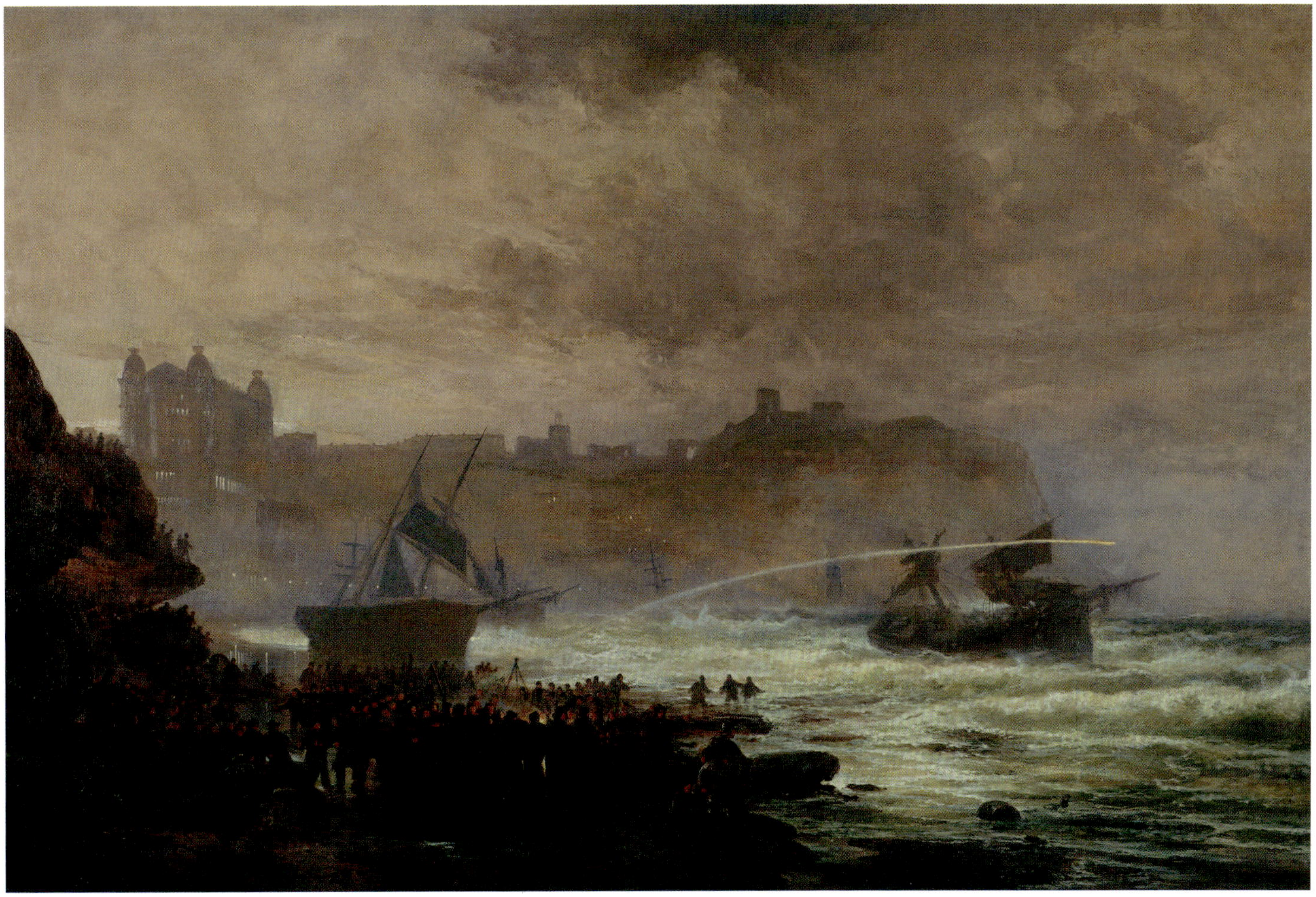

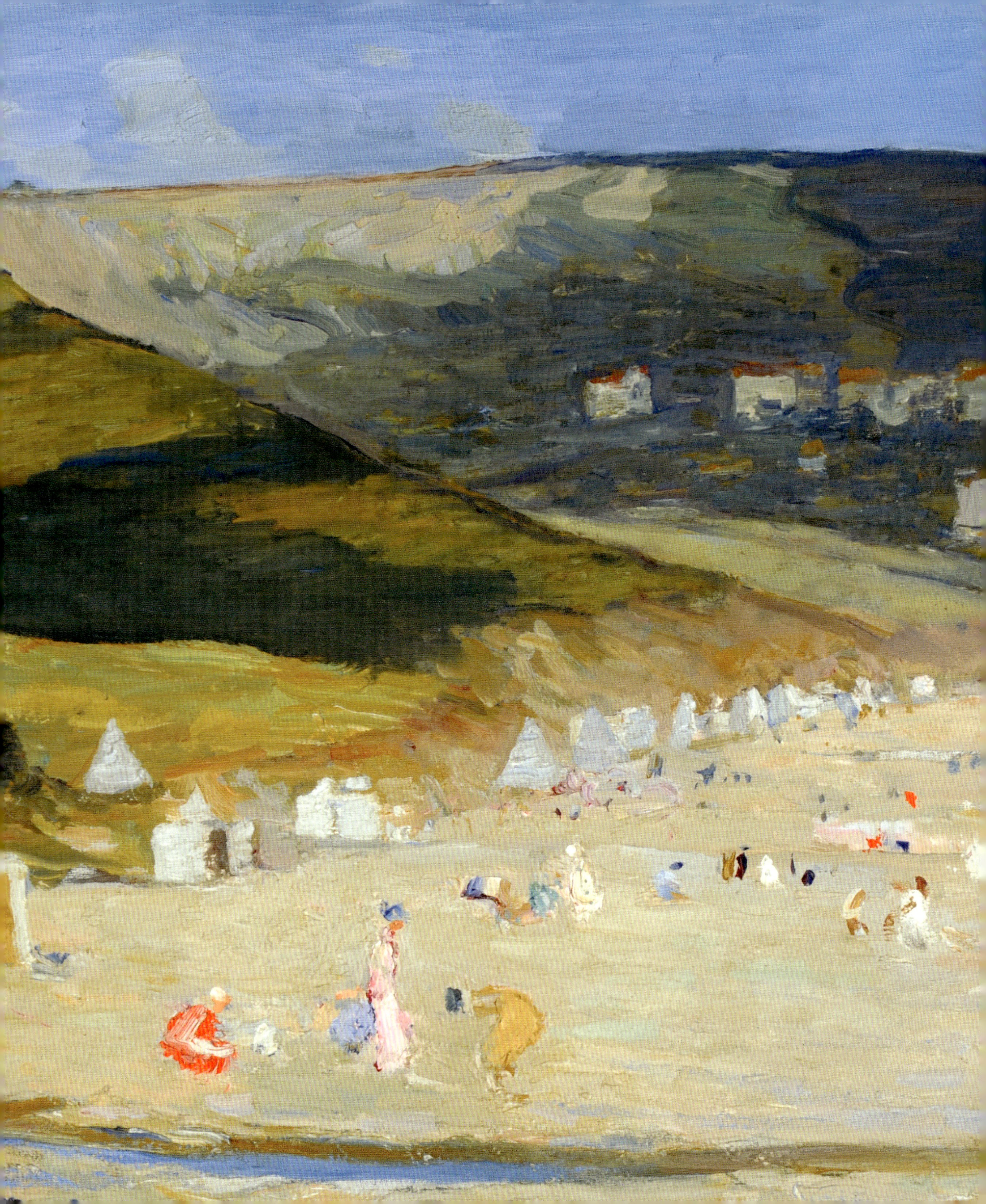

savagery, the wilderness. I loved the cold and northerly storms when no covering would protect you. I loved the strange race of people who lived there, whose stern almost forbidding exterior formed such contrasts to the warmth and richness of their nature.' In the first volume of her autobiography, *Oil Paint and Greasepaint*, published in 1936, Knight described how she became increasingly involved in village life as the years went by, going to weddings, wakes, chapel and joining in with the gossip, but the dark side of life in Staithes was never far away. In winter when the storms roared across the sea the women, wrapped in their shawls, would wait standing on the staithe for the boats to return. The gales could fling the boats violently onto the rocks then the sea would bring in the splintered wood and battered bodies of the men. Once the man's body had been returned to his home the women's eerie, grief-stricken wailing would begin. Whilst her sister, disturbed by the 'keening', shut herself inside Ebor Cottage where they lived, Laura would watch from her studio door as the funeral procession made its way up the steep cliff path to the churchyard. As she watched she memorised the figures so that she could draw them later.

In **The Fishing Fleet**, which Knight painted in 1900, she captures the grimness of working life in Staithes through her use of dark impasto paint, her palette a range of browns and grey. The fleet is clearly returning from sea because the women are there to help with the catch. Staithes was wreathed in superstition, and when the fleet departed the women kept indoors because it was considered unlucky by the men if they saw a woman on their way to work. The solitary figure of the woman in the foreground adds to the sense of isolation, a symbol perhaps of the widowhood that so often resulted from sea fishing in the treacherous waters. In contrast, Knight's many paintings and drawings of mothers and children display an understanding of the depiction of intimate domestic interiors, as in **Dressing the Children** from 1906. The artist was clearly welcomed into the village homes and the women were willing models. The style of such scenes is reminiscent of the work of Frank Holl, who described similar subjects in Cullercoats and Criccieth in Wales with the same Rembrandtesque palette and tenderness. In 1907, having enjoyed some success at the Royal Academy, Laura and her husband Harold Knight at last wearied of the tough life in Staithes and moved to Cornwall, where she entered a new world of light and colour that she was never to leave again.

Whitby has a highly significant cultural, literary and Christian heritage; the home of a seventh century abbey, the site of a synod which changed Christianity, the place where Captain Cook underwent his seaman's apprenticeship and an inspiration for Bram Stoker's novel *Dracula*. It is also the place that provided one of the masters of late nineteenth and early twentieth centuries with the everyday subject matter

Mark Senior, 1864 - 1927. Detail of *Runswick Bay* (1920). Oil on canvas, 50.7 x 60.8cm (University of Leeds Art Collection)

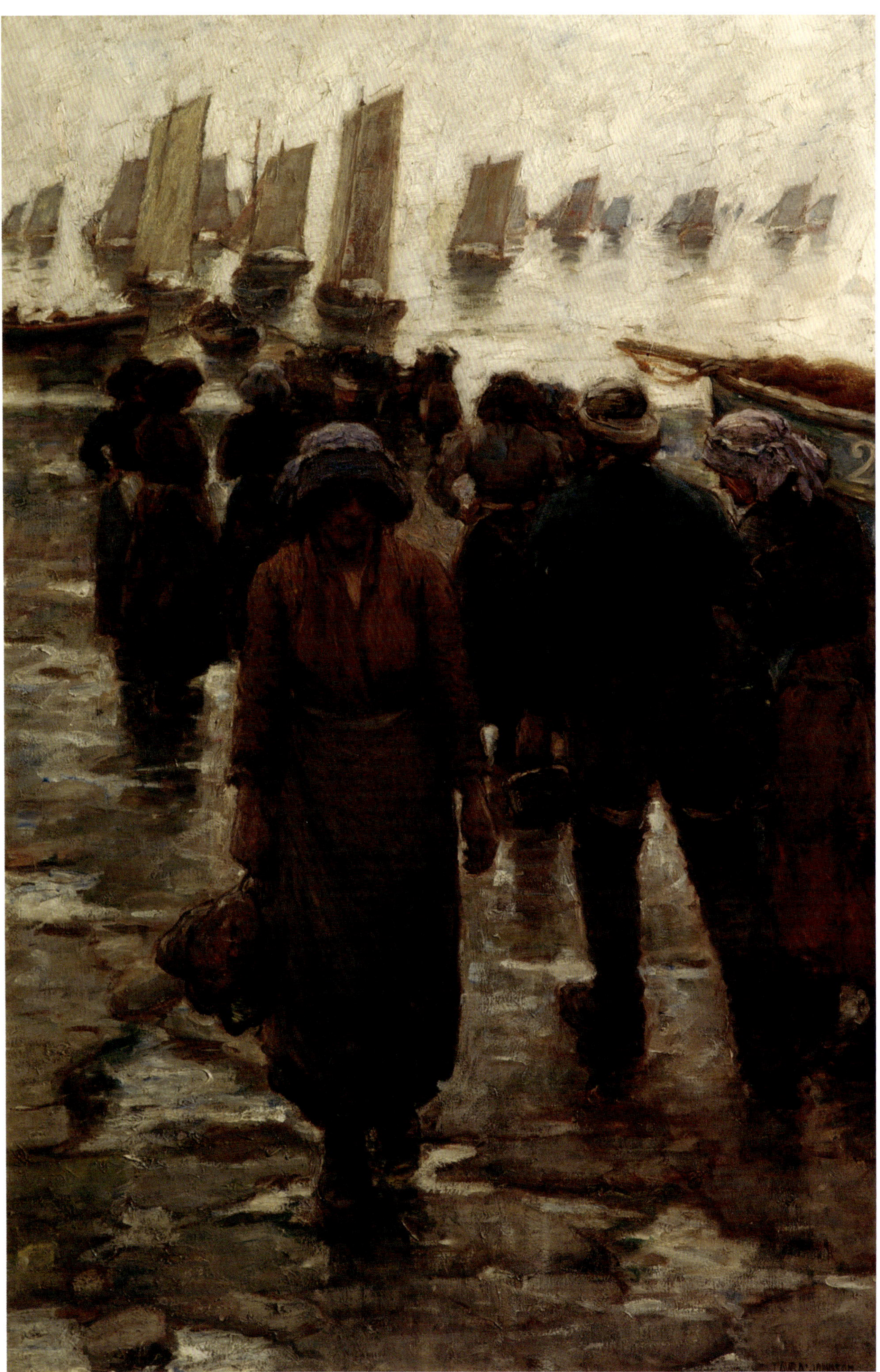

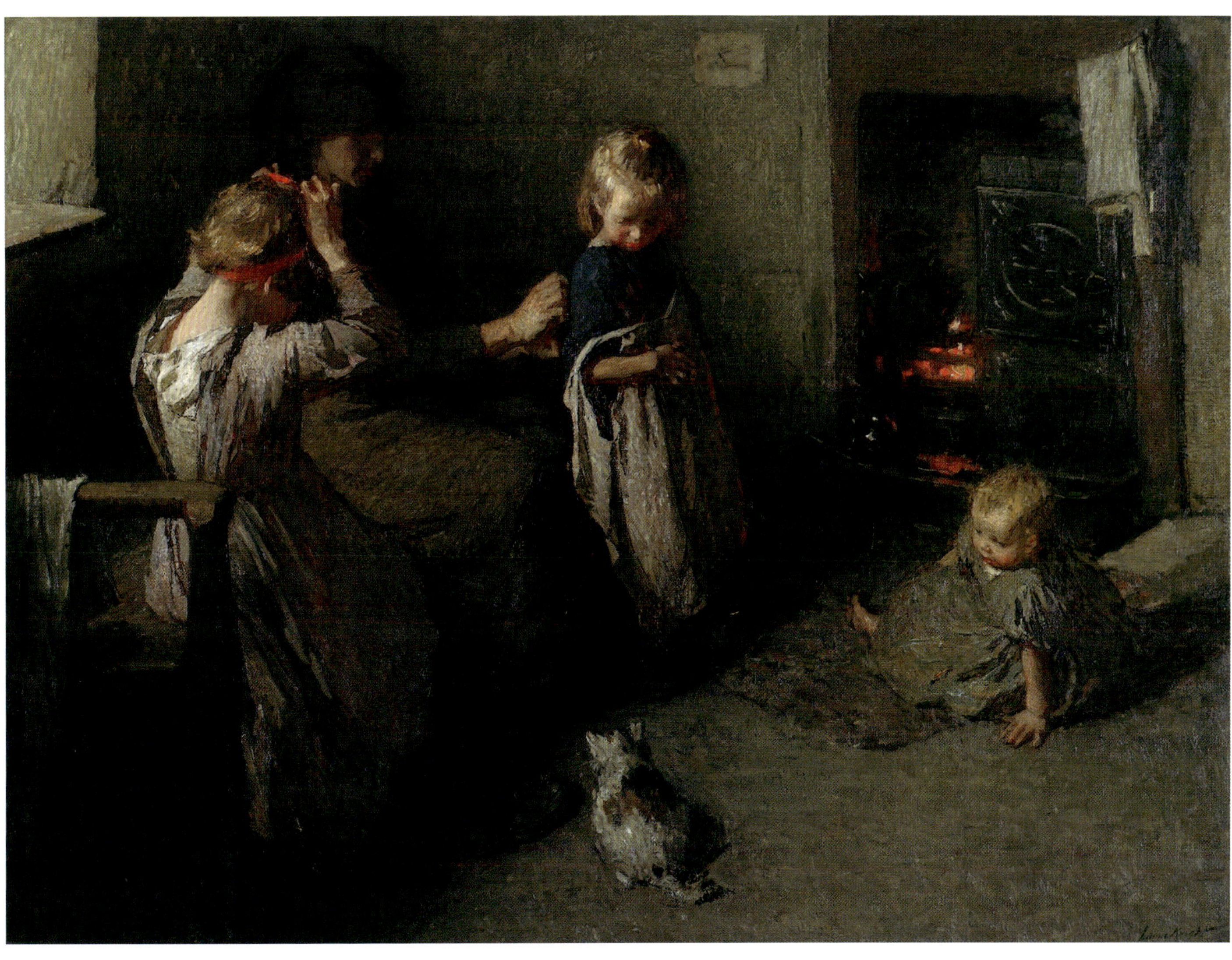

Laura Knight, 1877 - 1970. *Dressing the Children* (1906). Oil on canvas, 102.2 x 139.7cm (Ferens Art Gallery, Hull Museums and Galleries)

Opposite: Laura Knight, 1877 - 1970. *The Fishing Fleet* (1900). Oil on canvas, 123 x 84cm (Boltom Museum & Art Gallery)

that occupied his whole career. Frank Meadow Sutcliffe left a photographic record of the town that is not just an invaluable source of social history, but also the work of an artist that won him international acclaim. Frank was in fact the son of an artist, the Leeds-born watercolourist Thomas Sutcliffe, so he grew up with artistic ambitions. In 1869 Frank acquired his first camera, a mahogany stand camera that used large glass plates and the wet-collodion process, which meant that the plate was exposed before the light-sensitive coating dried. Taking photographs then was an awkward business and when, years later, Sutcliffe was invited by Eastman to experiment with the new Kodak pocket cameras he remarked, 'My only regret is that I didn't have it years ago.' Frank's father died when he was only eighteen and he had to become the breadwinner for his family, so his photographic career began in earnest.

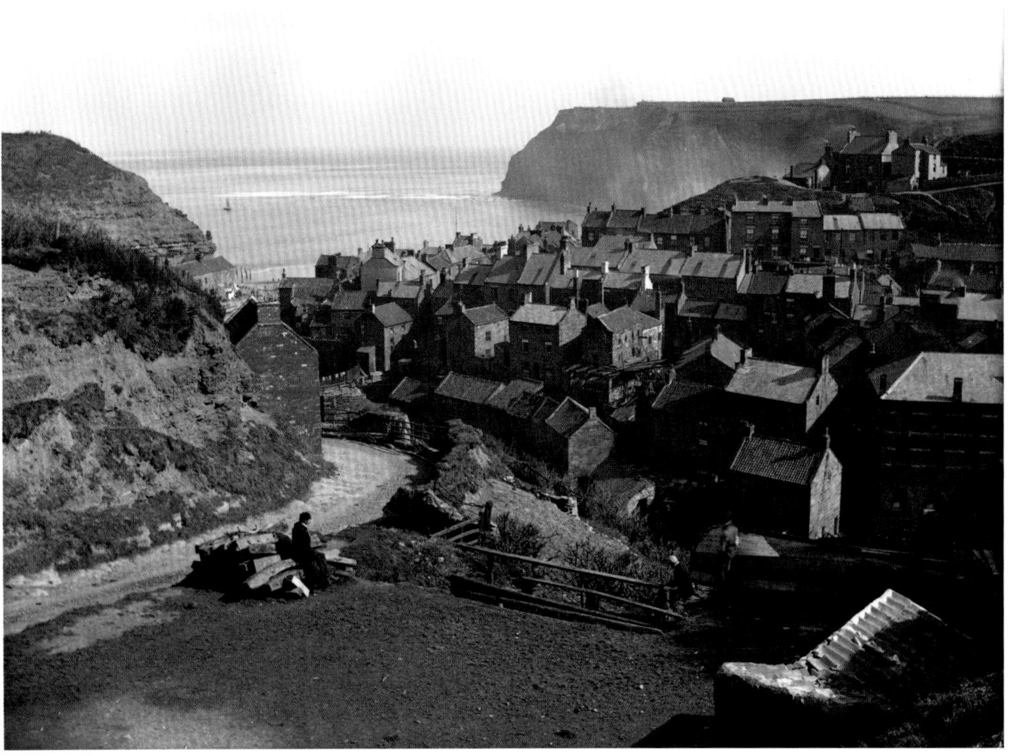

His first commission was to photograph abbeys and castles in Yorkshire for Francis Frith to be mass-produced and sold as postcards. However there was little money to be made from this so he decided to set up a portrait photography studio, initially in Tunbridge Wells, believing he would be more successful there, only to be disappointed. Sutcliffe moved to Whitby and opened up a much humbler studio there at the back of a jet workshop. He made a steady income from portraiture but his artistic ambitions were not satisfied; he had a desire to make work that was less formal, more naturalistic and of a better aesthetic and technical quality, thus he spent every spare hour walking purposefully around Whitby photographing the town, its industry and, above all, the people. Michael Hiley, in his book *Frank Sutcliffe: Photographer of Whitby* commented, 'Sutcliffe was able to produce striking photographs from very simple subject-matter – men leaning against a rail, sun streaming through the sail of a boat at the quayside, two women chatting in an alleyway... These scenes were there for all to see, but only Sutcliffe took notice of them and photographed them.'

Clearly, Sutcliffe came to know the life of Whitby intimately and he

Frank Meadow Sutcliffe, 1853 - 1941.
Staithes from Cowbar (c. 1880-1900)
Photograph. (Whitby Literary and Philosophical Society)

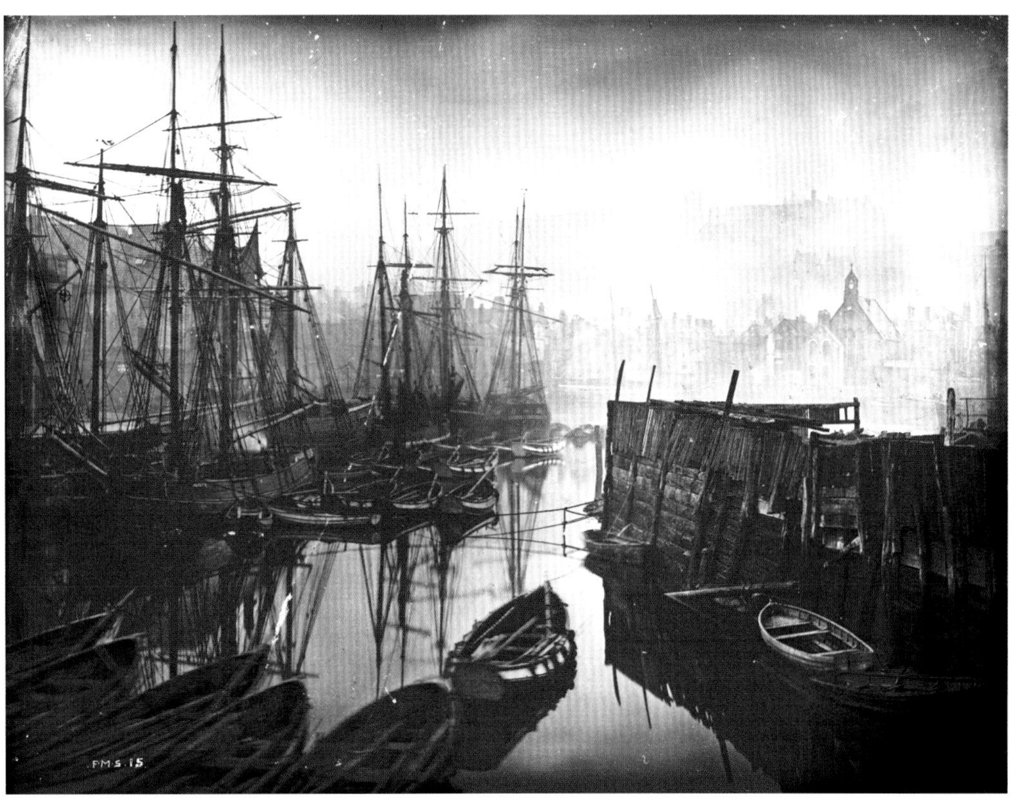

Frank Meadow Sutcliffe, 1853 - 1941. *Vessels in Dockend*, Whitby (c. 1880 - 1900) Photograph. (Whitby Literary and Philosophical Society)

knew where to find the most pleasing subjects and backgrounds, but he also had the skills to find the most perfectly balanced compositions in the group of fishermen leaning on the harbour rail, for instance, or the women around the fish-stall. On the other hand, quite a lot of the earlier images are more likely to have been posed, despite his search for spontaneity, because of the limitations of the long exposure he needed for his camera. A case in point may be his best-known image **The Water Rats** in 1886, a view of a group of young boys playing naked in the water out in the harbour. Sutcliffe himself tells us that he was wont to give the lads a few coppers to pose for him. **The Water Rats** created some controversy and caused him to be excluded from his local church because the clergy feared that the image would corrupt young girls. In other photographs he made of naked boys playing by the water there is much more a sense of the posed classic study of the nude. Sutcliffe was after all a founder member of The Linked Ring, a group of photographers who were dedicated to promoting photography as fine art. He was certainly keen to promote himself as well; he wrote about photography and he entered competitions across Europe and in the USA and Canada where he won prizes. In 1922 Sutcliffe gave up his studio and became curator of the Whitby Literary and Philosophical Society. The plates continued to be reproduced through

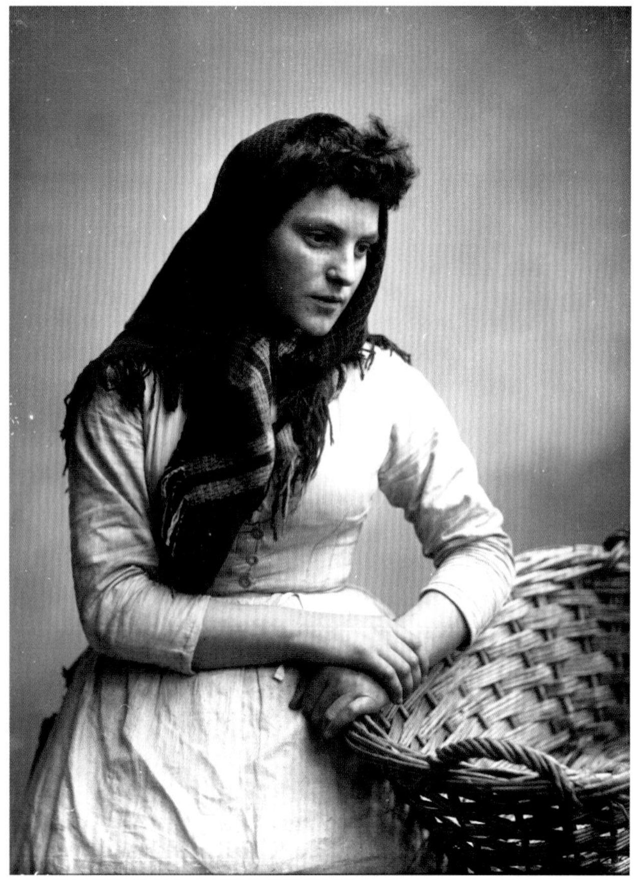

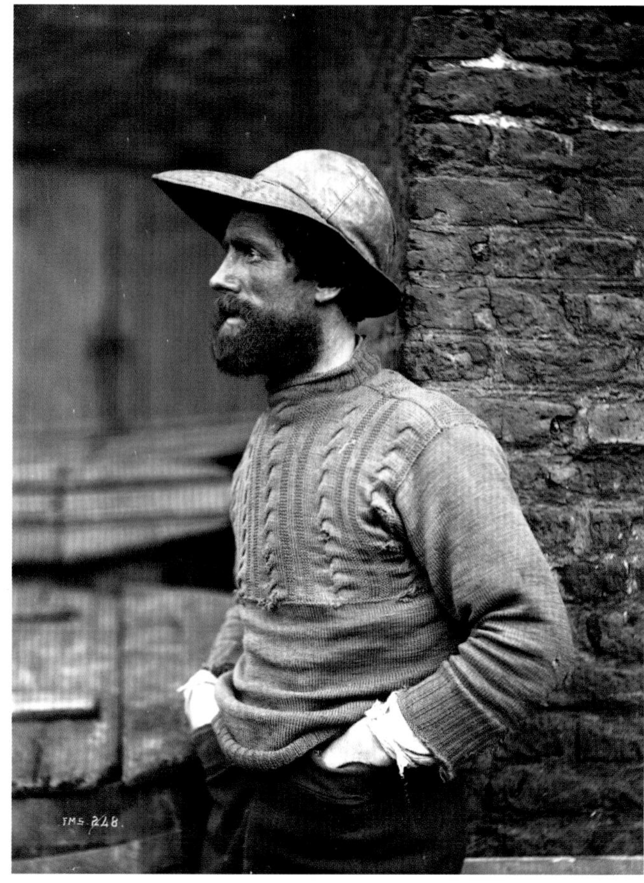

successive owners of Sutcliffe's Skinner Street studio, first Thomas Gillat and then Hugh Lambert Smith, then in 1959 the studio and the plates were purchased by Bill Eglon Shaw, who moved to Flowergate and set up the Sutcliffe Gallery. In 1967 the plates came to the Whitby Literary and Philosophical Society. Thanks to the museum and the Shaw family, Sutcliffe's photographs have survived to become some of the best-known images in British photography. Where Laura Knight gave us her sense of the hardship of life in Staithes in her sombre paintings, Sutcliffe left us with a more upbeat kind of realism in his photographic panorama of Whitby and its people.

Scarborough, Yorkshire's largest coastal fishing town, has attracted visitors since the early nineteenth century. At first regarded as a desirable health resort for the better off, with its spas and water treatments, and later reinventing itself as a brash and gaudy seaside town with funfairs, fish and chips and donkeys on the beach. Nowadays Scarborough's elegant history and beautiful wide sweeping bays manage to coexist with the holidaymakers' world. The Leeds painter Atkinson Grimshaw brought his family to live in the shadow of Scarborough Castle in 1876 in his unique

Frank Meadow Sutcliffe, 1853 - 1941. Photographs. (Whitby Literary and Philosophical Society)

Top left: *Portrait of a fishergirl, Nell 'Baccus'* (c. 1880 - 1900)

Top right: *Fisherman in a gansey* (c. 1880 - 1900)

Opposite page, top: *The Water Rats* (1886)

Bottom: *Fishstall at Whitby* (c. 1880 - 1900)

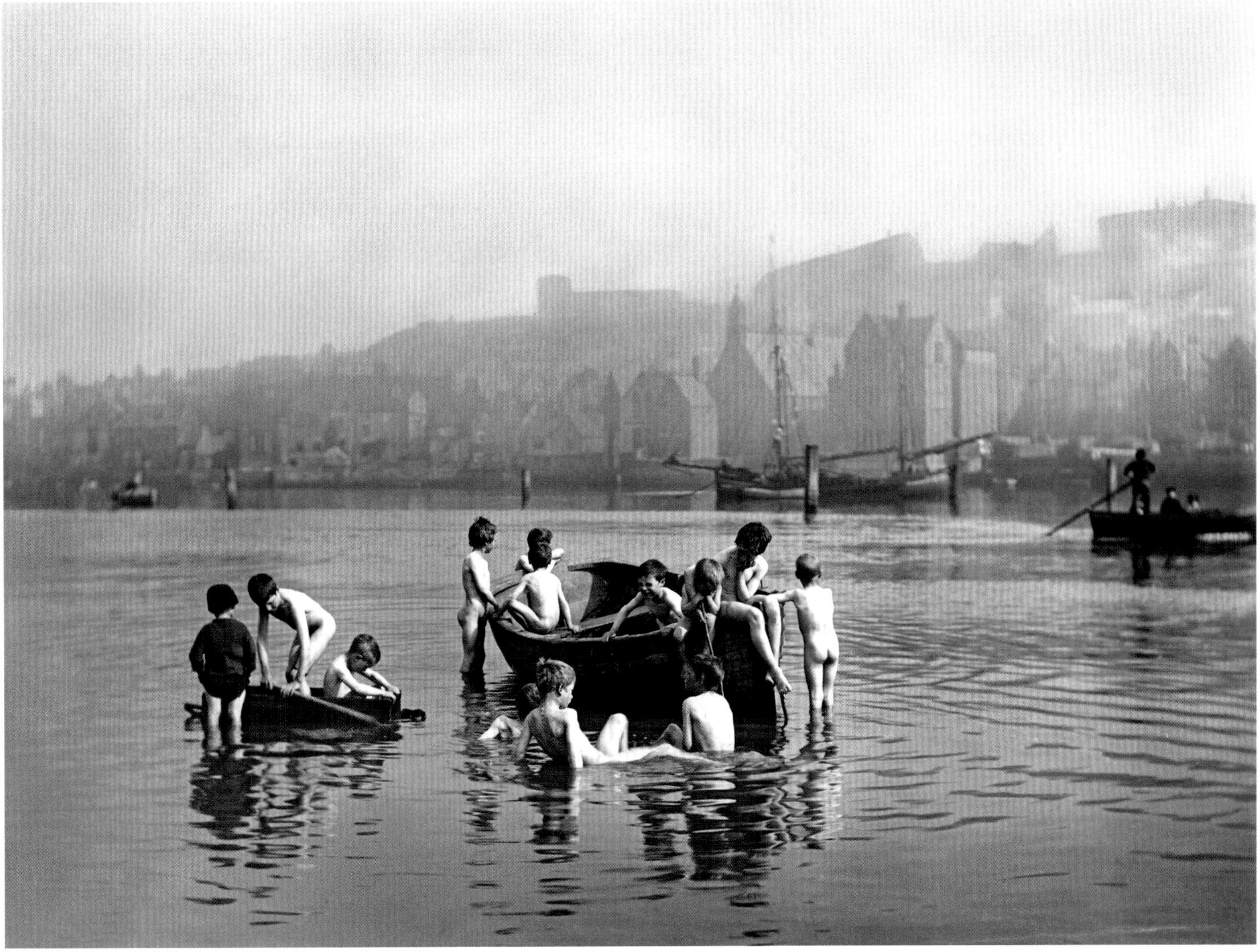

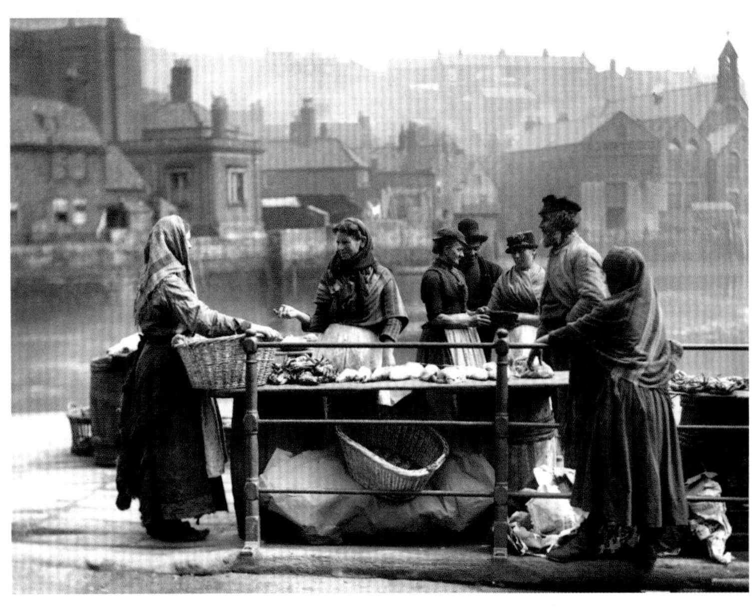

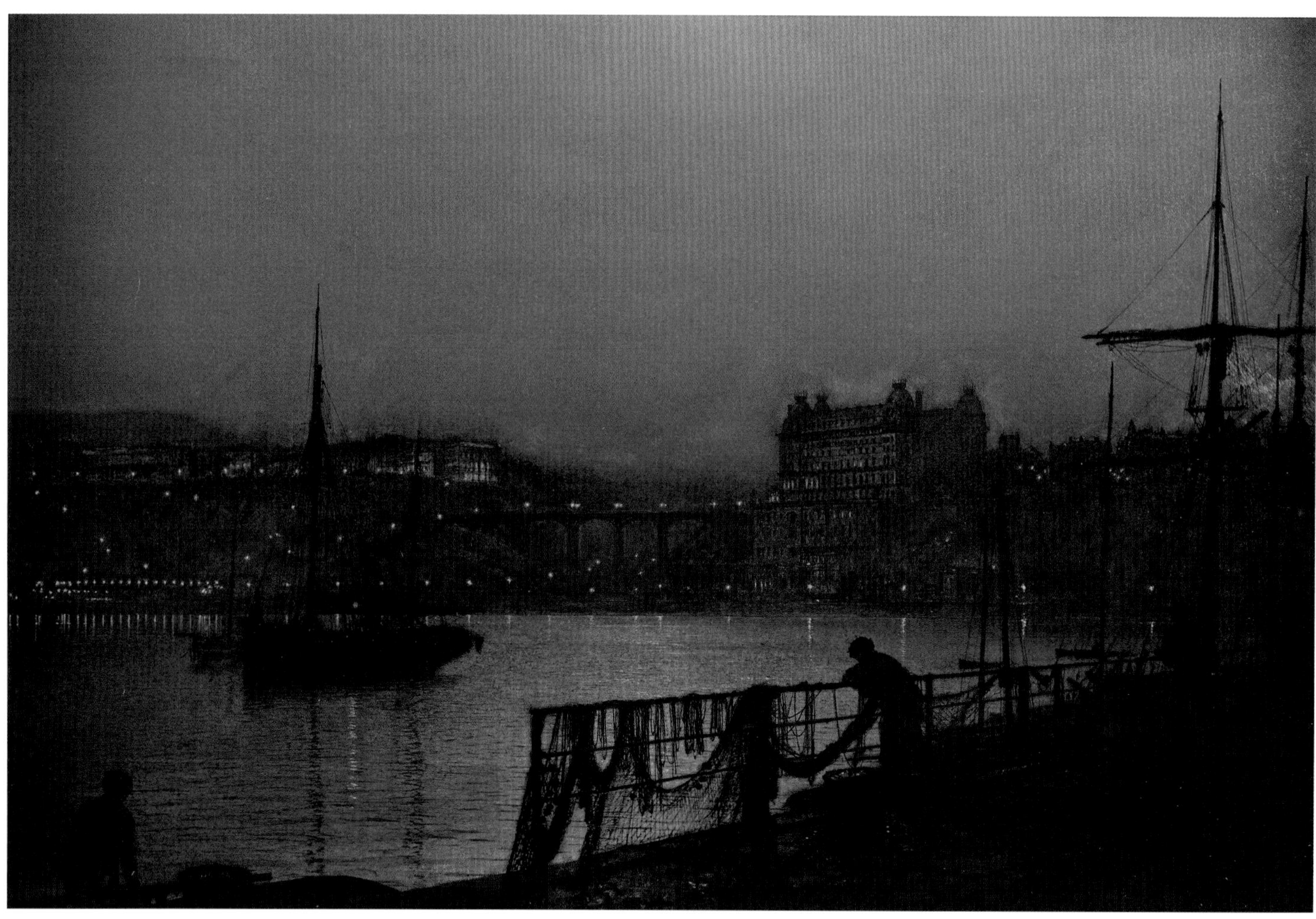

studio house, which he christened The-Castle-By-The-Sea. They moved there both for health reasons, after the deaths of three of their children from diphtheria a couple of years before, and to enable Grimshaw to paint his hugely popular sea and moonlight pictures. Grimshaw did in fact paint some of his most dramatic subjects at Scarborough, such as the night the Spa burnt down, but his inclination was more towards views of the harbour, with the ships sitting silently in the moonlight. Latter day painters, such as Andrew Cheetham, have concentrated more on the working life of the town and the splendour of the sea. Cheetham manages to combine both in the drawings he made out at sea with one of the last boats to go out there as the fishing industry met its ultimate decline in the first decade of this century, and his stunning mood-laden views out to sea. Cheetham belongs to a contemporary artistic community in Scarborough, which includes painters, print-makers, photographers, potters, textile artists and installation artists, all of whom bear witness to the extraordinary vitality of the cultural industries that have unrolled through time in one of Yorkshire's most inspirational areas.

Atkinson Grimshaw, 1836 - 1893. *Scarborough Lights* (1877). Oil on canvas, 58 x 89cm (Scarborough Museums and Art Gallery, Scarborough Museums Trust)

Opposite: Andrew Cheetham b. 1971. *Heavy Swell* (2011). Oil on board, 37 x 50cm (Courtesy of the Artist)

Andrew Cheetham b. 1971. *Running Tide* (2011). Oil on board, 23 x 37cm (Courtesy of the Artist)

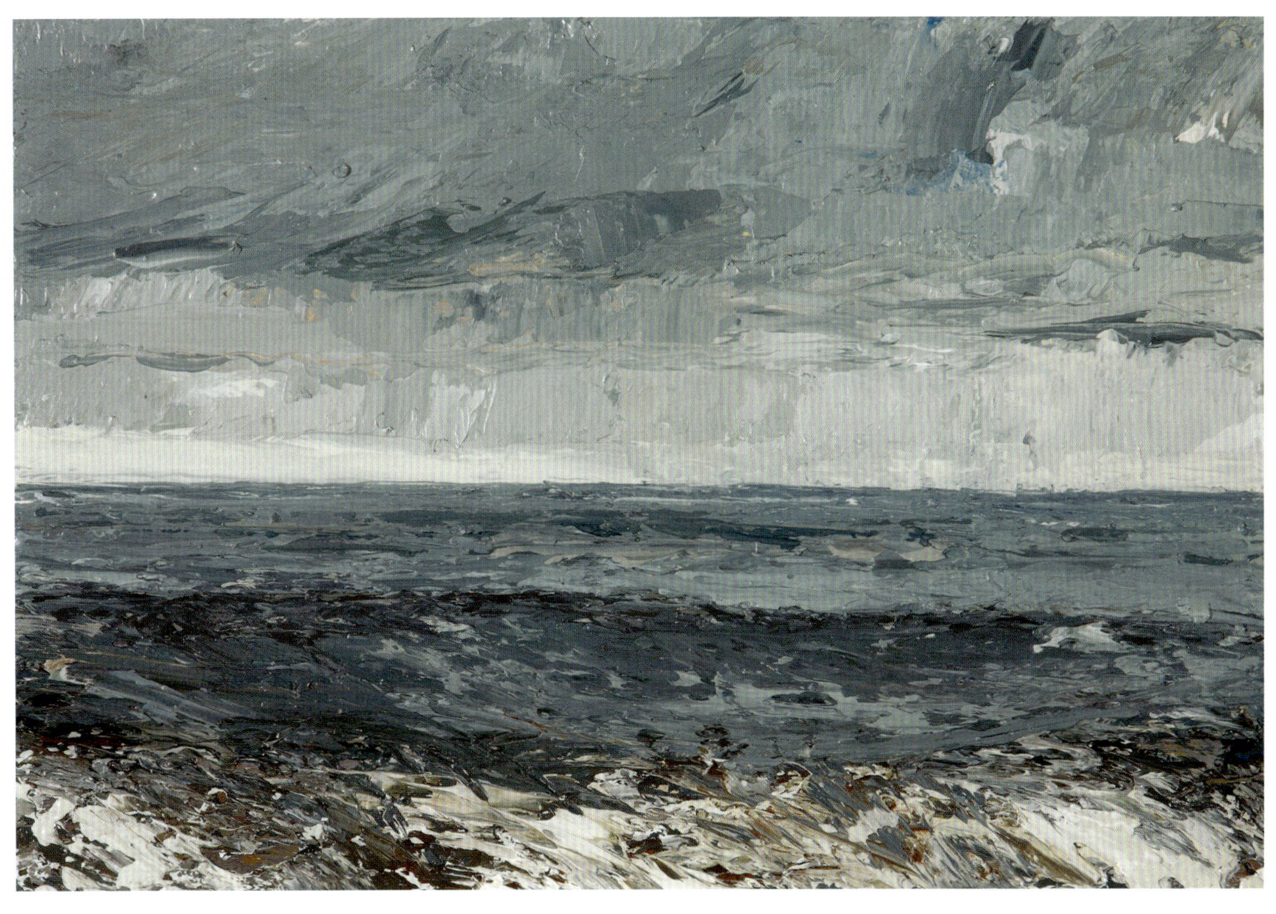

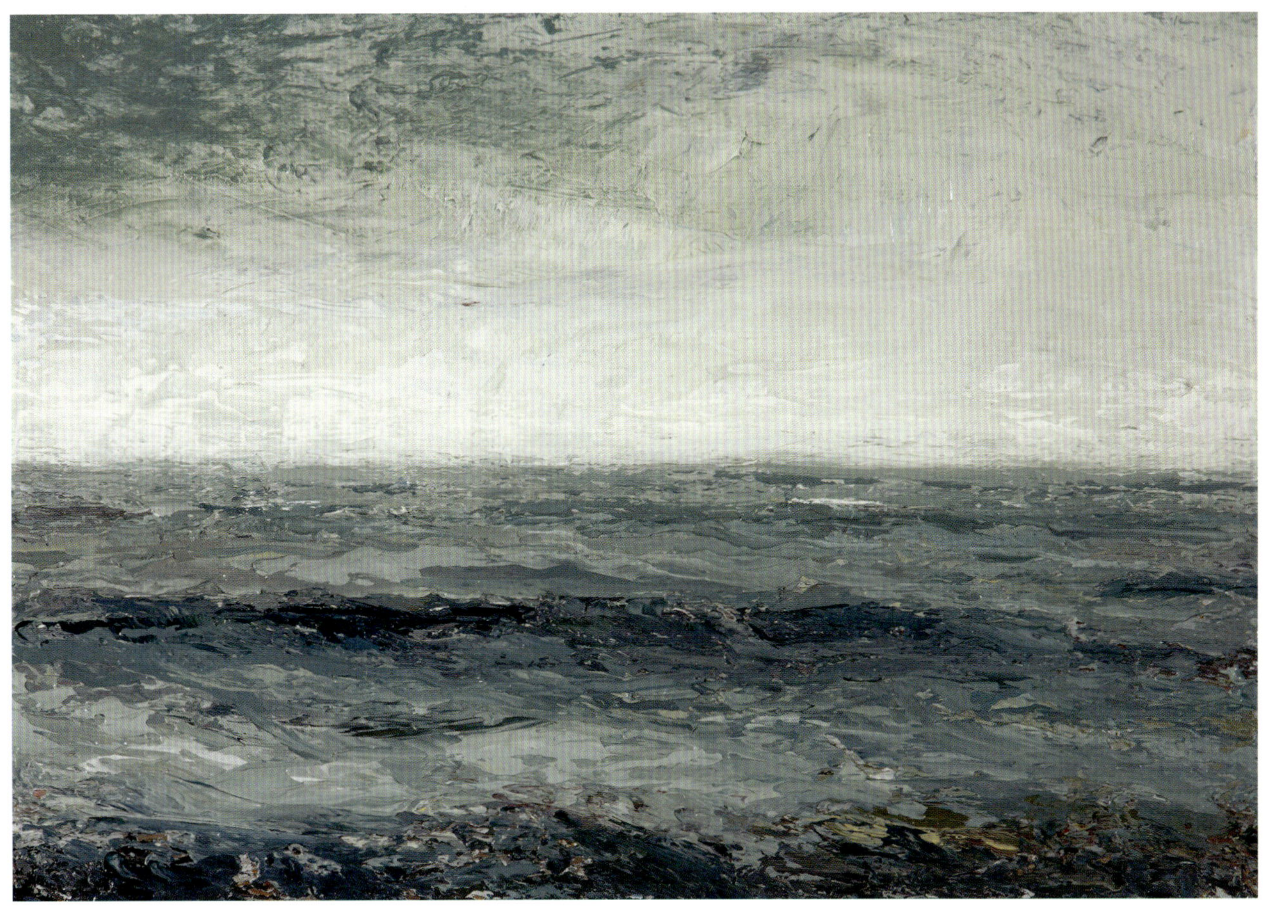

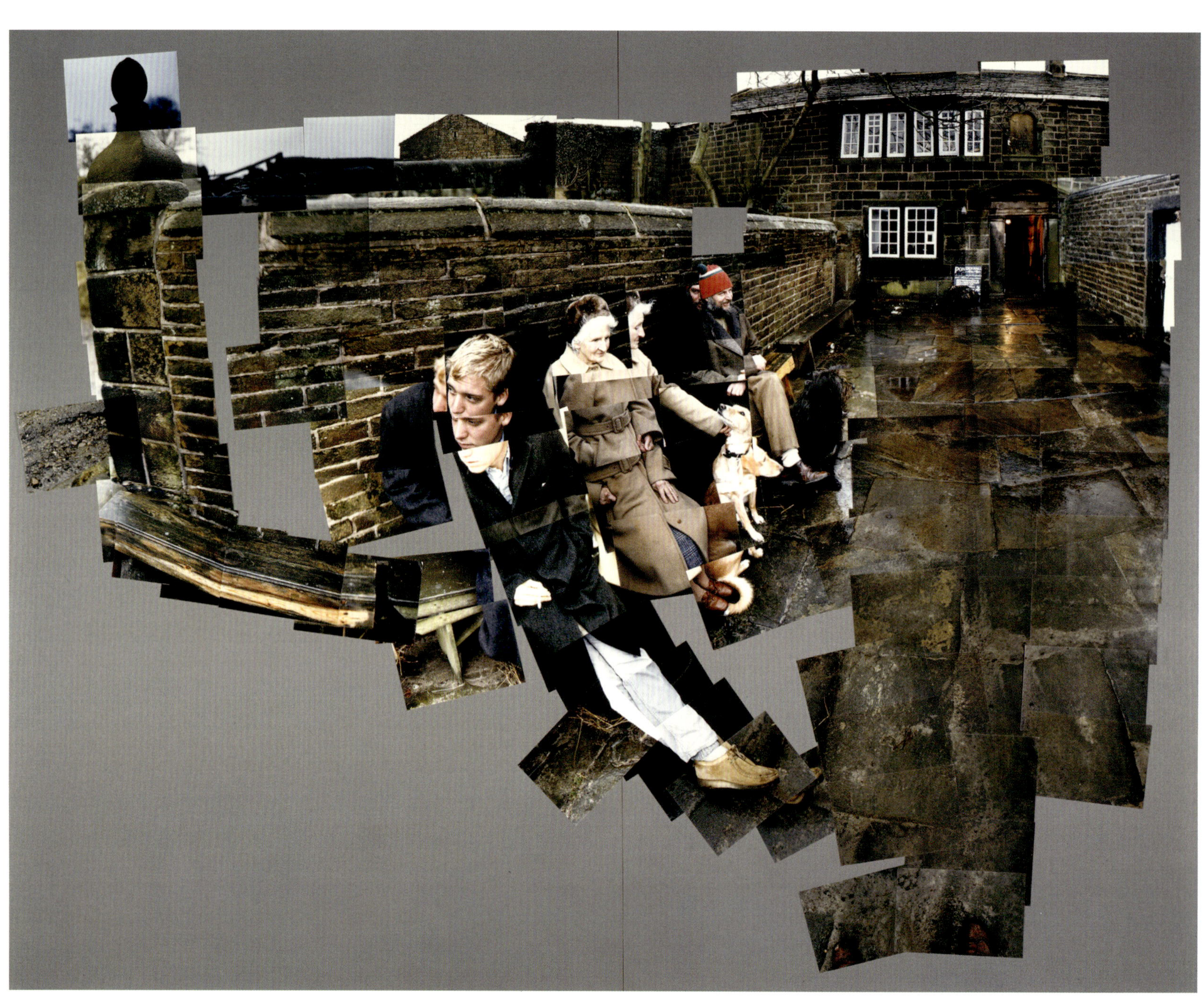

5. Yorkshire's People

Portraits have always been concerned with the subject's place in the world; their power, wealth, social status, aspirations and their physical beauty, or otherwise. In another dimension portraits are also about the artist's perception of that person, an aspect of the genre that intensified through the ages as the individuality of the artist became ever more significant, to the point where the artist is indisputably the more important figure in the relationship. Francis Bacon, Lucian Freud and David Hockney have always chosen whom they wish to paint and draw, rather than the other way round. Their paintings of people are as much about the artists' own lives as they are about the sitters. From the middle of the nineteenth century photography emerged as a favoured medium for portraiture, but the painted portrait remained, both as a prestigious and desirable art object and as a means to explore the psyche. The other side of the story, of course, is that not all paintings of people are deliberately posed; a candid camera shot or a privately observed sketch can tell us more about humanity than a gallery full of canvases of the great and the good.

David Hockney has always made portrait paintings and drawings of his friends and family, and when he began to experiment in the early 1980s with photo-collage, or 'joiners' as he called them, people appeared in these too. First he used Polaroid prints and subsequently 35mm commercially processed colour prints. The photographs were taken from different perspectives and at slightly different times then collaged together, resulting in work that was Cubist in appearance and, of most interest to Hockney that created a narrative all of its own. For a time he gave up painting altogether in order to explore the new opportunities this method provided for the exploration of human vision. On a cold day in January 1983 Hockney went with his mother Laura and friend Ian to visit friends who lived in Ponden Hall near Haworth, a seventeenth century hall rebuilt in 1801 that had connections with the Brontës. In the Brontës' day Ponden had belonged to the Heatons and it was one of the most impressive houses in the area. It is believed that Emily Brontë used the house as the inspiration for Thrushcross Grange, the home of the Lintons in *Wuthering Heights*. Hockney persuaded Laura and Ian to sit in the front courtyard with the artist Rob Taylor who lived at Ponden, and the family

David Hockney, b. 1937. *Ponden Hall (Thrush Cross Grange) Haworth Yorkshire Jan 1983 # 10* (1983). Photographic Collage on card, Edition 10/10, 126 x 164cm © David Hockney Private Collection

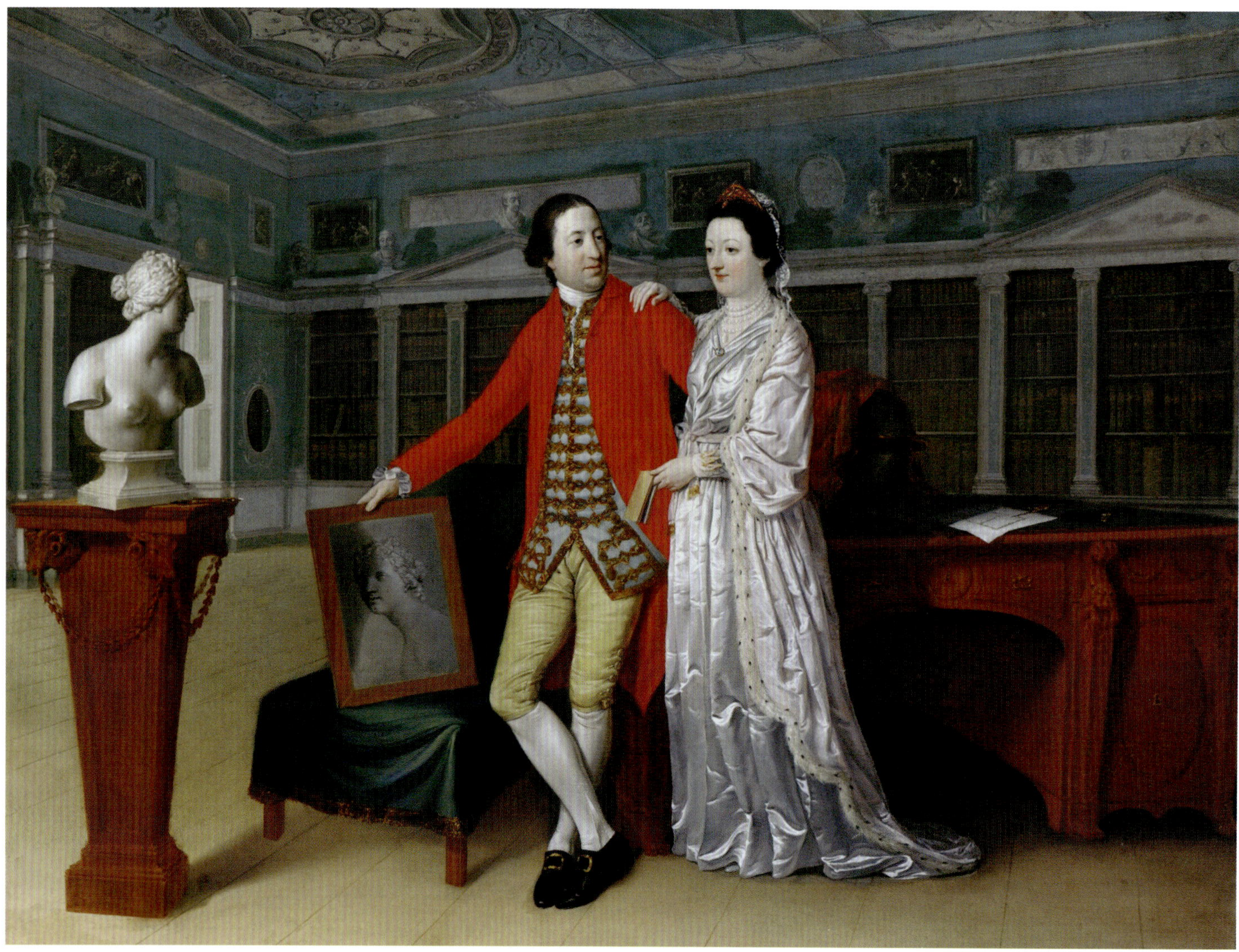

dog, and snapped a series of images from different angles. The resulting photographs were then assembled into a composition that captures the animation of this group of friends on a typically dark grey Haworth winter day. Eventually, frustrated with the limitations of photography, Hockney returned to painting.

Ponden Hall is extremely modest in contrast to Yorkshire's wealth of magnificent stately homes, which include Castle Howard, Harewood House, Newby Hall, Burton Constable and Nostell Priory near Wakefield. At Nostell there is a portrait of Sir Rowland Winn 5th Baronet and his French wife Sabine Louise d'Hervart painted by the Irish artist Hugh Douglas Hamilton in 1767. It epitomises the representation of the cultured, land owning upper classes in the eighteenth century. The Winns were originally textile merchants in London and the family subsequently owed its wealth to the rich seams of coal upon which their Yorkshire estate was built, and later from leasing land in Lincolnshire for mining iron ore

Hugh Douglas Hamilton Dublin, 1739/40 - 1808. *Sir Rowland and Sabine Winn* (1767). Oil on canvas, 100.3 x 125.7cm (Nostell Priory, The National Trust)

during the Industrial Revolution. Sir Rowland Winn was responsible for bringing the architect Robert Adam to Nostell to design neo-classical extensions to the house and Thomas Chippendale to create grand suites of furniture for every room. Winn was well read and took enormous pride in his vast collection of books. Rowland and Sabine pose in a casually elegant manner beside the Chippendale desk in the setting of the library with its Adam plasterwork and walls lined with bookshelves. Not content merely with displaying the extravagant evidence of their literary leanings, the Winns contemplate a drawing of the classical bust that stands before them, indicating their appreciation of art. The painting is a work of self-aggrandisement, not intended to convey anything about the couple's personalities. In their day it hung in their London house in St James Square to show off their fashionably refurbished country house in Yorkshire and themselves as people of wealth and good taste.

Behind every grand Yorkshire family there was an invisible army of servants whose lives were dedicated to the comfort of their employers, in exchange for which they were given board and lodging and some small remuneration. Servants usually appeared in British nineteenth century paintings on the sidelines of the scene. Sometimes they appeared as humorous, moralistic or decorative characters in narrative or genre painting, a tradition that dates from seventeenth century Netherlandish painting. Rarely did they become a subject in their own right. In 2003 the National Portrait Gallery in London staged *Below Stairs*, a groundbreaking exhibition that explored the history of portraits of servants in British art, featuring portraits commissioned by employers who had formed a close attachment to their servants, perhaps in recognition of the loyalty or the eccentricity of those who worked for them. Outstanding among these is a group of small paintings of the servants at Bramham Park, Yorkshire.

The portrayer of the Bramham Park servants was George Garrard, a sculptor and painter of multifarious subjects. Although he showed early promise as an animal painter Garrard was described as ambitious and vain, his talents dissipated by trying to work in too many different areas. When Garrard died in 1826 he left his wife and disabled child in poverty, so maybe the 1822 commission to paint the Bramham Park servants, an unusual one for any artist at the time, was taken in some desperation to earn money. Whatever the reasons, these little portraits remain as an extraordinary document of the working class in the early nineteenth century. They include William Fox, coachman, Mrs Brown the housekeeper, the gatekeeper William Wright, an unnamed man whose smart dress suggests that he may have been the butler and one of the many gardeners who kept the miles of hedges, acres of grass and Versailles inspired water cascades of the classical parkland at Bramham Park in immaculate working order. Each person poses in an appropriate setting and stares at the artist with the self-conscious stare of one who is unaccustomed to such attention. Mr Fox, for instance, stands clutching his pitcher of beer in a spartan room. His coachman's hat lies on a bench and his red cloak hangs on the wall, above which we can make out a painting of a horse, all of these the essentials of his life. Mrs Brown, with a grimly fixed expression, stands in the laundry, with flat irons and other equipment lined up on a table beside her. Mr Wright the gatekeeper adopts a slightly affected pose, hand raised to shield his eyes as he looks out for arrivals at Bramham Park. Only the mystery man, standing on a richly patterned carpet surrounded by paintings and fine furniture, manages a slight smile. One is left to wonder exactly why the Lane Fox family, renowned for their sporting pastimes and splendid park, chose to have their servants' portraits painted when they did. The incumbent of Bramham Park in 1822 was George Lane Fox, known as 'the gambler', who was a member of the gambling, hard-drinking set that collected around the Prince Regent. Several times his father had to settle his debts and when he inherited in 1821 he was again deep in debt. George, although described as prone to violent tempers, was generous and much loved by the country people, which could explain the existence of the portraits of his servants. Sadly, it was whilst George was away in 1825 that fire largely destroyed the house and there was no money left to rebuild it until 1906.

There has always been a close connection between Bramham Park and Harewood House because the former was the home of the Bramham Moor Hunt and both the Lane Fox family and the Lascelles family rode with the hunt. In 1922 Princess Mary, the only daughter of King George V and Queen Mary, married Henry Viscount Lascelles who became the 6th Earl of Harewood on the death of his father in 1929. In 1930 the couple moved into Harewood House, Leeds, which thus became Yorkshire's royal residence. Princess Mary had a great love of the outdoors, and although the house contains a number of portraits of her, the image that stands out is an equestrian portrait by Sir Alfred Munnings painted about 1930 when the 6th Earl was the master of the Bramham Moor Hunt, which depicts Princess Mary as the elegant country lady. Munnings was celebrated for his paintings of horses and riders, a talent that found him many upper class clients. In 1930, when his **Portrait of HRH Princess Mary, The Princess Royal on Portumna** was painted, he was at the height of his popularity and was often invited to the grandest country houses to paint the owners with their horses. Princess Mary's portrait is exceptional for the setting of horse and rider against a beautifully painted autumnal setting of the trees in Harewood park.

In the 1940s Munnings was president of the Royal Academy where he became notorious in 1949 for the speech he made at the annual dinner, a no holds barred attack on modern art that was broadcast to the nation

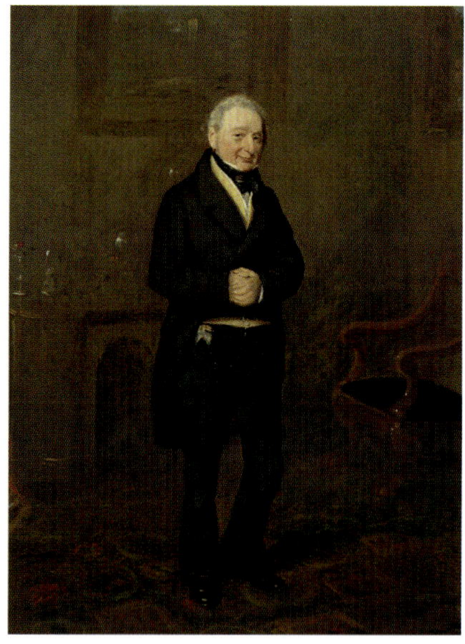

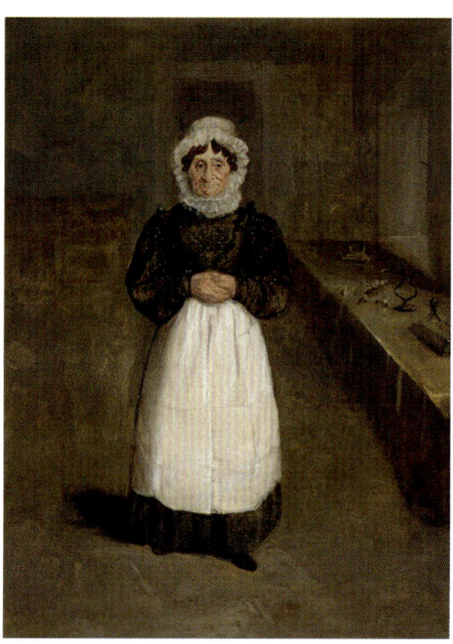

George Garrard, 1760 - 1826. *Portrait of Household Steward of Bramham Park* (identified as John Pollock), c. 1822. Oil on canvas, 46 x 36.2cm (Leeds Museums and Art Galleries, Temple Newsam House)

George Garrard, 1760 - 1826. *Portrait of a Housekeeper at Bramham Park*, c. 1822. Oil on canvas, 46.4 x 36.2cm (Leeds Museums and Art Galleries – Temple Newsam House)

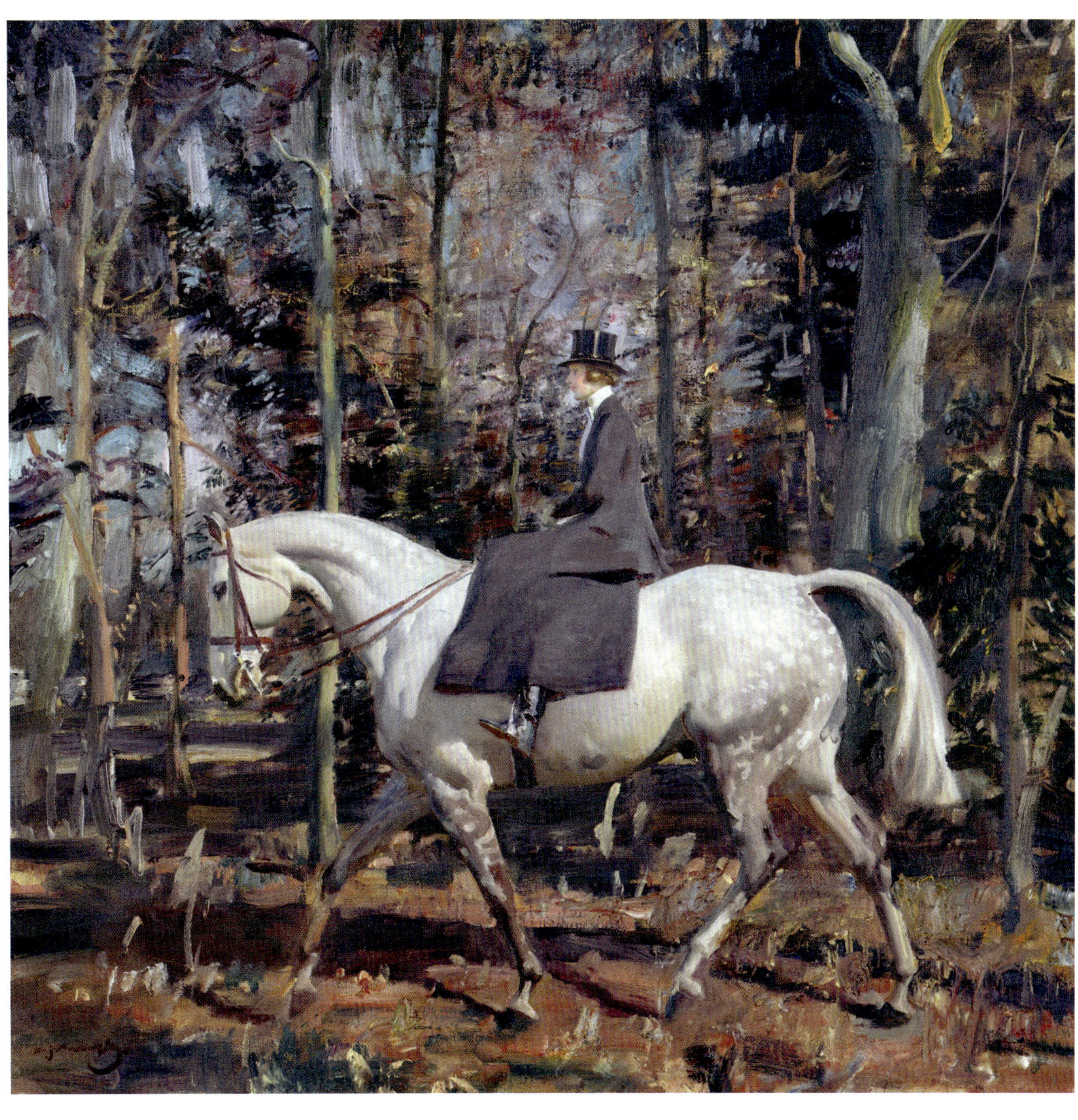

Alfred Munnings, 1878 - 1959. *H.R.H. Princess Mary, the Princess Royal, on Portumna* (c. 1930). Oil on canvas, 72.5 x 75cm (Harewood House Trust)

and caused a scandal. Ironically, Harewood in the later twentieth century was to become home to an outstanding collection of modern art acquired by Princess Mary's son George, the 7th Earl of Harewood, and Patricia, Countess of Harewood. In the 1990s Harewood also became a centre for contemporary art with a gallery created in the undercroft that led onto Charles Barry's Victorian terrace. In 2001 the figure and portrait painter Jason Brooks was invited to make new work for an exhibition there, which included his monochromatic **Harewood Castle Self Portrait** executed in his highly photo-realist airbrushed style. The artist's face stares straight at us from his rendition of Turner's painting of Harewood Castle from

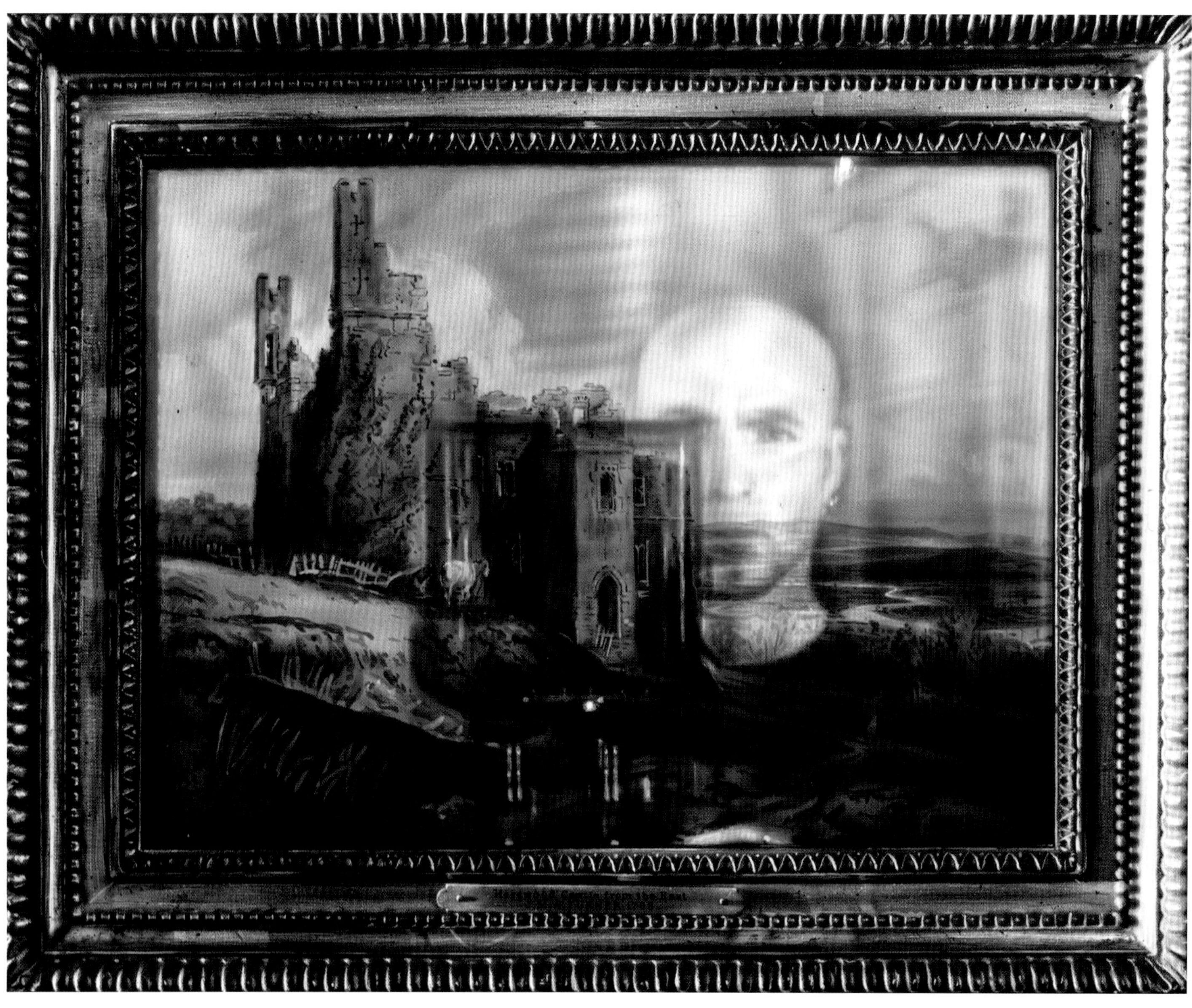

the South East of 1798, framed in its elaborate gilt frame and set against a black background. In recent years, many artists have appropriated the paintings of old masters for use in their own work. Here, Brooks' face can be read as a reflection in the glass protecting the picture, yet at the same time he seems to place himself within the painting itself, a process of engagement with Harewood's art collection which is in fact what he was commissioned to do. Munnings of course would have seen this as an act of audacity that would have had him choking with indignation.

Jason Brooks, b. 1969. *Harewood Castle Self Portrait* (2001). Airbrushed oil on canvas, 85.5 x 101cm (Ferens Art Gallery, Hull Museums and Galleries)

Yorkshire has always been the home to contemporary art collectors; Atkinson Grimshaw, for example, was supported in his career by many wealthy locals, notably Walter Battle of Harrogate. Victorian art collectors usually bought art off the walls at the Royal Academy exhibitions, but the more discerning were inclined to commission work directly from the artist. Samson Fox was the classic Victorian giant of industry; he was born in Bradford and grew up in Leeds, started work at the age of eight in a textile mill, at fifteen became an apprentice at a tool-making and foundry company and by his twenties he was running his own business. Fox went on to make his fortune from mechanical and chemical engineering in Leeds where his companies were responsible for many innovations in manufacture, notably in steamships and railways. He moved to live in desirable Harrogate where he was elected Mayor for three years in a row between 1889 and 1891, made many gifts to the town, founded the building of the Royal School of Music in London and lived in palatial style at Grove House, Harrogate, a mansion that survives to this day. Fox had his own art gallery in Grove House and he was a great lover of music. Over the centuries artists from all over Europe have come to Britain and played their part in enriching our art and culture. In the nineteenth century art dealers made a good living from importing European art and artists to the wealthy Victorian middle classes. The Croatian artist Blaho Bukovac was one of these. He first visited Fox in Harrogate in 1888 and his commanding yet introspective portrait of Fox was painted in 1890 and exhibited at the Paris Salon in 1891, one of a series of pictures of family and friends that the artist painted as Fox's guest in Harrogate.

Bukovac is well known in Central Europe and the Balkans as one of the founders of a modern, Western tradition of painting in that region in the late nineteenth century. He trained in Paris at a time when Impressionism was catching the public imagination, an influence that can be seen in the brushwork of the green leafy background that he creates for the dark bulky form of his sitter. Bukovac learnt English when living in America in his early teens and he first visited England aged sixteen when he docked in Liverpool on board a merchant ship. From the mid-1880s until the First World War he regularly came to England, where his pictures were imported by the London dealers, Vicars Bros. Fox was not only one of Bukovac's most important patrons, he also helped to change the artist's image in England. Vicars had marketed Bukovac rather crudely as a painter with 'Parisian' morals. Fox treated him as a gentleman, lavished hospitality on him and introduced him to his family and circle of friends. The portrait of Fox reveals Bukovac at his best, as a sensitive and technically accomplished artist. This is seen in the skilful composition of the portrait, with the man's impressively large body filling most of the canvas to convey a sense of Fox as the powerful businessman. Equally compelling is the delicate painting of Fox's hands, his right wrist revealed

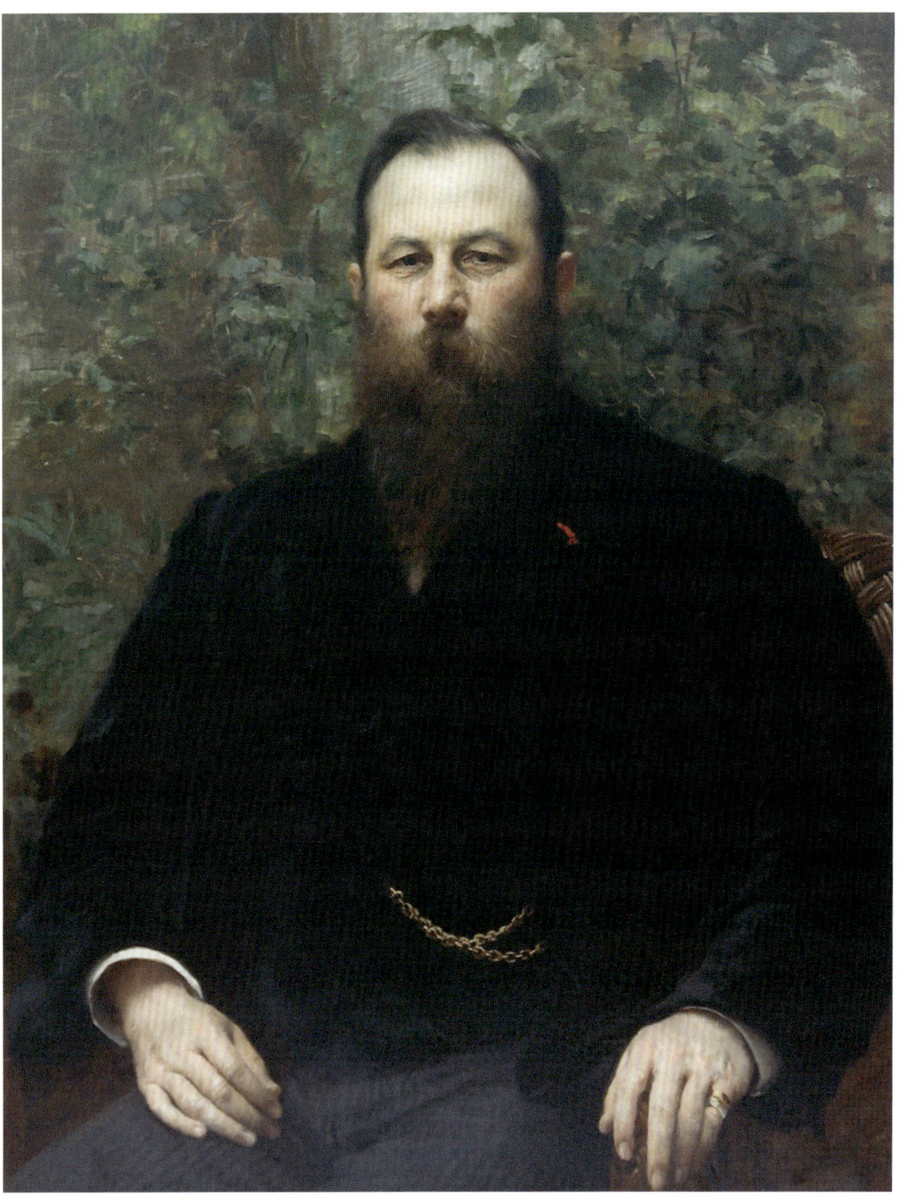

in a way that hints at the man's human vulnerability so that we get an understanding of Fox as a kindly benefactor and a lover of art and music. Fox collected many other paintings by Bukovac, including several of the exhibition pictures of female nudes that had made his reputation such as *The White Slave* and *Potiphar's Wife*. Since the posthumous auction of Fox's paintings in 1911 most of this remarkable private Harrogate art collection remains untraced.

Since the end of the Second World War both public and private art collecting has expanded and enriched the visual arts in Yorkshire and made them available to an ever increasing audience. To mention just a

Blaho Bukovac, 1855 - 1922. *Samson Fox* (1890). Oil on canvas, 99.7 x 76.2cm (Mercer Art Gallery, Harrogate Borough Council)

few: Helen Kapp, Arthur Haigh, Terry Freidman, Jeffrey Sherwin, Ronnie Duncan, Ernest Hall, Jonathan and Margaret Silver and Greville Worthington have all contributed in quite different ways to the appreciation of art in Yorkshire galleries. Helen Kapp, born in 1901, was a painter, illustrator, wood engraver and an art curator. In 1951 she became the director of the Wakefield Art Gallery where she faced down local resistance to build up a fine representation of modern British art in the Wakefield collection through astute buying, good relationships with artists with Yorkshire connections, especially Hepworth and Moore, and the curatorship of such groundbreaking exhibitions as *Vision and Reality* 1956, which introduced abstract painting and sculpture to the people of Yorkshire. Kapp went on to became the director of Abbot Hall Art Gallery in the 1960s, where she achieved her ambition of creating a gallery in an eighteenth century house that was, in her own words, 'stimulating and vibrating… a place where clashes of ideas and feeling generate new thought and ideas that will reverberate in our lives'. In Halifax in 1983 Ernest Hall and Jonathan Silver bought the redundant mill buildings at Dean Clough and set about transforming them into a huge centre for commerce and cultural industries with artists' studios and galleries. Jonathan Silver and his wife Margaret went on to convert Salts Mill in Saltaire near Shipley into a thriving cultural and business centre that is remarkable for its custodianship of the largest collection of David Hockney's pictures in the world. Silver went to Bradford Grammar School and first encountered Hockney, an old boy of the school, when he asked him to design a cover for the school magazine. Silver studied art and textiles at Leeds University followed by a highly successful career with a string of stylish men's fashion shops that brought the swinging sixties to the north of England. Travelling with his family in America in the 1980s, Silver met Hockney again, they became firm friends and Silver enthused the artist with the idea of showing his work in an old Bradford Mill. He bought Salts Mill in 1987 and the Silvers made it into a place of beauty: its bookshops and galleries always scented with the perfume of lilies, Mozart's music playing in the background and Hockney's art on the walls.

In 2009 Leeds Art Gallery staged *British Surrealism in Context: A Collector's Eye*, an exhibition of Jeffrey Sherwin's extraordinary collection of British surrealist art. Sherwin, a retired Leeds doctor, and his wife Ruth have spent over twenty-five years putting together their collection of over 220 paintings, drawings and sculpture. Sherwin's mother was an amateur artist and she encouraged his awareness of art as a child, but it was not until 1986 that he found the art that he really wanted to collect in a surrealist show at Leeds Art Gallery; he was intrigued by the way it took the everyday and turned it on its head. Sherwin was inspired in his collecting by visiting artists' studios and by taking advice from Leeds

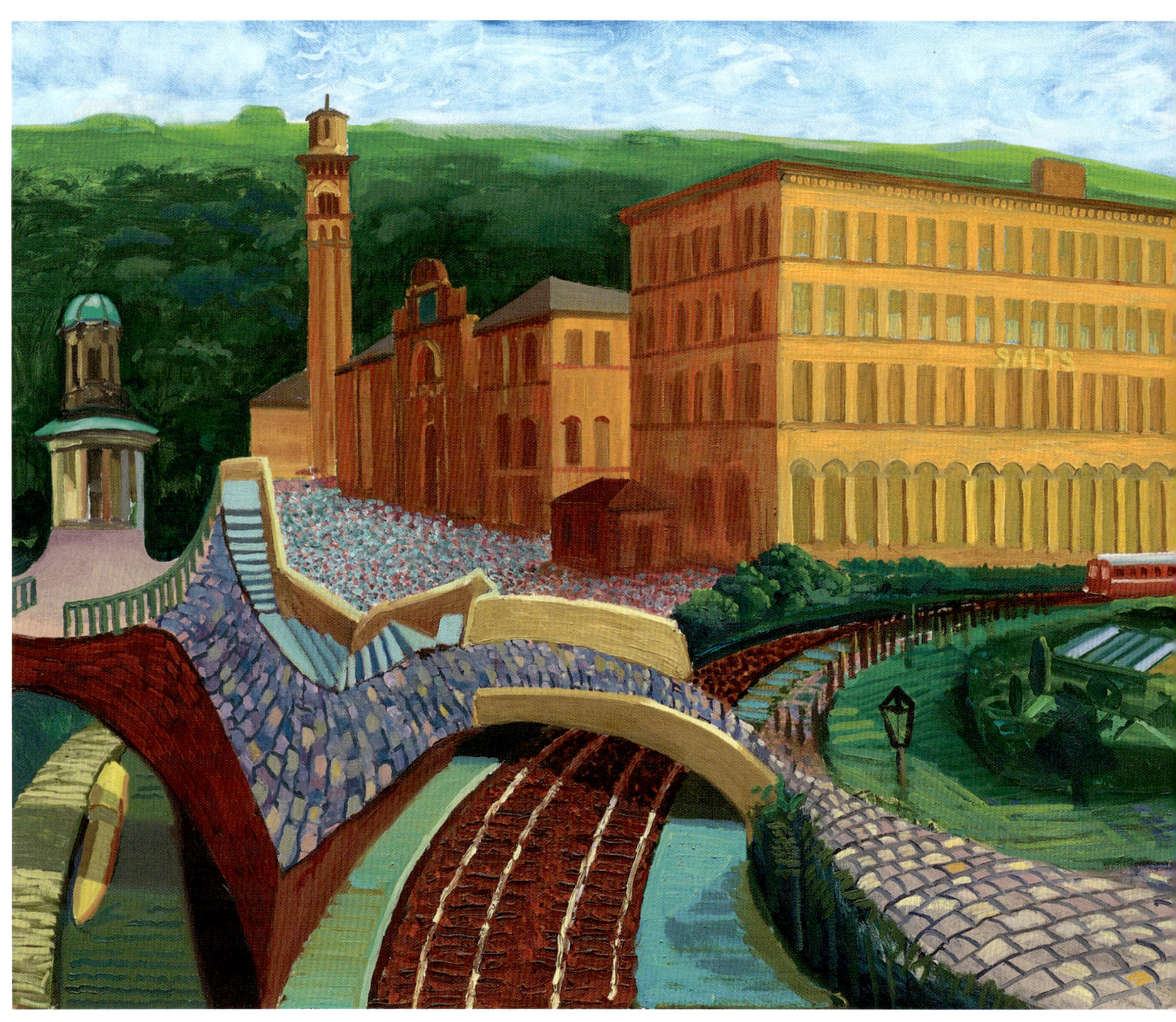

David Hockney, b. 1937. *Salts Mill, Saltaire, Yorkshire* (1997). Oil on 2 canvases, 121.9 x 304.8cm
© David Hockney
Photo Credit: Prudence Cuming Associates

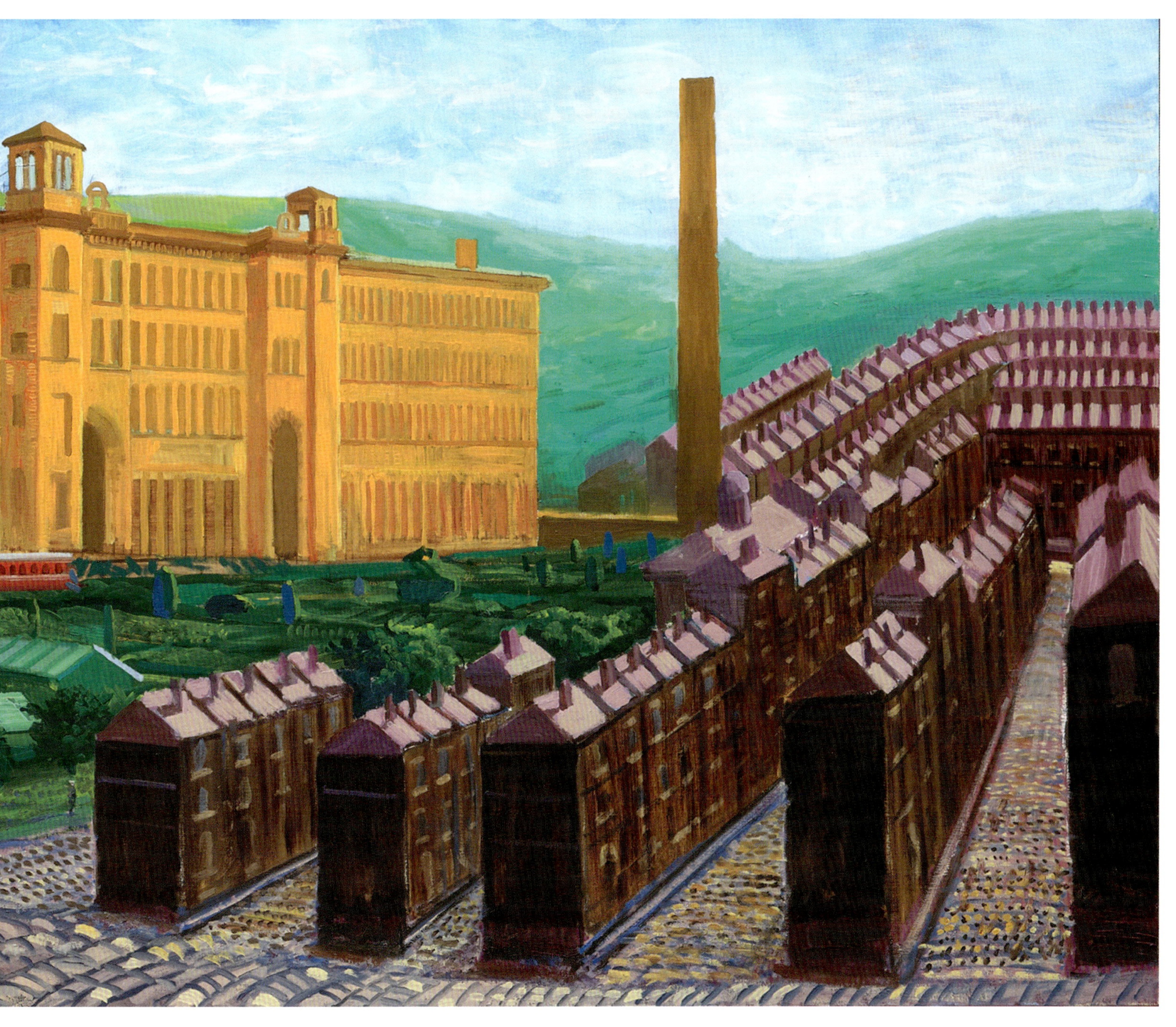

curators such as the American architectural historian Terry Freidman whom he came into contact with through his work as a city councillor with an interest in the arts. Indeed, it was Freidman, the mastermind behind the foundation of the Henry Moore Institute in the city, who organised the British surrealism show that piqued Sherwin's interest, along with many other hugely influential Leeds exhibitions including expositions on the work of Jacob Epstein and Herbert Read. Sherwin has always been a staunch supporter of Yorkshire connected artists ranging from Henry Moore, Kenneth Armitage, Anthony Earnshaw and Harry Thubron to Damien Hirst. Every room of his house is crammed with art, even hanging from the banisters. In Sherwin's view his collection is one of national importance, of which he considers himself 'only a temporary guardian.'

A quality that features very strongly in the collecting activities of all of these Yorkshire private collectors is their dedication to helping artists develop their careers and to share their collections with others. Terry Freidman played a key part in helping the sculptor, photographer and environmentalist Andy Goldsworthy on his path to international fame; Ronnie Duncan, formerly an Otley mill owner, opened a gallery in a barn at his own home so that visitors can come and enjoy his art collection; and Greville Worthington, who lives in a converted Victorian church in Brough Park near Richmond in North Yorkshire, uses his home not only as a spectacular backdrop for his collection but also to stage public exhibitions. Among this illustrious group, Arthur Haigh stands out for a lifetime of devotion to art and artists that he managed to achieve on the salary of a clerk at a carpet works. Haigh lived a frugal life in Brighouse near Huddersfield in a small terrace house, which over the course of his lifetime was hung from floor to ceiling with contemporary art. He toured the small galleries, art college shows and studios of Yorkshire and built up an impressive art historical knowledge and aesthetic sensitivity that enabled him to pick out art talent long before the commercial dealers got there. Haigh not only bought work and presented it to public collections, he also helped struggling artists with money for materials. His reputation for being able to talent spot earned him invitations to judge competitions and sit on museum buying panels. Haigh's collection was distinguished by his distinctive preference for Yorkshire artists such as Tom Wood – who painted more than one portrait of Haigh – Peter Brook, Mary Lord and Marie Walker Last.

Tom Wood first painted Haigh in a double portrait with the art critic Bill Oliver in 1984. The two men sit across the table from each other surrounded by swirls of expressionist colour and impasto, happily talking about their shared passion for art. Wood has described the painting as being 'conceived along the lines of a Kitaj meets Holbein kind of painting.' Much of Haigh's collection, such as this work, was given to galleries before

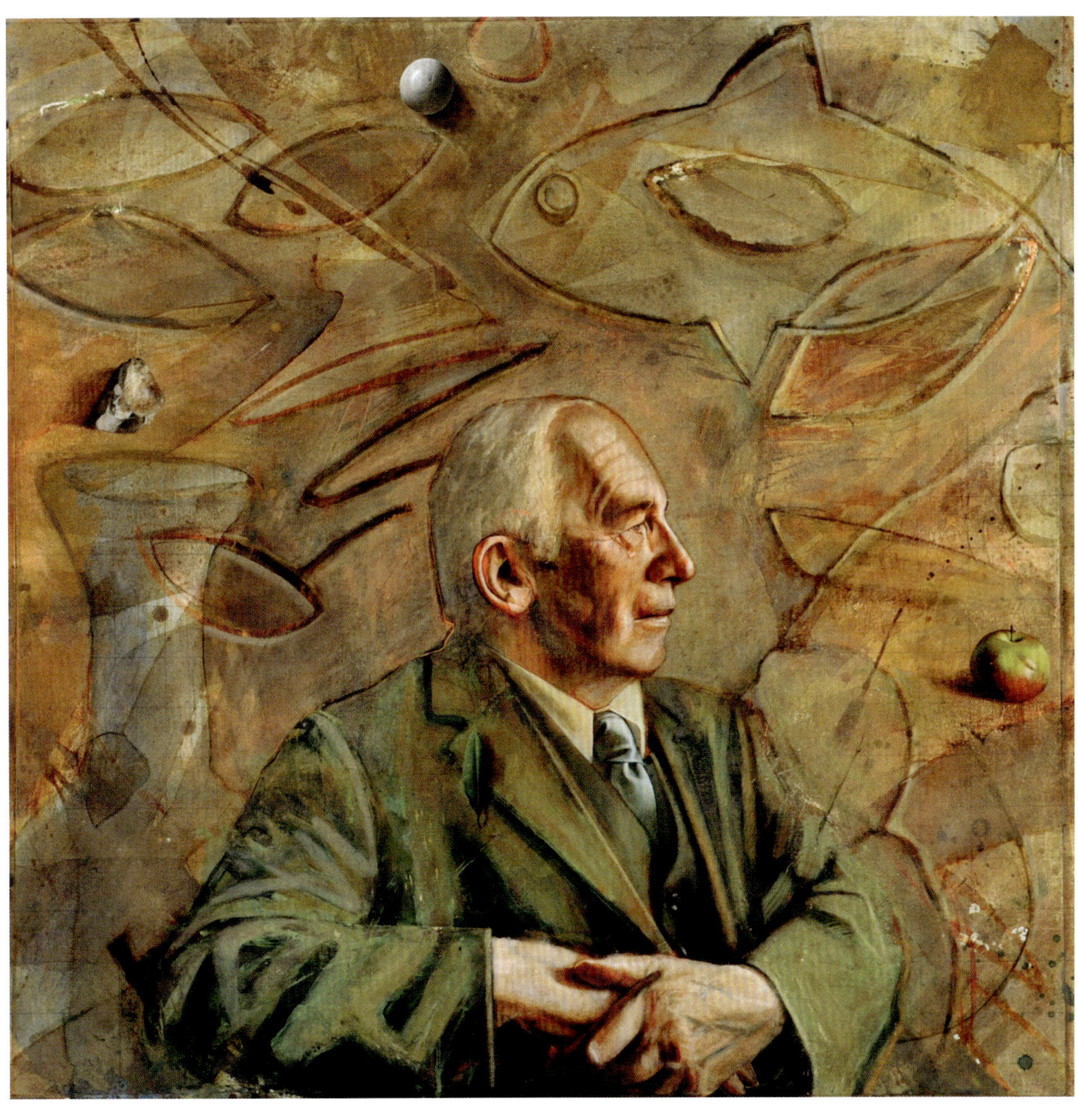

Tom Wood, b. 1955. *Arthur II (Arthur Haigh)* (1983). Oil on canvas, 110.5 x 110.9cm. (University of Leeds Art Collection)

his death in 1999 at the age of eighty-two, including more than 150 paintings and pieces of modern sculpture to Cartwright Hall Art Gallery in Bradford. Tom Wood recalls, 'Arthur and Bill would often visit exhibitions together. Bill had a car whereas Arthur never learnt to drive, he only had a television late in life and often watched it with the sound off in case the neighbours heard it. Both Arthur and Bill were loyal supporters of my work and when Cartwright Hall commissioned the double portrait it was to commemorate most importantly their friendship and I hope my friendship with them.' A single portrait, Arthur II, was commissioned by Arthur Haigh, not to glorify himself but to help Tom Wood at a time when the artist was struggling financially. 'He was a bit shocked when he saw how big the painting was and for a long time it

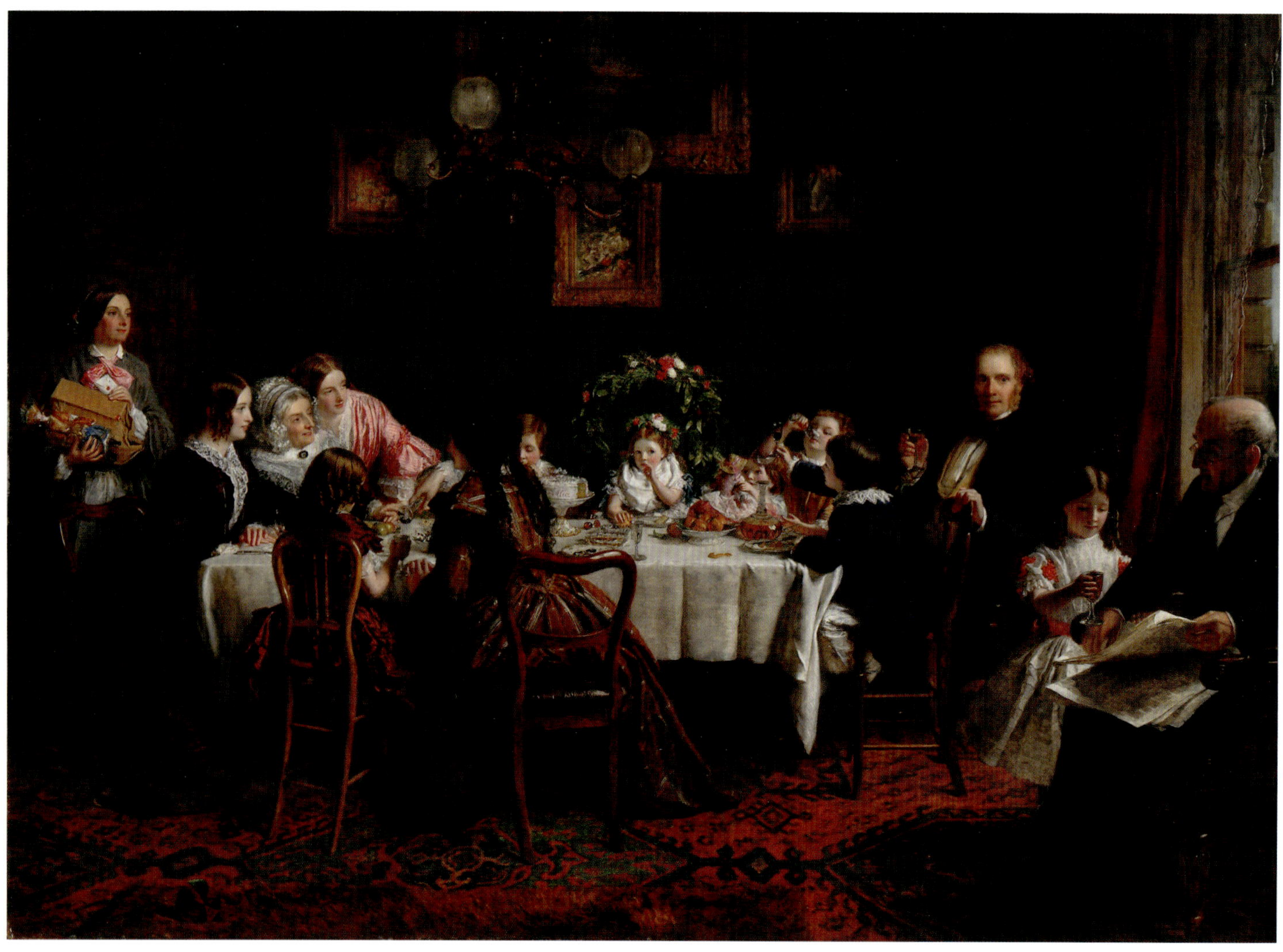

remained with me as he worked out where he could fit it in to his already cluttered house. A lot of it was painted from life including all of the hands and most of the face. The background was influenced by Egyptian hieroglyphics, which I had been studying in the Egyptian collection at the British Museum. One of the hieroglyphs is of a fish signifying Arthur's insatiable appetite for fish.'

Self-portraits fascinate us with what they tell us about the artist. The artist is not setting out to flatter somebody who is paying him to produce an appealing image, although pre-twentieth century artists made self-portraits as a form of advertisement for their skills and social acceptability. In British art of the Victorian period, artists were much inclined to use their own family as models, especially their children, not only for convenience but also for economic reasons. William Powell Frith was one

William Powell Frith, 1819 - 1909. *Many Happy Returns of the Day* (1856). Oil on canvas, 81.3 x 114.4cm (Mercer Art Gallery, Harrogate Borough Council)

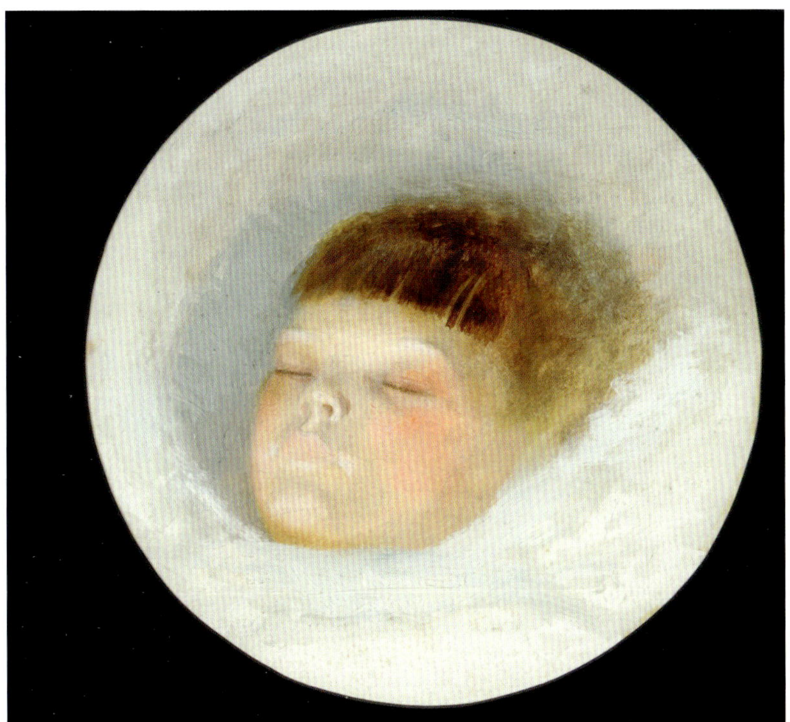

of the most celebrated artists of the Victorian age, known for his panoramic views of Ramsgate Sands, Derby Day, the railway station and the private view at the Royal Academy in 1881. Frith was born near Ripon and spent his early years in Harrogate where his father was an innkeeper, after which he went to study at the Royal Academy of Arts and spent the rest of his life in London. The Mercer Art Gallery in Harrogate therefore has an outstanding collection of Frith's work. His art was about Victorian people of all classes, and although some gallery goers took a snobbish attitude to his interest in depicting the working classes, most people were captivated. Frith's major works had to be cordoned off with a policeman to hold back the crowds when they went on show at the Royal Academy, after which they toured this country and the United States of America. Frith's highly populated pictures required an extensive, and expensive, use of professional artists' models, so he often resorted to employing his own family as models. In *Many Happy Returns of the Day*, on the surface a celebration of respectable middle-class family life, Frith included his wife and children and cast himself as the paterfamilias in the scene at Alice's birthday party tea. The maid brings in an armful of presents, his young sons are drinking sherry with great gusto and he looks fondly at his daughter as she hands a glass of wine to the grandfather figure, actually an old man brought in to model from the local workhouse. Domestic bliss is the theme, yet in reality at the time the picture was painted Frith's first child by his mistress Mary Alford was born at a house just a walk away from his own home. The artist wrote a popular autobiography published in 1888 in which he recounts in fascinating detail his life as an artist, although sticking strictly to the double standards of the day and omitting to mention his second family.

The Leeds artist Atkinson Grimshaw and his wife Fanny had sixteen children, although sadly only six of them survived into adulthood. Although Grimshaw's children were very much loved, he painted only a few pictures of them, including a deeply moving watercolour study of his daughter Gertrude just after her death from diphtheria, which in the space of one month in 1874 took away three of his children. Elaine, another of Grimshaw's daughters who survived into her nineties, wrote an unpublished memoir of her father in which she included a poignant

Atkinson Grimshaw, 1836 - 1893. *Gertrude*, 1874. Watercolour, 17.5 x 17.5cm. (Leeds Museums and Galleries)

description of the making of the Gertrude's posthumous portrait: 'There came a day when the mother sat on the wide oaken staircase outside a darkened room – just a corner of a blind lifted, maybe, to help the painter see his work and the still, still little model... Here on this foot-square scrap of pasteboard is the painter's work: the aureole of fever-tangled hair on the pillow, the smooth-cut fringe, the closed eyes and rosy cheeks – but when he came to those silent lips, they are unfinished, a blur.'

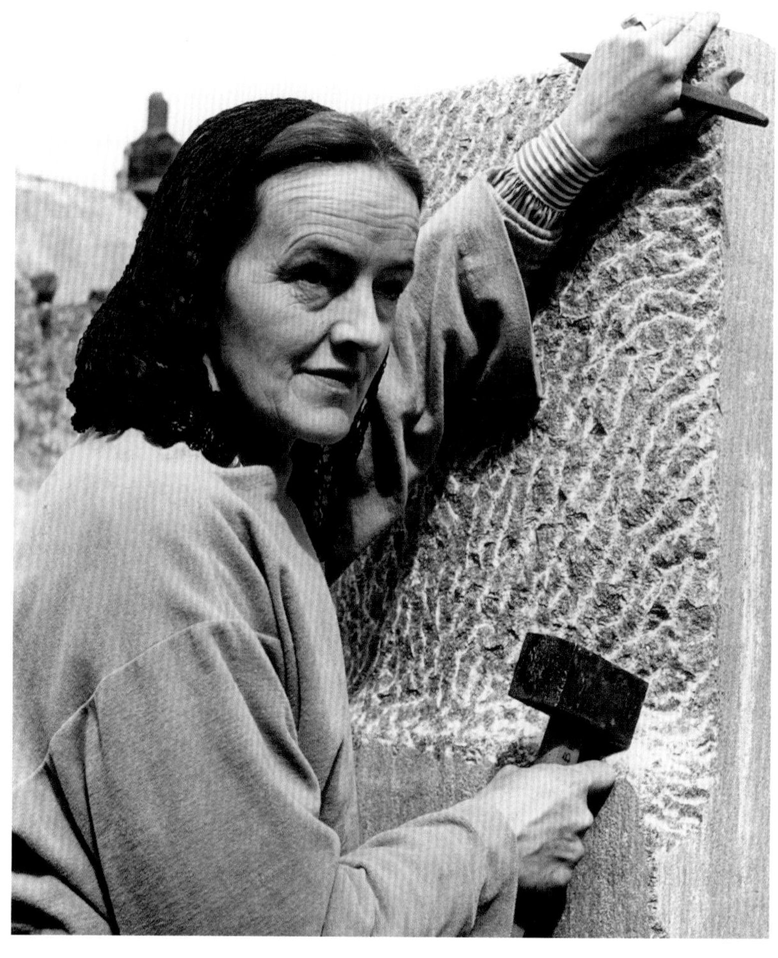

Barbara Hepworth. Photo portrait by Peter Keen. (© estate of Peter Keen / National Portrait Gallery, London)

Modern and contemporary women artists often make profound self-scrutiny the subject of their work. The sculptor Dame Barbara Hepworth has always been known as one of Yorkshire's most famous and accomplished women. Indeed, there is now an art gallery in her birthplace of Wakefield named after her. Hepworth was of the same generation as Henry Moore and studied at Leeds School of Art and at the Royal College of Art in London at the same time as him. Whilst Moore was the son of a coal miner, Hepworth came from a middle-class background; her father was the Yorkshire County Surveyor and an Alderman. Hepworth was one of the few women artists of her generation to achieve international prominence, above all for her groundbreaking work in the pursuit of abstract form. Although Hepworth eventually made Cornwall her home rather than Yorkshire, the West Riding was good to her, awarding her a county scholarship to the Royal College of Art and a Travel Scholarship to Italy in 1924, which spurred her on in her career. In London in the late 1920s she joined other artists in a new movement of direct carving, and her work began to be noticed and purchased. She was constantly experimental in her search for abstraction, piercing the stone and trying out ideas in prints, collages and photograms. Hepworth was fiercely intellectual and her life was devoted to her work, possibly at the cost of two marriages. She had a slight figure and a strong face with a high forehead accentuated by the scarf that she wrapped round her hair when working in the dust of the studio. With her cut-glass accent and permanent cigarette in hand, in film and photographs she is often physically dwarfed by her own creations. In the 1950s the photographer Peter Keen posed Hepworth at work on her carving, an energetic and liberated figure. In contrast the celebrated Armenian Ida Kar, who specialised in images of writers and artists and made a series of photographs of Hepworth, presents her in a more passive feminine pose, encircled by her sculpture with hands neatly clasped. In 1971 the photographer Bob Collins captures more of her energy and style, posing her leaning forward to the viewer with behind her a piece of her own sculpture. Drawing for Hepworth was a less usual activity than carving. During the Second World War she worked for the War Artists' Advisory Committee recording hospital operations. Later in life when her second marriage to the artist Ben Nicholson had broken down she found drawing to be a therapeutic as well as a creative exercise. In her self-portrait drawing of 1950, she captures the intensity of concentration in her eyes as she presents us with a view of how she saw herself.

Yorkshire has produced some fine women artists working in many different media. Photography is the medium chosen by Tessa Bunney, who followed the reverse path to Hepworth: she grew up in Cornwall and later adopted North Yorkshire as her home. The idea of introducing artists in residence into different environments has now enjoyed great success for several decades in Yorkshire, as it has across Britain. Not only have painters, sculptors, textile artists, photographers, ceramicists and many other makers working in different media been invited to base their studio in museums, art galleries and heritage sites, but also in places of work across rural and industrial Yorkshire. Tessa Bunney has a specific interest in people's working lives, especially in the rural environment. Her work in fact takes her around the world to explore the ways in which ancient ways of living off the land are fast disappearing with the encroaching tide of mass-industrialisation. However, in 2004 she stayed closer to home, spending time up on the moors of Nidderdale, a designated Area of Outstanding Natural Beauty, working with the hill farming communities and the gamekeepers on a country estate to record their way of life and the relationship between landscape and people. Bunney's photographic compositions are remarkable in that they manage to convey so much of a person and his or her life without necessarily including the person's face. For example, in the Nidderdale project she conveys the harshness of winter up in the hills by portraying a farmer's back view, his head slightly bent against the flurry of snow. Lambing is described in an image of a newborn lamb wobbling to its feet with just the hand of the shepherd extended towards it. All we see of the gamekeeper is his hand holding a dead grouse against a background of clear blue sky and the green hills of Nidderdale. These anonymous people's lives are perfectly described to us by the perceptiveness of the artist's composition and her implicit understanding of their world. In 2009 Bunney spent time as artist in residence at Newby Hall, a private Georgian family home near Ripon that opens both house and garden to the public. Although the house stewards

Over: Tessa Bunney, *Newby Hall* (2009). Photo (courtesy of the Artist)

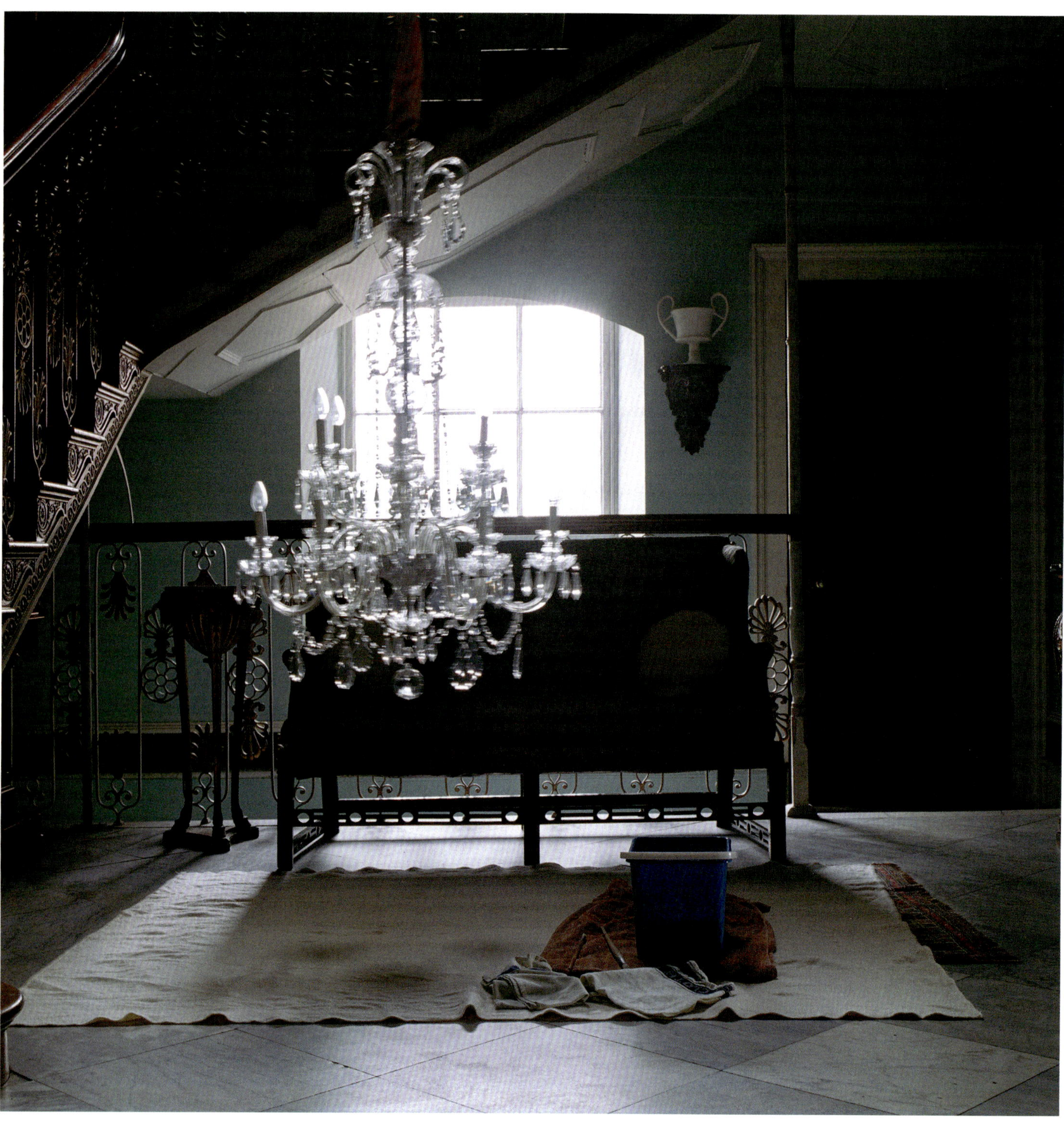

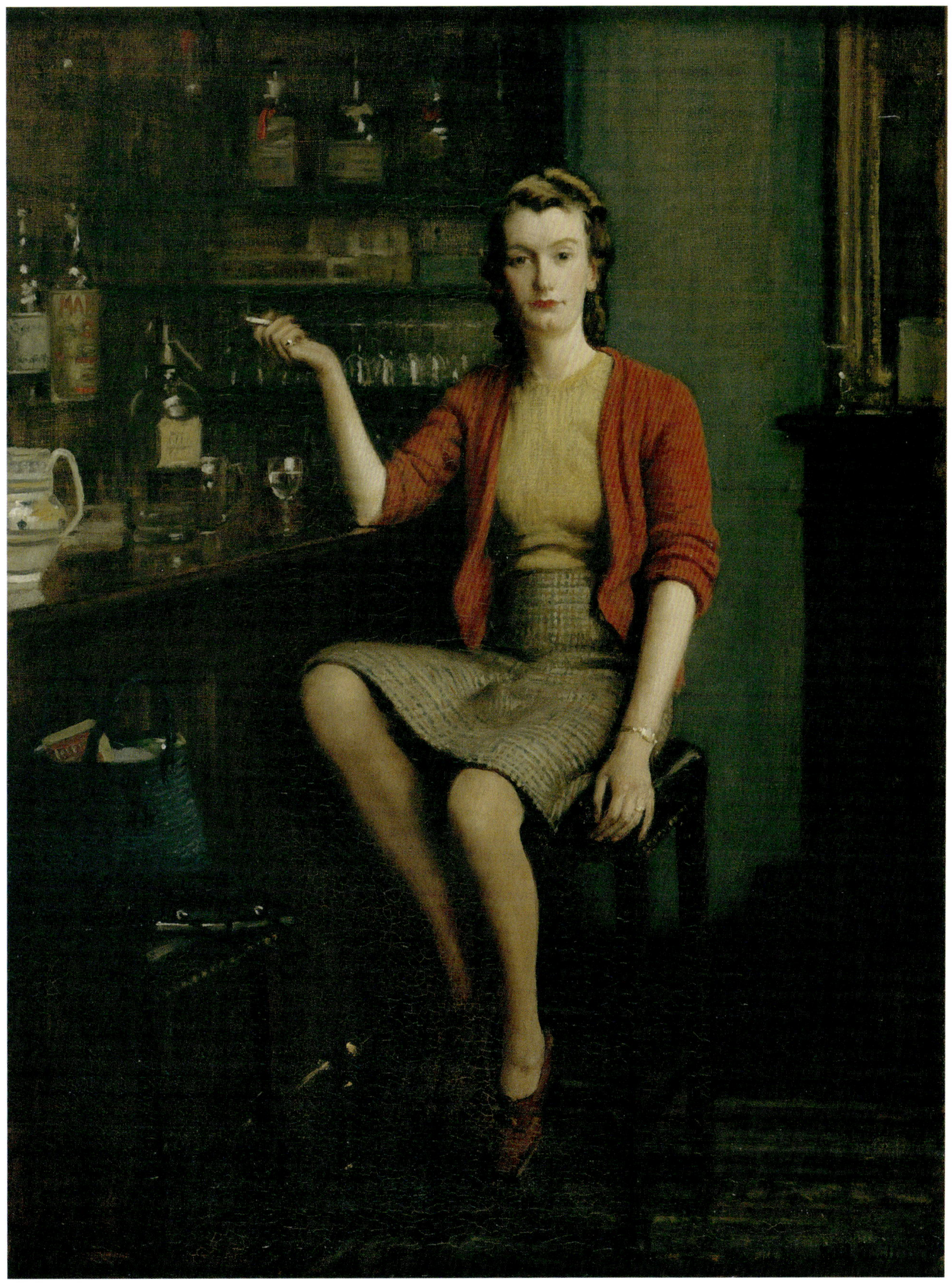

and gardeners barely figured in her photographs, the human presence is keenly felt. For example, a splendid chandelier, lowered to the floor for cleaning, hangs incongruously beside the cleaner's blue plastic bucket, almost a metaphor for the relationship between the house owner and the servant.

Portraiture is more usually associated with celebrity, but the east Yorkshire painter Frederick William Elwell, painting in the first half of the twentieth century, like photographer Tessa Bunney in this century, made the working classes his subject. Elwell, whose wife Mary was also a painter, was born in Beverley near Hull and studied at Lincoln School of Art, where he found his interest in the French Impressionists, then in Antwerp and Paris where he developed his skills in portraiture and still life. Having failed to make his mark on the London art world, Elwell returned to Beverley where he set up his portrait studio. Mary had considerable personal wealth, which gave Fred more freedom to travel, to paint what he wished, and to mix with fashionable artists such as Laura Knight and Alfred Munnings. Elwell took as his theme working life in Beverley, producing numerous atmospheric and closely observed interiors featuring kitchen maids, woodcarvers and other local craftsmen. His most compelling works include a number of single portraits of anonymous characters posed in their place of work that are surprisingly reminiscent of the Bramham Park portraits of the family's servants. **The Landlord**, 1935, bought the same year by the Ferens Art Gallery in Hull, has the man looking directly at the artist, stiffly posed holding a funnel over a ceramic urn as he decants the sherry. The dark atmosphere of the pub with bottles and glasses catching vestiges of light in the gloom emulates the Dutch genre scenes that Elwell admired. **In a Bar**, 1943, captures the same setting only from the other side of the bar. It is wartime and the woman with her Victory roll hairstyle, tweed skirt and cardigan, perches rather unsurely on the high stool, cigarette held aloft. Hull was bombed constantly throughout the Second World War. The constant anxiety and dread of that time could explain the woman's resigned expression as she gazes out of the canvas.

Yorkshire is by no means short of celebrity, and writers are outstanding amongst its most famous people. Branwell Brontë's portrait of his sisters

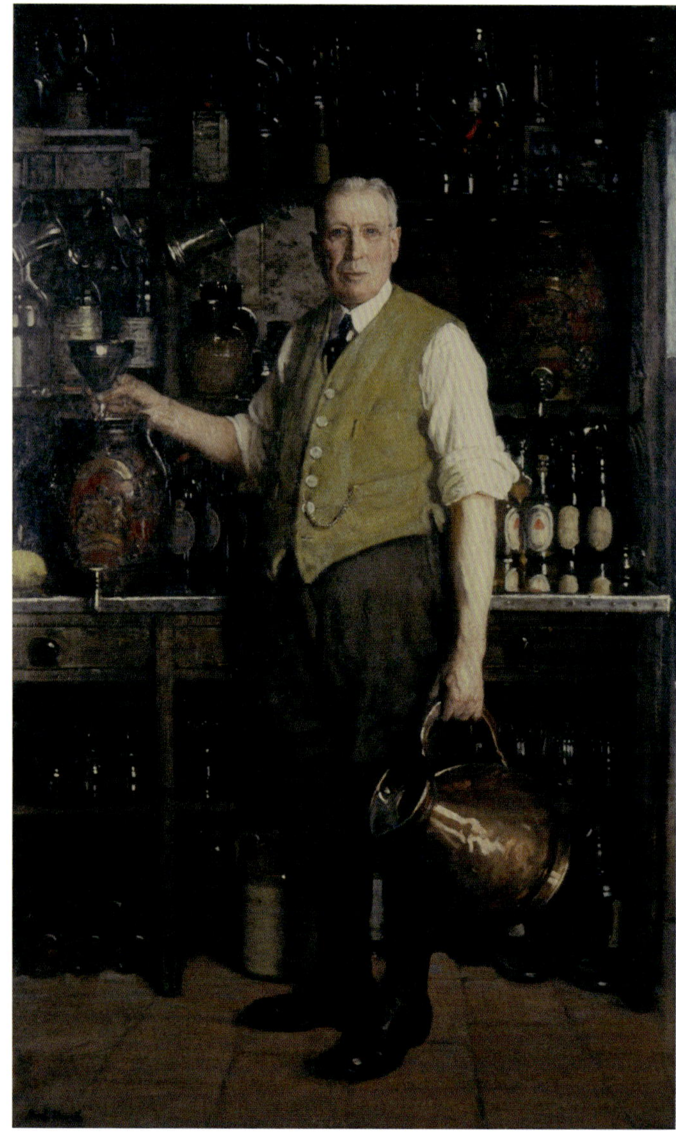

Fred Elwell, 1870 - 1958. *The Landlord* (1935). Oil on canvas, 163.5 x 103cm (Ferens Art Gallery, Hull Museums and Galleries)

Previous page: Fred Elwell, 1870 - 1958. *In a Bar* (1943). Oil on canvas, 102 x 82.5cm (Ferens Art Gallery, Hull Museums and Galleries)

Opposite: Branwell Bronte, 1817 - 1848. *The Brontë Sisters (Anne Brontë; Emily Brontë; Charlotte Brontë)* (1834). Oil on canvas, 90.2 x 74.6cm (© National Portrait Gallery, London)

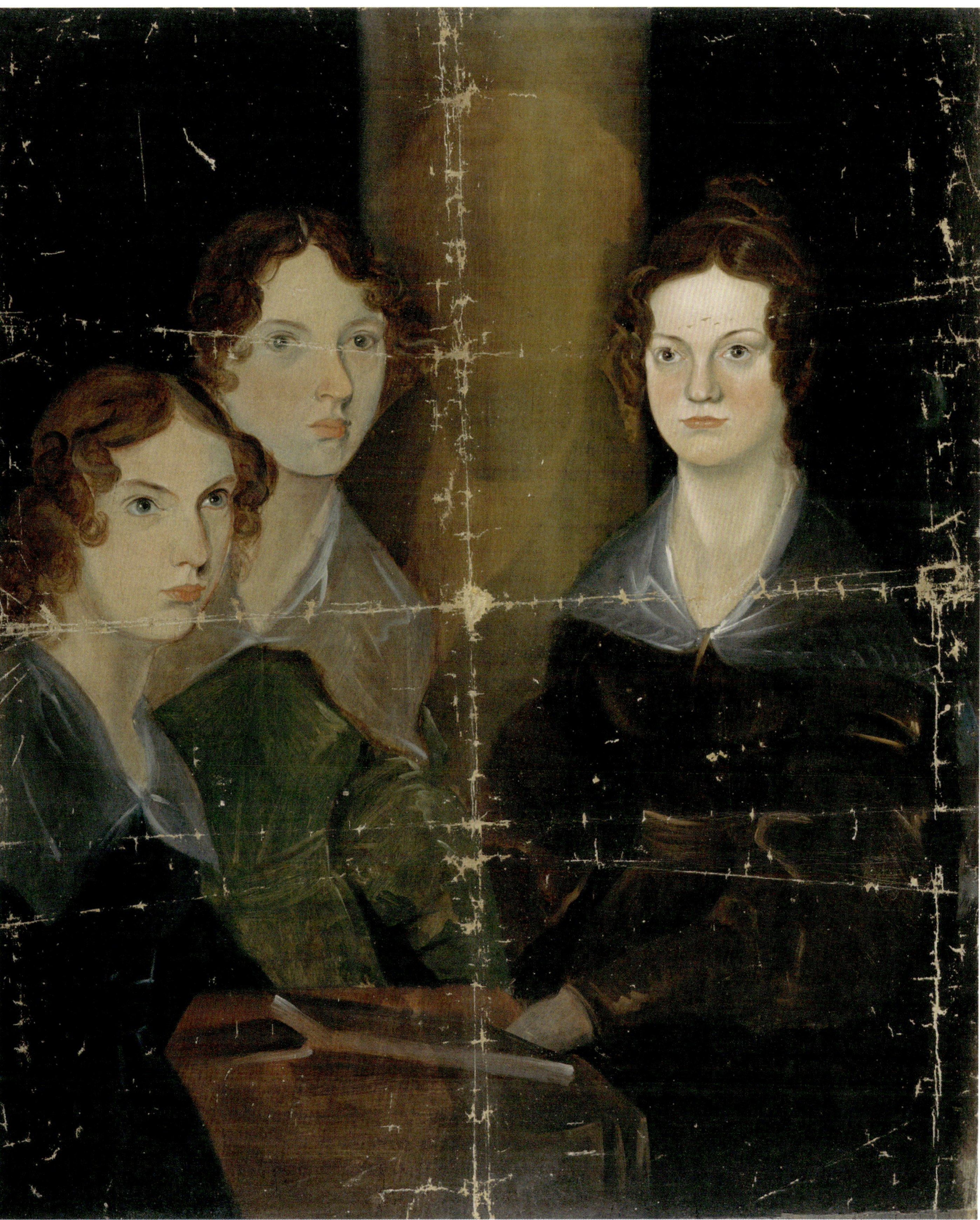

Charlotte, Emily and Anne, with himself – or could it be the Reverend Patrick Brontë? – painted out in the centre of the group is arguably the best known literary image in the world. Executed in 1834 when he was just seventeen, years before his sisters found fame as writers, it is a work of considerable aspiration. Branwell portrays his family in the manner of a group of aristocratic ladies, with a pile of books on the table to indicate their literary leanings. Charlotte loathed the picture, Mrs Gaskell described it as 'not much better than sign painting' and Arthur Nicholls folded it up and hid it in a wardrobe until it was found after his death, scarred by neglect, by his second wife Mary and bought by the National Portrait Gallery in 1914. George Richmond's conventional 1850 chalk drawing of Charlotte, in contrast, was approved of by her widower, so much so that he bequeathed it to the National Portrait Gallery on his death in 1906, where the two portraits now hang in close proximity. J B Priestley, the Bradford-born dramatist, novelist and essayist, famous from the 1930s for such plays and novels as *The Good Companions*, *Angel Pavement* and *An Inspector Calls*, appears in ninety drawings, photographs and oil portraits under the same roof. James Penniston Barraclough's portrait of Priestley at Cartwright Hall Art Gallery in Bradford presents him as the self-confessed archetypal Yorkshireman, a solid figure packed into an armchair, regarding us with a knowing look.

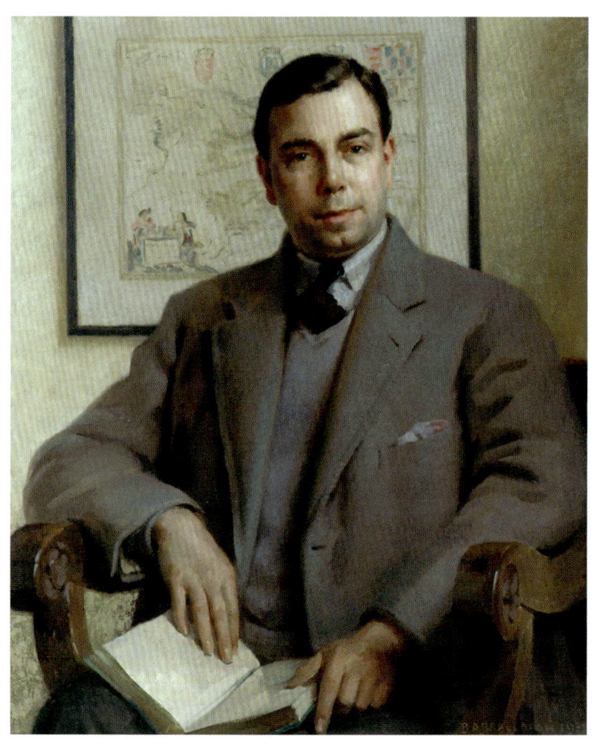

In 1850 it would have been essential for Charlotte Brontë to have her portrait drawn by Richmond for the purposes of promoting her books. The sitting, indeed, was instigated by her publisher George Smith, who wanted an appealing image of her to print on the flyleaf of *Jane Eyre*. Priestley would have been equally aware of the importance of getting his face well known. Other writers were perhaps not so willing, and went into a portrait sitting with some reluctance, or, as in the case of the novelist A S Byatt who hated images of herself, with strictly unconventional ideas about how she wanted to be painted.

The artist Damien Hirst, on the other hand, has never displayed any reluctance to put himself in the spotlight. Hirst was born in Bristol but grew up in Leeds, where he managed to run wild and develop a passion for art at the same time. Hirst made it to Goldsmith's College in London where he channelled his rebellious nature into astonishing works of creativity. In the early 1990s Hirst had his first solo exhibition and also participated in the Young British Artists show at the Saatchi Gallery the following year. There he displayed *The Physical Impossibility of Death in the Mind of Someone Living*, a 14-foot-long glass tank with a shark preserved in formaldehyde. At the 1993 Venice Biennale he showed *Mother and*

James Penniston Barraclough, 1894 - 1984. *J B Priestley* (1932). Oil on canvas, 91.7 x 77.2cm (Bradford Museums and Galleries)

Opposite: Jonathan Yeo, b. 1971. *Damien Hirst* (2013). Oil on canvas, 153 x 153cm (Jonathan Yeo Studio)

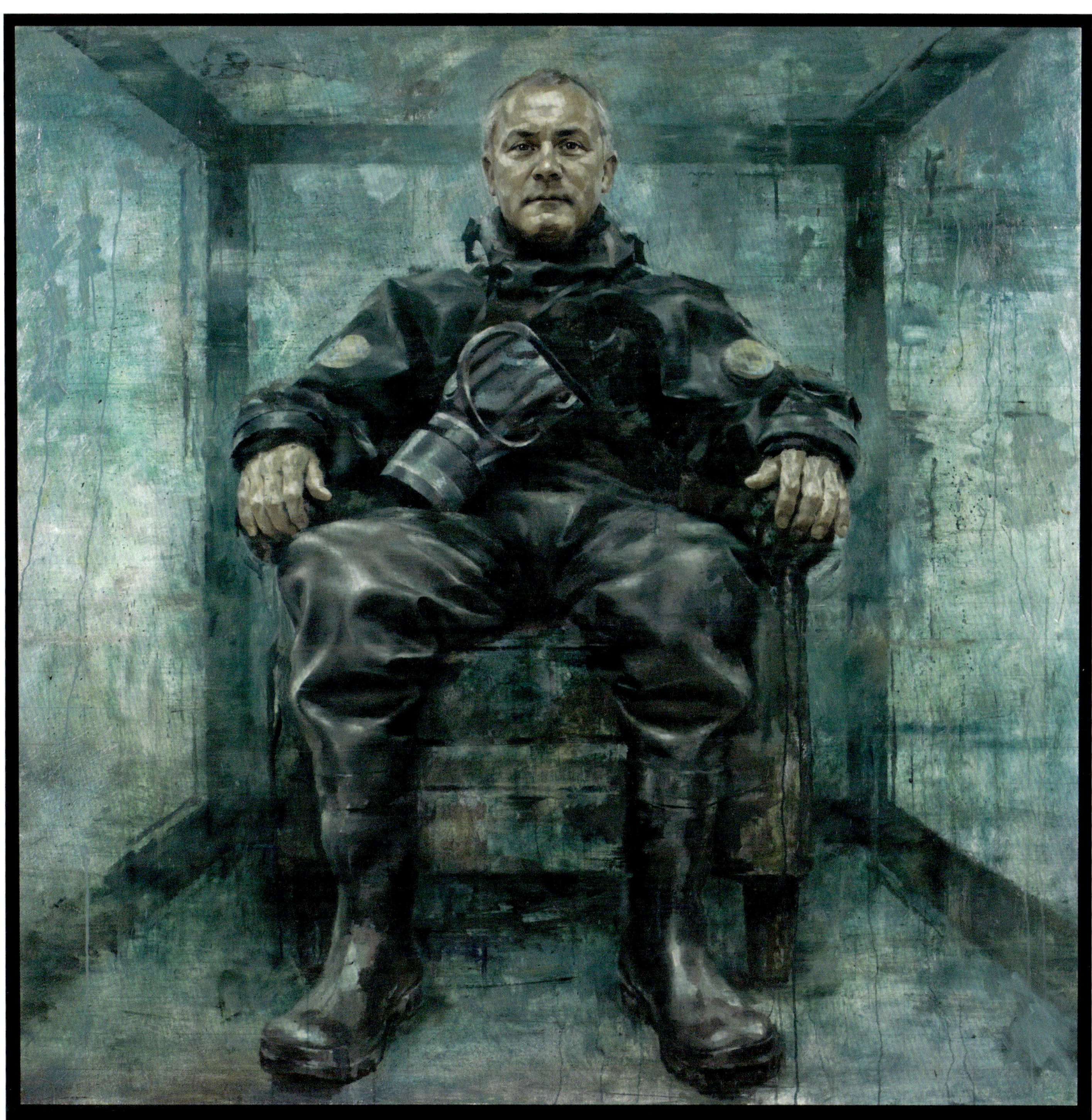

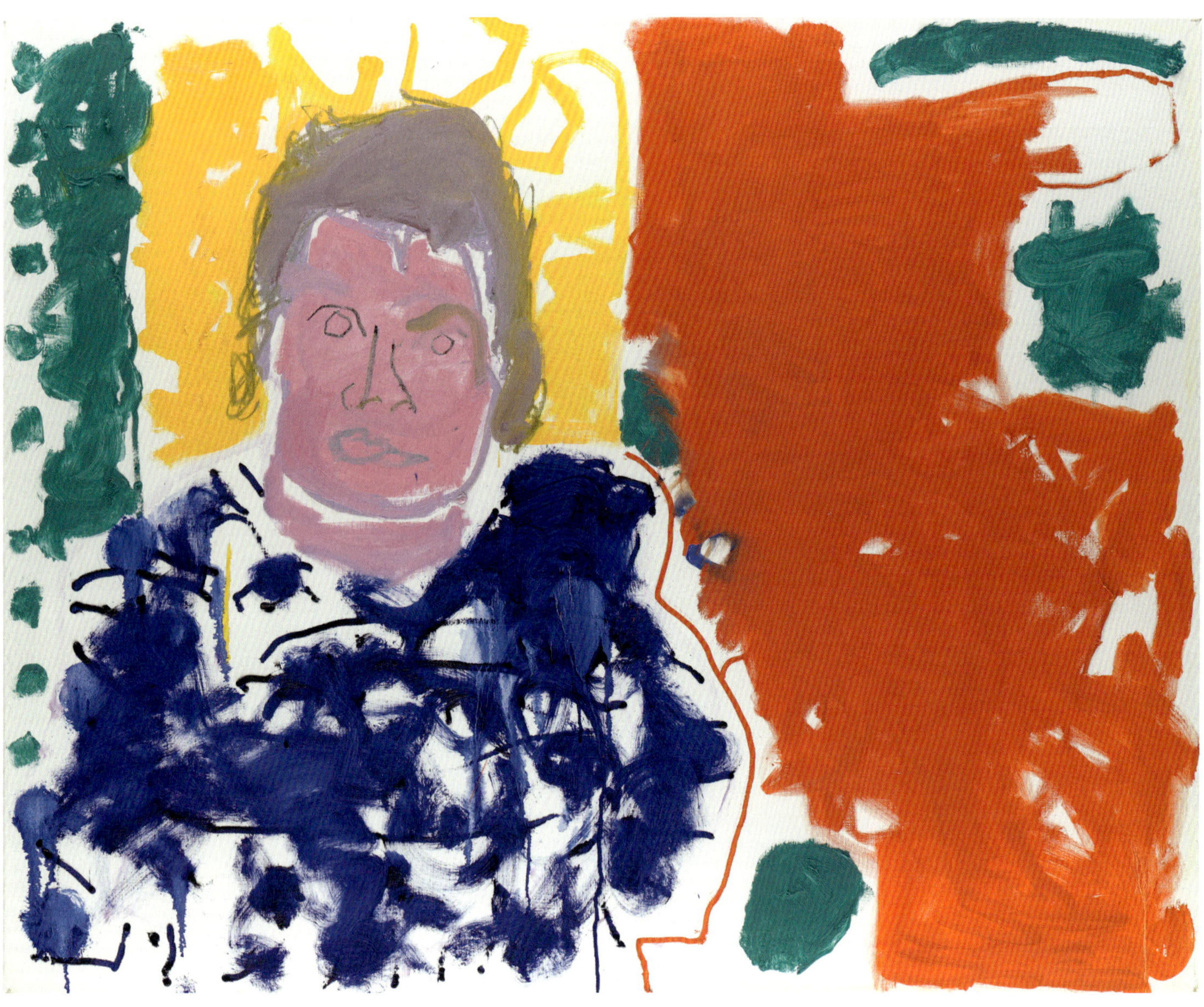

Child Divided, an installation that featured a bisected cow and her calf displayed in four vitrines, or glass cases, filled with formaldehyde. With his controversial and sometimes gruesome works, Hirst soon became one of the best-known artists in Britain. In 2013 Jonathan Yeo made a six-foot tall portrait of Hirst in a chemical protection suit enthroned inside one of his own vitrines. Yeo, in collusion with the artist, presents the middle-aged *enfant terrible* of British art as a commanding almost regal presence, whilst at the same time not letting us forget Hirst as an artist who played with dangerous materials.

When the trustees of the National Portrait Gallery commissioned a portrait of A S Byatt in 1995 – the only painting of her in the collection

Patrick Heron, 1920 - 1999. *A.S. Byatt (Portrait of A S Byatt : Red, Yellow, Green and Blue)* (24 September 1997). Oil on canvas, 96.8 x 121.6cm © The Estate of Patrick Heron. All rights reserved, DACS 2014. (© The estate of Patrick Heron. All Rights Reserved, DACS, [2014])

– she chose Yorkshire artist Patrick Heron to paint it because she admired his early semi-cubist image of T S Eliot, also in the gallery. Byatt gave Heron two reasons why she wanted an abstract portrait of herself, 'One is that I do not like looking at images of myself, the second reason is because I don't like, to be truthful, most representational portraits I see nowadays. What I wanted was the presence of the idea of me, not of a record of the whole of my face that I don't much like.' The work took three sittings with the artist at which Byatt observed the shared anxiety of painter and sitter as they both faced a blank sheet of paper for the preparatory sketches. The finished oil on canvas, Portrait of **A S Byatt : Red, Yellow, Green and Blue : 24 September 1997**, was at first a shock to the author, but then, she recalled, as she looked at it she saw a sense of herself as a writer emerge from the energetic splashes of colour, '... of how I feel when I start work, a vanishing, watching body in a sea of light.' The experience of being drawn by Heron prompted Byatt to write an erudite collection of essays *Portraits in Fiction*, 2001, in which she delves into the complex relationship between portraits and fictional characters, exploring the idea that 'Portraits in words and portraits in paint are opposites rather than metaphors for each other. A painted portrait is an artist's record, construction, of a physical presence... A painting exists outside time and records the time of its making.'

Alan Bennett appears in many stylish photographs from the 1960s onwards, documenting his career as a playwright, screenwriter, actor and author. He tends to retreat to the edges of the group pictures but on the whole looks happy and moderately relaxed. There is a page of pencil sketches of Bennett by Cecil Beaton from 1969, in which Beaton aims to capture the animation of the writer's face, but, tellingly, there is only one portrait in oils commissioned from the Yorkshire artist Tom Wood in 1993. It must be difficult to turn down the honour of having one's portrait painted for the national collection, although no doubt it has happened. In Tom Wood's portrait of Bennett there is a sense of uneasiness as the sitter, famous for the self-effacing unworldliness of his memoirs, adopts a reflective pose with tea mug in hand and an electric plug and paper bag on the table in front of him. In 2006 a correspondence with the writer emerged in records at the National Portrait Gallery that revealed that the portrait was in fact a second attempt. Bennett wrote, 'I had a session with him [Wood] just last week in which he had to capture more of my 'youthful charm', poor sod.' Tom Wood commented on his reaction, 'I was upset at the time because it was the first time a commission of mine had ever been rejected. But Alan was wonderful about it. He said the theatre was all about rejection and I should think of the second painting as a rewrite.' The artist goes on to describe the symbolism behind the objects on the table, 'The man who was building the frame for the painting happened to stand behind Alan Bennett in the market at Settle

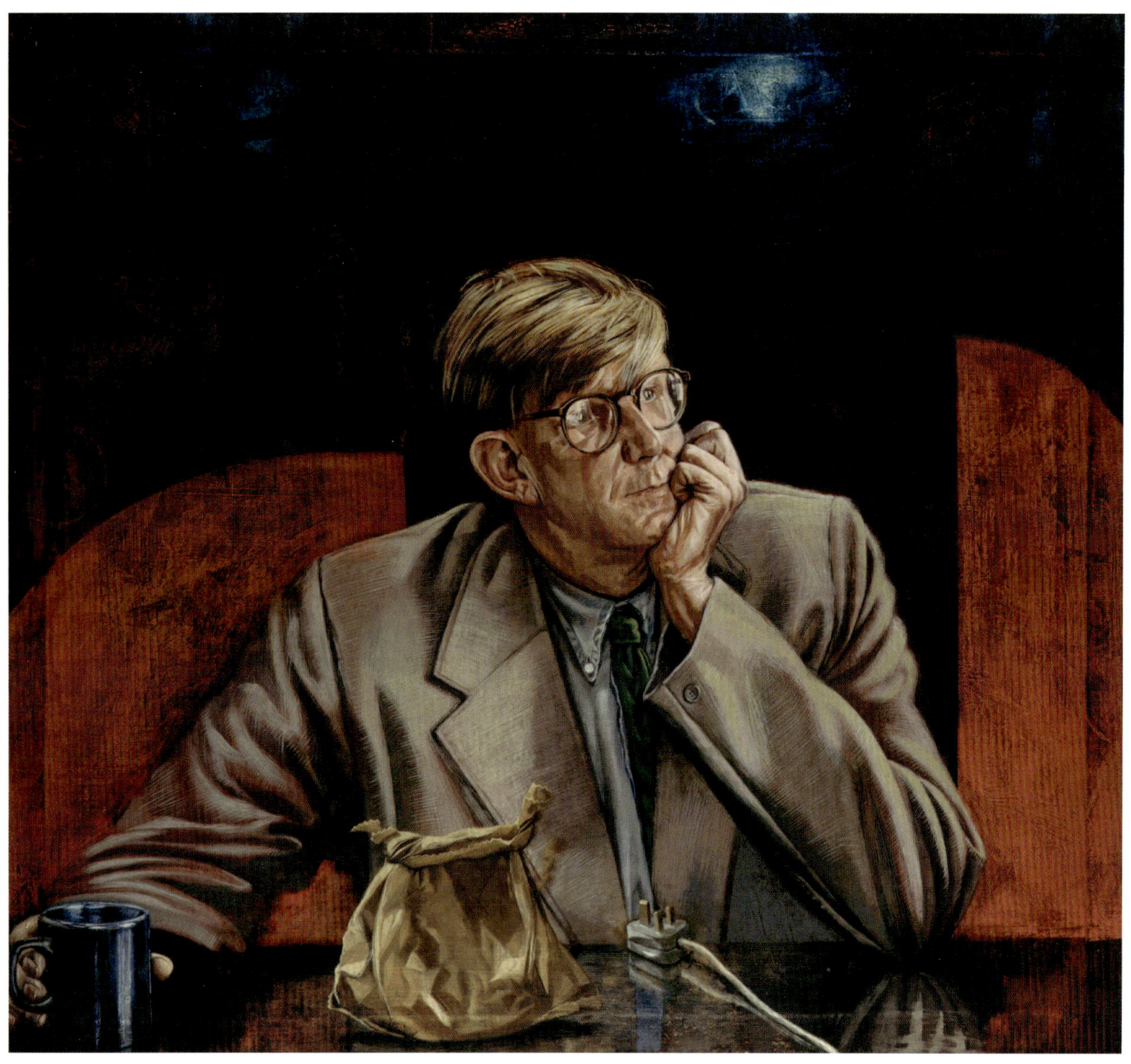

as he bought a bag of apples and was very tempted to tap him on the shoulder and introduce himself as the framer of his forthcoming portrait but he never did. It also suggests something old fashioned, traditional and wholesome in contrast to the plug which was placed there as a contrast … Despite Alan Bennett's public persona there was also an element of him that was very modern and sharp, for example when I knew him he drove a large, high powered Audi saloon car, good for the motorways as he said, something people might not expect of him.' In 2013 a new portrait of Alan Bennett appeared at the Royal Society of Portrait Painters Annual Exhibition at the Mall Galleries in London. Bennett agreed to the commission from North Yorkshire artist Sam Dalby because the oil

Tom Wood, b. 1955. *Alan Bennett* (1993). Oil on canvas laid on panel, 110.5 x 122cm (© National Portrait Gallery, London)

painting was to be sold to raise funds for the historic building and arts centre the Folly in Settle, no doubt comfortable with the idea that in this case his portrait was not being saved for the nation.

Alan Bennett has written extensively about growing up in Leeds in the 1930s and 1940s and his family's close relationship with their local communities. Yorkshire has a strikingly multi-cultural population with many different ethnic groups, some of which have been established for several generations in Yorkshire's big cities of Bradford, Leeds and Sheffield and the large industrial towns. There has been a strong, tight-knit Jewish community in Yorkshire – mostly living in Leeds – for more than a century, and many of its sons and daughters have gone on to become leaders in their field, including the law, business, science and the arts, and to become great benefactors to Leeds. Many families sought sanctuary here from the persecution of the late nineteenth century pogroms in Eastern Europe, and more found safety before or during the two world wars. The Leeds Jewish community is the second largest provincial community in Britain exceeded only by Manchester, currently numbering over 8,000. The community became established in 1840 and the first dedicated synagogue opened in the city in 1863. By the 1870s most of the Jewish people lived in a Jewish ghetto in a poor part of the city, later settling in the more affluent areas of north Leeds, including Chapeltown, Moortown and Alwoodley. The community produced some major Jewish artists, including Jacob Kramer and Joash Woodrow.

Jacob Kramer was born in Russia in 1892 into an artistic middle class family, his father a painter and his mother a singer. When Kramer was still a baby his family fled Russia to escape the country's virulent anti-Semitic policy. They settled in Leeds and lived in poverty, which caused Kramer to run away to sea when he was just ten years old. He returned to attend Leeds School of Art and joined the radical Leeds Arts Club, which introduced him to new ideas in art and encouraged him to make paintings that were informed by his spiritual beliefs, thus becoming an English expressionist artist. A scholarship from the Jewish Educational Aid Society sent Kramer to the Slade School of Art just before War broke out, where he befriended other leading artists of the day, including Augustus John, David Bomberg and William Roberts and became involved in the Vorticist movement. In the early 1920s Kramer returned to Leeds where he was lauded as a local artistic celebrity. He set up a group of artists called the Yorkshire Luncheon Club, which met regularly at Whitelock's public house in Leeds but Kramer's return to Leeds was not a triumph and he became alcoholic, living in poverty and producing poor quality portraits of local figures to pay for his drinks. However, Kramer's earlier work, such as **The Jew (Meditation)**, 1916, was of great quality, imbued with his unique interpretation of the Jewish race and religion in an inimitable Expressionist style.

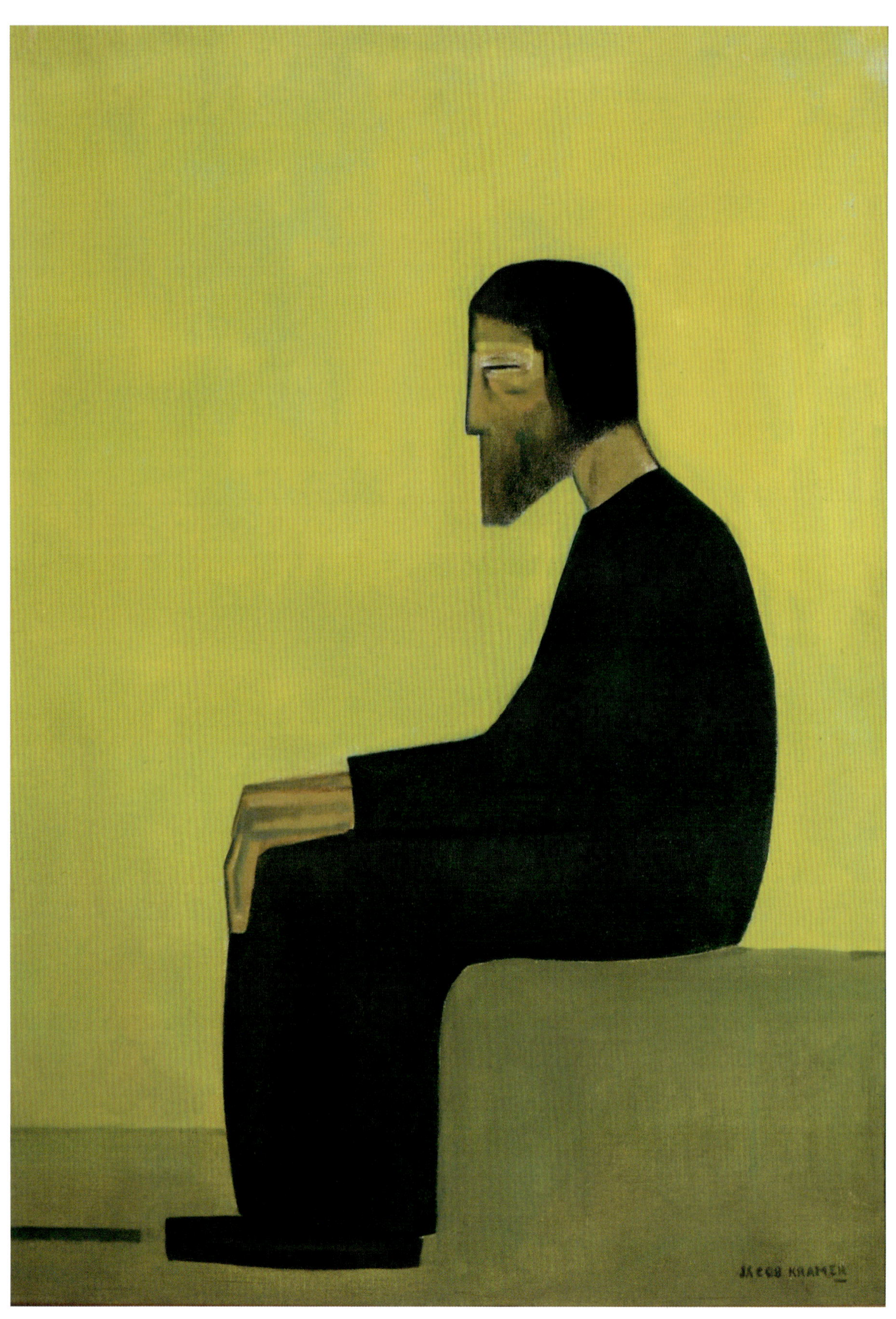
JACOB KRAMER

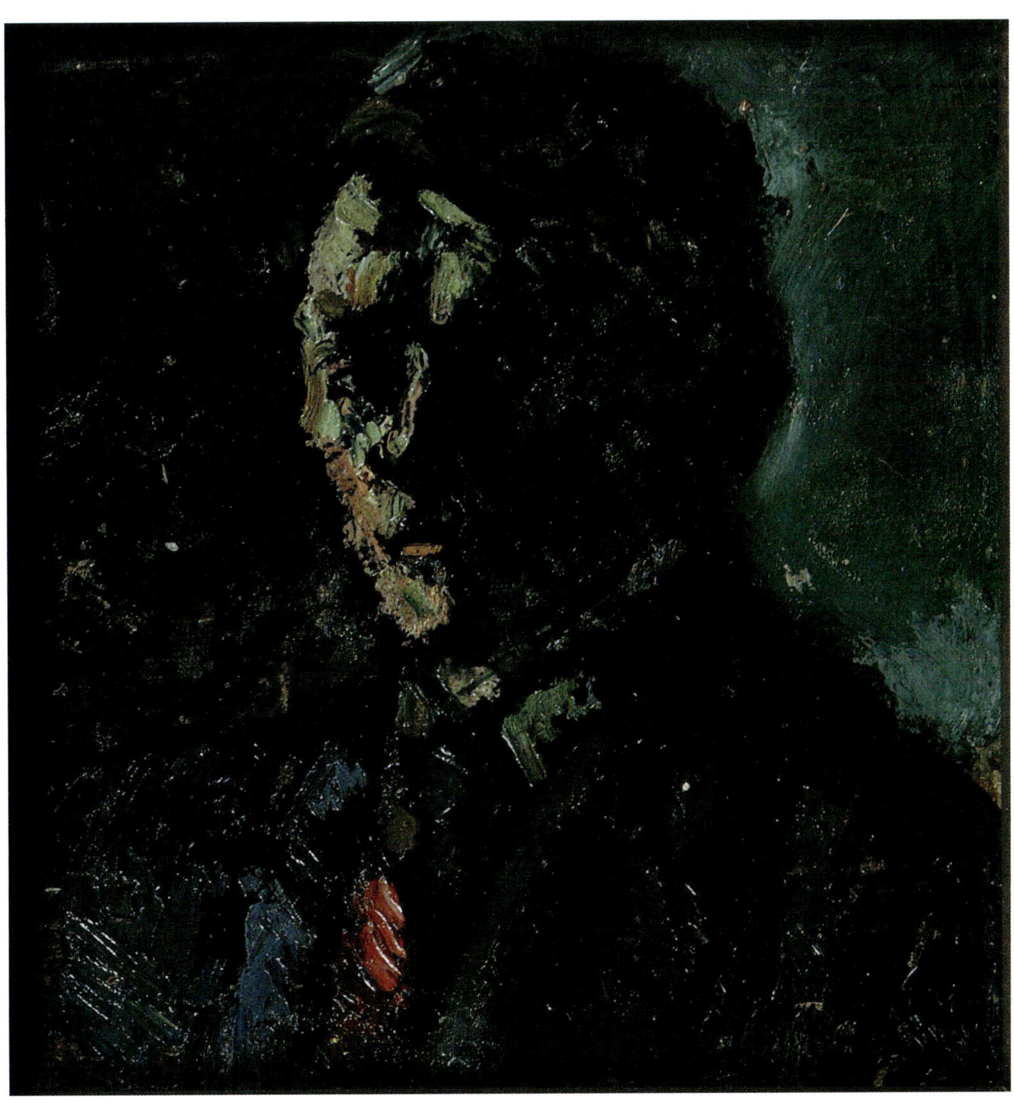

Joash Woodrow, 1927 - 2006. *Self Portrait (1)* (c. 1950). Oil on board, 34 x 31cm (108 Fine Art / Private Collection – reproduced courtesy of the Woodrow Family and the Bridgeman Art Library)

Opposite: Jacob Kramer, 1892 - 1962. *The Jew (Meditation)* (1916). Oil on canvas, 101.6 x 76.2cm (University of Leeds Art Collection)

Joash Woodrow was a forgotten Jewish painter who was rediscovered by chance in 2001 when he became too ill to cope alone in his small Leeds house where he had lived for over twenty years. The house was filled with 750 works on canvas and 4,000 works on paper, the product of a lifetime of constant, solitary artistic production. Rescued by Leeds artist Christopher P Wood and art dealer Andrew Stewart, the works identified Woodrow as one of the most significant artistic figures in postwar British art. Woodrow was the seventh of nine children in a poor but cultured Jewish family that had escaped the pogroms in eastern Poland of the early 1900s. Joash trained at Leeds School of Art and in 1950 won a scholarship to the Royal College of Art where he was a contemporary of John Bratby, Leon Kossoff and Frank Auerbach. His intense shyness meant that he could not cope with the competitive atmosphere in London

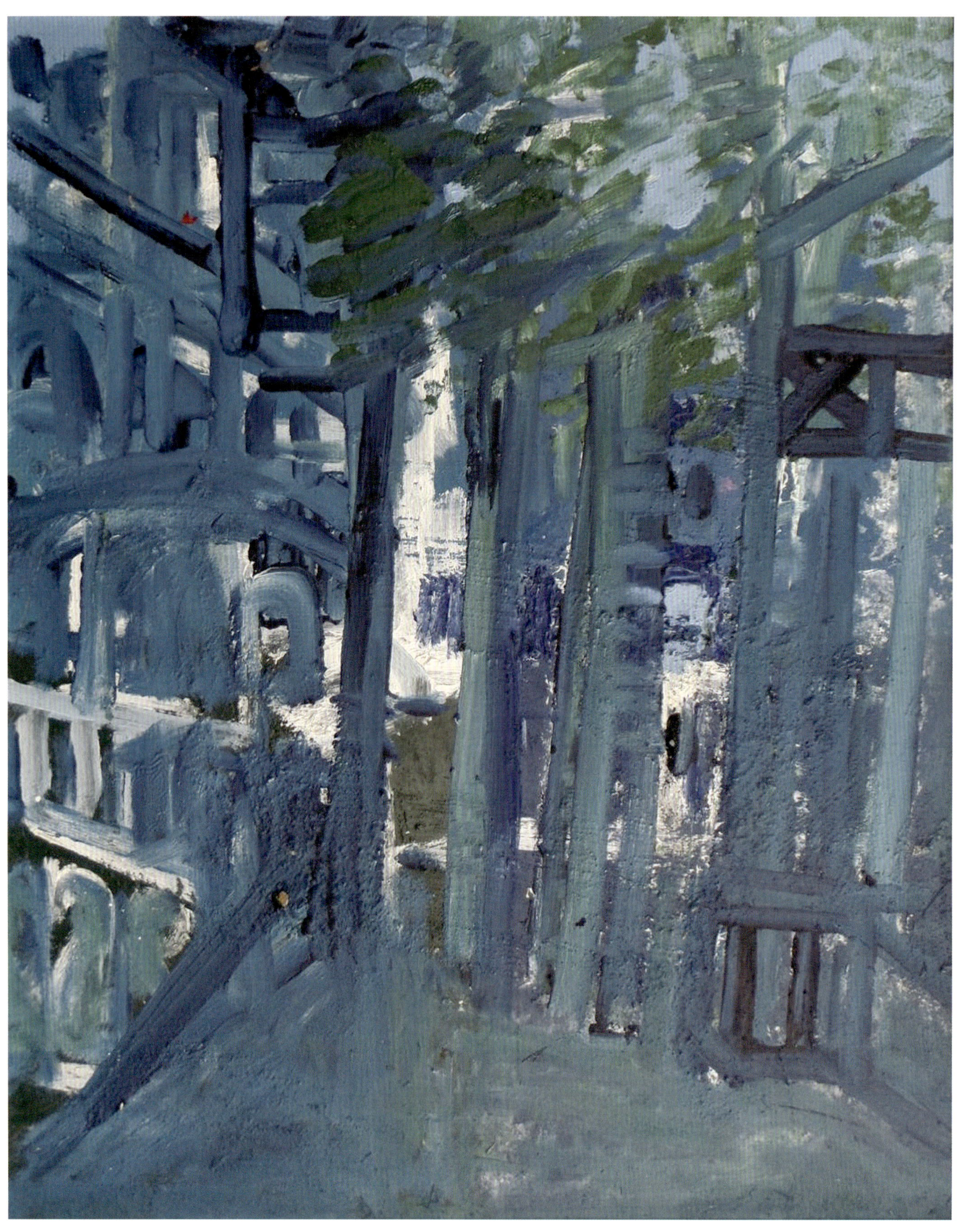

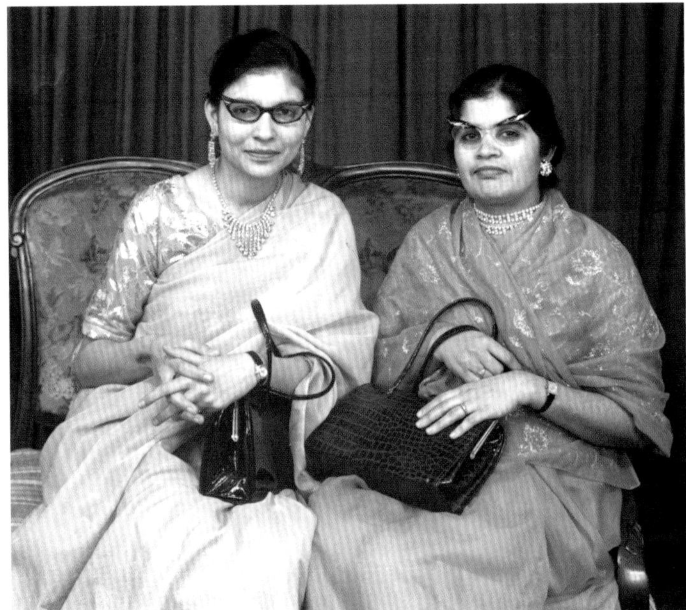

Belle Vue Studio, Bradford. Portrait photographs, c. 1970s. (Bradford Museums and Galleries)

Opposite: Joash Woodrow, 1927 - 2006. *Crown Place, Harrogate* (c. 1980). Oil on board, 84 x 68cm (108 Fine Art / Private Collection – reproduced courtesy of the Woodrow Family and the Bridgeman Art Library)

and in 1953 he suffered a nervous breakdown and went back to Leeds. He moved back in with his mother and two brothers and never stopped making art until ill health overcame him. European art was his inspiration and his small landscapes and portraits of the 1950s, dark with streaks of colour, bore the influence of Rouault. But it was a number of visits to the Picasso exhibition at the Tate in 1960 that had the greatest impact on Woodrow's art. Picasso gave him an insight into his Jewish heritage, and the realisation that the roots of his art lay not in England but in Europe. Looking further afield he found a fierce expressionism in the work of Karel Appel, Asger Jorn and the Cobra group, and Jean Dubuffet and the Art Brut circle. Texture and mark making came to the fore, giving Woodrow the extraordinary energy to paint with intense activity for three decades. Paintings became huge and drawings emerged at a furious rate, made outdoors on his tours of north Leeds and neighbouring places, including Harrogate. He turned his back on the art world and painted for himself alone. When he became incapacitated and went to live in sheltered housing he lost all interest in his work, including his later life fame, and died aged seventy-eight in 2006.

Bradford was once a rich city, with its wealth built on the processing of wool in the great mills that grew up there. In the second half of the twentieth century Bradfordians began looking for better-paid jobs than those available in the city's mills. In their place in the 1950s a new wave of workers were recruited from India, Pakistan and Bangladesh. The largest numbers arrived from Pakistan and specifically from the Mirpur district of Azad Kashmir. The immigrant workers came from very poor rural areas and for them Bradford presented an opportunity to improve their lives. The men went to work in the mills and on the buses, and were later joined by their wives and families. Aspiring Asians working in Bradford earned enough money to send some home, and with the money they sent indisputable evidence of just how wealthy and successful they had become. This was achieved by a visit to the Belle Vue Studio in Manningham Lane, where the photographer Sandford Taylor had first set up business in 1902. It was there that the Edwardian middle-classes used to go to be photographed in style, wearing their best clothes and sitting in front of a painted backdrop of a room in a stately home, with props of potted palms and grand furniture. By the 1950s well-heeled people had their own small portable cameras and photography studios began to disappear, but the Belle Vue Studio welcomed Bradford's new

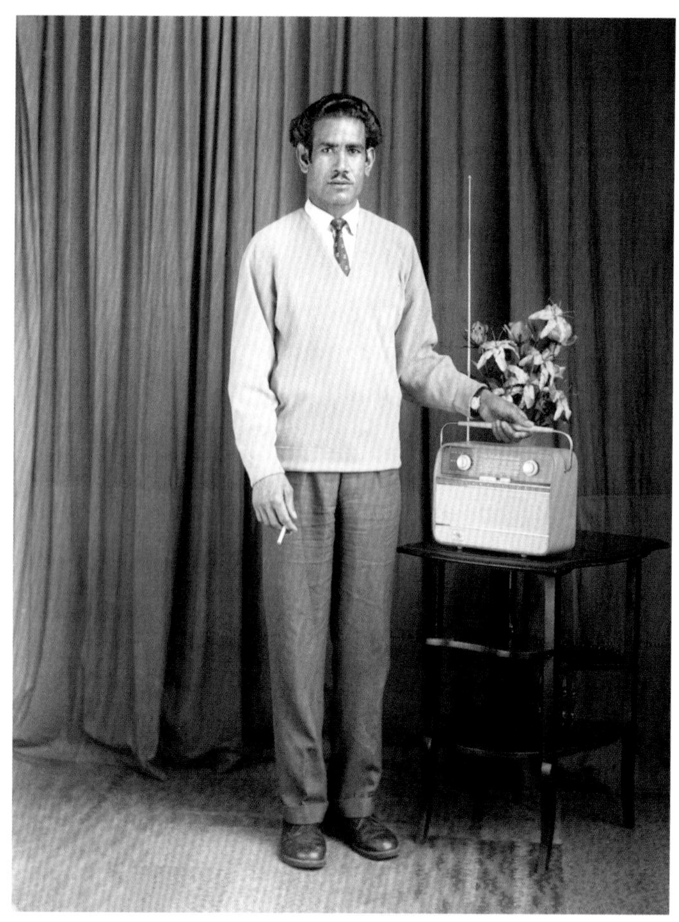

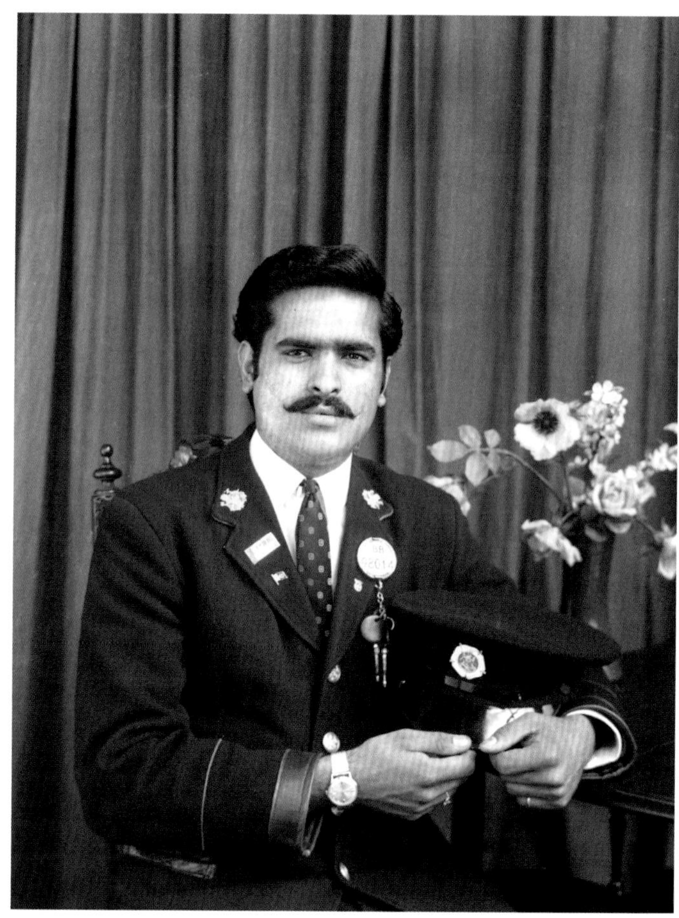

residents who were only too delighted to put on their best clothes and pose with the whole family against the aspirational setting. Transistor radios were placed on side tables, the men wore smart suits with pound notes tucked into their breast pockets and the women clutched large leather handbags on their laps. The photographs were sent home to admiring families who wasted little time in finding their own way to Yorkshire. As well as the Asian customers post-war migrants from Poland, Ukraine and Latvia, and from the Caribbean, also found their way to the Belle Vue Studio and kept business going until 1975 when the owner retired and shut it down. Ten years later he decided to sell up, and started to dispatch the old glass negatives into a skip, but local curators and photographer Tim Smith arrived in time to rescue 17,000 negatives of portraits from the 1950s to the 1970s, now in the Bradford Museums.

Documentary photographer Tim Smith has made Bradford his adopted home. 'A very cosmopolitan city,' is how he describes Bradford. 'You can almost travel the world on the city circular bus and I've always taken an interest in communities in Bradford whose origins lie overseas. For many years, I centred the work I did with them actually in the city,

Belle Vue Studio, Bradford. Portrait photographs, c. 1970s. (Bradford Museums and Galleries)

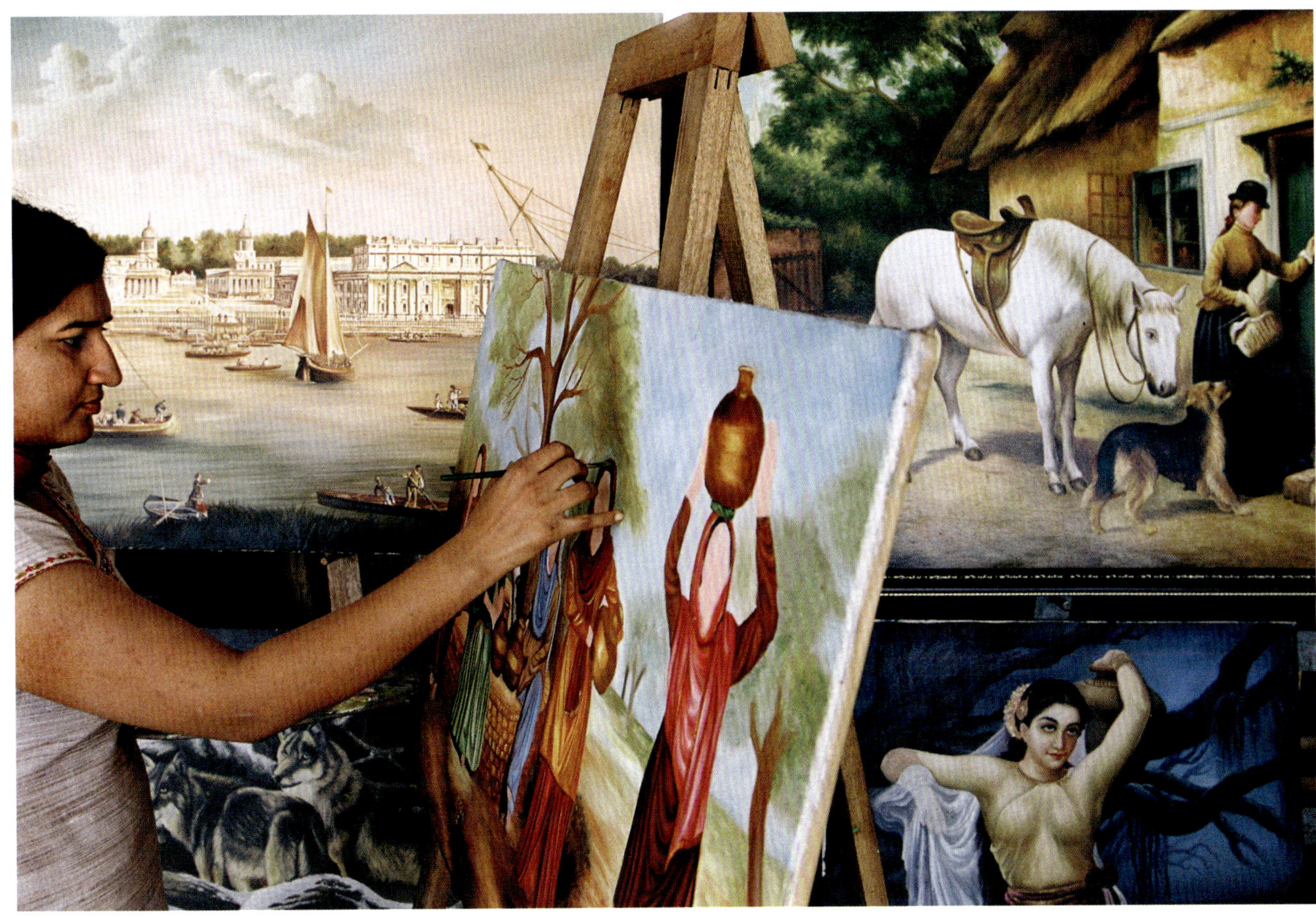

Tim Smith, b.1959 . *The Star Art Studio on the Grand Trunk Road, Ludhiana*. Photograph (Courtesy of the Artist)

then it expanded to doing work in other British towns and cities with similar communities. I also started going to the places where they had come from – Pakistan or India, Ukraine or wherever, to look at the other end of the story.' Tim's travels have led to a number of bodies of work to be seen in both exhibitions and books, such as *Here To Stay* in which the Belle Vue Studio photographs are complemented with more recent photographs of local Asian communities and individuals' testimonies about their lives in Bradford. *In Home From Home* he visited Mirpur and for *The Grand Trunk Road* he travelled along the eponymous highway, as he believes in putting stories of migration in their historical context. 'The story of Asian migration in Britain is the story of the British Empire. All those trade and military links that go back centuries, the history of the First World War and the Second World War, and the Partition of India in 1947, all are partly responsible for very particular groups of people coming to settle in Britain. I think it's important to understand that.' Tim Smith's photographs capture the social history and character of huge swathes of Yorkshire's people, all of which add richly to the culture of Yorkshire.

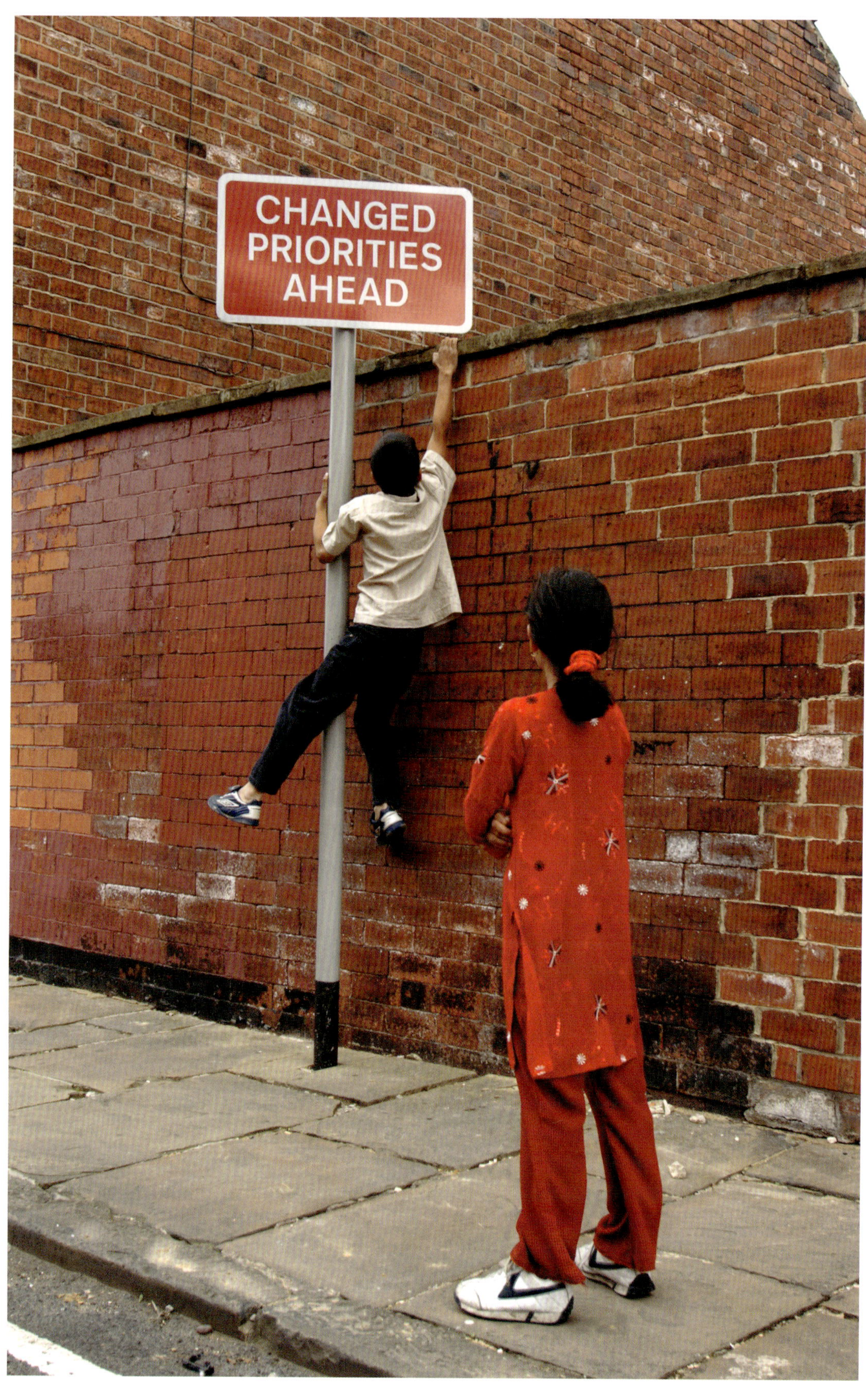

Tim Smith, b.1959
Children playing with a traffic sign in Beeston, Leeds (2005). Photograph (Courtesy of the Artist)

Acknowledgements

I would like to thank the following individuals and organisations for the help they have given me in producing this book.

Jane Sellars

Jake Attree
Mark Bills
Layla Bloom, the Stanley and Audrey Burton Gallery, University of Leeds
Bradford Museums and Art Galleries
The Brontë Society
Andrew Cheetham
Andrew Clay
Ann Dinsdale
Mark Edwards, Keeper of the Whitby Museum
Lara Goodband
Emily Green, National Museum of Coal Mining
James Huntington-Whiteley, JHW Fine Art
David Joy
Nicholas Lane Fox
Myles Linley
Marco Livingstone
Richard Macfarlane, Calderdale Museums
Messum's, London
Frank Milner
Simon Palmer
Grant Scanlan, Kirklees Museums
Debbie Seymour, Karen Snowden, Scarborough Museums Trust
Jeffrey and Ruth Sherwin
Margaret Silver
Kirsten Simister, Ferens Art Gallery, Hull Museums and Galleries
Tim Smith
Andrew Stewart
Brenda Taylor
Lois Toyne
Kate Whiteford
Jane Winfrey, Bonhams
Ted Wilkins, Leeds Museums and Galleries
Tom Wood

Thanks are also due to the following for the supply of images:

Bridgeman Art Library
David Chalmers Photography
Paul Harris – Photographer
Simon Miles Photography

Bibliography

Alexander, Christine and Sellars, Jane, *The Art of the Brontës*, Cambridge University Press, 1995

Attree, Jake, Messum's, 2013

Barker, Juliet, The Brontës, Weidenfeld and Nicolson, 1994

BBC Archive, Henry Moore: One Yorkshireman Looks at his World, 1967

Bradbury, Malcolm, The Atlas of Literature, De Agostino Editions, 1996

Brandt, Bill, Arts Council of Great Britain Touring Exhibition, c. 1973

Brooks, Jason, Harewood House Trust, 2001

Diaper, Hilary and Green, Lynne, A Malham Family of Painters, the Stanley and Audrey Burton Gallery, University of Leeds, 2009

Diaper, Hilary ed., Letters from Malham: Wartime Life at High Barn Cottage, the Stanley and Audrey Burton Gallery, University of Leeds, 2009

Dunbar, Janet, Laura Knight, Collins, London, 1975

Feather, Jessica, British Watercolours and Drawings: Lord Leverhulme's Collection in the Lady Lever Art Gallery, National Museums Liverpool, 2010

Fox, Caroline, Dame Laura Knight, Phaidon Press Limited, 1988

Hill, David, Harewood Masterpieces: English Watercolours and Drawings, Harewood House Trust, 1995

Hill, David, Thomas Girtin: Genius in the North, Harewood House Trust, 1999

Hockney, David et al, David Hockney: A Bigger Picture, Thames and Hudson, 2012

Joy, David ed., The Yorkshire Dales: A View from the Millennium, Great Northern Books, 1999

Knight, Laura, Oil Paint and Grease Paint, Penguin, London, 1941

Landscape in Britain 1850 – 1950, Arts Council of Great Britain, 1983

Livingstone, Marco, David Hockney: My Yorkshire, Enitharmon Editions, 2011

Milner, Frank, Adrian Henri: Paintings 1953 – 1998, National Museums Liverpool, 1998

Moncrieff, Elspeth, The Art of Simon Palmer, 2011

Morris, Susan, Thomas Girtin, Yale Center for British Art, New Haven, 1986

Parker, Cornelia, Brontëan Abstracts, The Brontë Society, 2006

Parris, Leslie, Landscape in Britain c. 1750 – 1850, The Tate Gallery, 1973

The Pre Raphaelites, The Tate Gallery, 1984

Sellars, Jane ed., Kate Whiteford: Sitelines Harewood, After Chippendale, Harewood House Trust, 2000

Sellars, Jane ed., The Art of Thomas Chippendale: Master Furniture Maker, Harewood House Trust, 2000

Sellars, Jane ed., Atkinson Grimshaw: Painter of Moonlight, The Mercer Art Gallery, Harrogate Borough Council, 2011

Shanes, Eric, Turner: The Great Watercolours, Royal Academy of Arts, London, 2001

Whiteford, Kate: Land Drawings/ Installations/ Excavations, Black Dog Publishing, 2008

Whone, Herbert, The Essential West Riding, E P Publishing Ltd, 1975

Wilton, Andrew and Lyles, Anne, The Great Age of British Watercolours, Royal Academy of Arts, 1993

Index

Illustrations in bold type

Abbot Hall Art Gallery 115
Ackroyd, Norman **32, 33,** 34
Adam, Robert 109
Adel Crag 64
Almscliffe Crag 11, 32
Anderson, Sophie 19
Armitage, Kenneth 118
Attree, Jake 88, **89,** 90

Bacon, Francis 107
Barden 38, 42, **43**
Barraclough, James Penniston **128**
Battle, Walter 42, 113
Beaton, Cecil 131
Beeston **140**
Belle Vue Studios **137, 138**
Bennett, Alan 4, 131, **132,** 133
Bentley, Phyllis 60
Beverley 126
Bingley 59
Bolton Abbey 5, **21, 26,** 27, 30, **38,** 40, **41,** 42
Blackwell, Su 62
Bomberg, David 133
Bradford 46, 48, 49, 59, 60, 62, 68, **70,** 75, **80,** 86, 115, 133, 137, 138, 139
Bradford Industrial Museum 80, 86
Bradley, John **61,** 62
Bramham Park 109, **110,** 126
Brandt, Bill 63, 79
Bridlington 6, 68
Brighouse 118
Brimham Rocks 64
Brontë, Anne 21, **22,** 61, 62, **127,** 128
Brontë, Branwell **20,** 21, 61, 62, 126, **127**
Brontë, Charlotte **20, 21,** 27, 61, 62, **127,** 128
Brontë, Emily 20, 21, **22,** 61, 62, 107, **127,** 128
Brontë Parsonage Museum 20
Brontë, Patrick 60, 128
Brook, Peter **88,** 118
Brooks, Jason **112**
Brown, Capability 30, 36
Bukovac, Blaho **114**
Bunney, Tessa 123, **124,** 126
Burton Agnes Hall 6
Burton Constable 108
Byatt, A S 128, **130,** 131

Cartwright Hall Art Gallery 119, 128
Castleford 64, 76, 79
Castle Howard 86, 108
Cheetham, Andrew 104, **105**
Chippendale, Thomas **34, 35,** 109
Coldstones Cut **56,** 57
Collins, Bob 123
Cory, Charlotte 62
Cowen, William **70**

Dalby, Sam 132
Davies, Hunter 85
Dean Clough **89,** 90, 115
Doncaster **78,** 79
Dracup, Liza **46**
Duncan, Ronnie 115, 118

Earnshaw, Anthony 118
Eccleshill 80, **81**
Elwell, Fred 16, **17, 125, 126**
Epstein, Jacob 118
Evans, Walter Bernard 53, **55**

Farnley Hall 6, 12, **37,** 38
Fell, Sheila 19, **84**
Ferens Art Gallery 16, 126
Foster, Gilbert 94
Fountains Abbey 5, 7, 8, 10, **11,** 30, 51, **53, 54, 55**
Fox, Samson 113, **114**
Freidman, Terry 115, 118
Freud, Lucian 7, 107
Frith, Francis 100
Frith, William Powell **120,** 121
Fryston Colliery **79,** 80

Gabain, Ethel 19
Garrard, George 109, **110**
Gaskell, Mrs 27, 128
Giggleswick **85**
Gilman, Harold 75
Ginner, Charles 75, **77**
Girtin, Thomas 12, **14, 38,** 40, 47, 51, **54**
Goldsworthy, Andy 118
Grantley Hall 82
Green, Lynne 90
Grimshaw, Atkinson 6, 7, 24, **25,** 42, **43, 45,** 46, 71, 72, **73, 74,** 75, 102, **104,** 113, **121**
Grimshaw, Elaine 72, 121
Grimshaw, Gertrude **121,** 122

Haigh, Arthur 88, 115, 118, **119,** 120
Halifax 59, 76, 86, **87, 88,** 89, 90, 115
Hall, Ernest 115
Hamilton, Hugh Douglas **108**
Harewood Castle 30, **31, 32,** 33, **112**
Harewood, Earls of 30, 33, 34, 112
Harewood House 6, 13, 15, **29, 30,** 36, 40, 86, 108, 110
Harrogate 7, 24, 42, 46, 53, 90, 113, **136,** 137
Hartley, Marie 48
Haworth 20, 22, 59, 60, 61, **62, 63**
Hawsker 93
Hebden Bridge 59
Henri, Adrian **63**
Henry Moore Institute 118
Hepworth, Barbara 27, 115, **122,** 123
Heron, Patrick 7, **130,** 131
Hiley, Michael 100
Hirst, Damien 118, **129,** 130
Hockney, David 7, 16, **18,** 19, 27, **66, 67,** 68, **69, 80, 81,** 82, 90, **106,** 107, 108, 115, **117**
Holl, Frank 97
Holmes, Katharine 7, 47, **51, 52**
Holmfirth **60**
Horton-Fawkes family 12, 37, 38
Huddersfield 59, 60, 71, 76, 82, **83, 84,** 85
Hull 16, 90, **91**

Inchbold, John William **41,** 42
Ingilby, Joan 48
Ingleborough 42, **45**

Jackson, Fred 94
Jervaulx Abbey 7, 57
John, Augustus 133

Kapp, Helen 115
Kar, Ida 123
Keen, Peter **122,** 123
Keighley 59, **61**
Kirkstall Abbey 5, **21**

Knaresborough **28**
Knight, Laura 19, 94, 97, **98, 99,** 102, 126
Knostrop 72
Kramer, Jacob 47, 133, **134**

Lane Fox, George 110
Lascelles family 30, 33, 34, 40, 110
Lawson, Fred 47
Leeds 5, 7, 22, 24, 28, 59, 64, 72, **73, 74,** 75, **77,** 85, 86, 113, 122, 133, 135, 137
Leeds Art Gallery 6, 7, 22, 24, 42, 75, 115
Leighton Bridge **4**
Linley, Myles 90, **91**
Lord, Mary 118
Lotherton Hall 24
Lowry, L S 10, **82, 83,** 84, 85
Ludhiana **139**
Lumb, Edna **85,** 86

McCullin, Don **78,** 79
MacGregor, Jessie 19
Malham 47, **48,** 49, **51**
Malkin, Henry **79,** 80
Marr, Laurie 55
Marr, Leslie **11**
Mercer Art Gallery 24, 46, 121
Methley 6, 7, 64
Mirfield 62
Moore, Henry 6, 7, 27, 64, **65, 76,** 115, 118, 122
Munnings, Sir Alfred 110, **111,** 112, 126

National Coal Mining Museum 76
Newby Hall 108, 123, **124**
New Stubbin Pit **79**
Nicholls, Arthur Bell 62, 128
Nicholson, Ben 123
Nidderdale **55,** 57, 123
Nostell Priory **108,** 109

Oliver, Bill 118, 119
Otley 34

Palmer, Samuel 59
Palmer, Simon **4,** 7, 8, **57, 58**

Parker, Cornelia 62
Pateley Bridge 57
Pearson, Constance 47, **48, 49,** 51
Pearson, Philippa **49, 50,** 51
Pevsner, Nikolaus 57
Pighills, Joseph **62**
Piper, John 58, 86, **87,** 88
Ponden Hall **106,** 107, 108
Pontefract, Ella 48
Pool in Wharfedale 10
Priestley, J B 60, **128**
Princess Mary (Princess Royal) 33, 110, **111**

Rae, Henrietta 19
Ravilious, Eric 59
Read, Herbert 118
Rego, Paula 22, **23,** 62
Renishaw Hall 86
Reynolds, Joshua 42
Richmond, George 128
Ripon **27,** 28, 55
Roberts, William 133
Robertson, Alex 42
Robin Hood's Bay 10, 20, 93, 94
Roe, Robert Ernest **92,** 93, 94, **95**
Rose, David **55,** 57
Rotherham 71
Roundhay Park **73,** 74
Runswick Bay 48, **96**
Ruskin, John 12, 27, 40, 42
Rutter, Frank 75

Sabin, Andrew **56,** 57
Sadler, Michael 75
St Ives (Yorkshire) **46**
Salts Mill 80, 115, **117**
Scarborough 61, **92,** 93, 94, **95,** 102, **104**
Senior, Mark 94, **96**
Settle 131, 133
Sherwin, Jeffrey 115
Silver, Jonathan & Margaret 80, 115
Smith, Tim 138, **139, 140**
Staithes 48, 93, 94, 97, **100,** 102
Stewart, Andy 135

Stoker, Bram 97
Sutcliffe, Frank Meadow 99, **100, 101, 102, 103**
Sutcliffe, Thomas 99

Tadcaster 9, 10, 15
Tadema, Alma 74
Taylor, Sandford 137
Taylor-Wood, Sam 62
Temple Newsam 5, 7, 24
Thubron, Harry 118
Turner, J M W 5, 7, 8, **12,** 13, 15, 21, **26, 27, 28, 29, 30, 31,** 32, 33, **36, 37,** 38, **39,** 40, 47, 51, **53,** 112

Wakefield 49, 76, 122
Wakefield Art Gallery 115
Walker, Ethel **19,** 20
Walker Last, Marie 118
Washburn Valley 11, **36**
Watson, Peter 76, **79**
Weight, Carel **60**
Wheldale Colliery **76**
Whitby 93, 97, 100, **101,** 102
Whiteford, Kate **34, 35,** 36
Whone, Herbert **59**
Winn, Sir Rowland & Sabine **108,** 109
Wolds, the **66, 67,** 68, 69, 90
Wood, Christopher P 135
Wood, Tom 118, **119,** 131, **132**
Woodrow, Joash 133, **135, 136,** 137
Wordsworth, William & Dorothy 21, 40, 42
Worthington, Greville 115, 118

Yeo, Jonathan **129**
York 76, **82,** 86, 90
Yorkshire Luncheon Club 135
Yorkshire Sculpture Park 64, **65**